100 THINGS
LAKERS FANS
SHOULD KNOW & DO
BEFORE THEY DIE

To Jayden and Hudson:
At ages eight and six, you have already carved out
your own special place in our family. Your curious
minds, captivating personalities, and wondrous joy
will take you far. God gives each of us a unique
talent. Figure out what your special gift is, use it to
pursue your dreams, and the future will be yours.

Contents

Foreword *by James Worthy* xi

Kobe: Memories of a Player for the Ages xv

1 Showtime 1

2 Magic-Bird 4

3 The Shaq/Kobe Dynasty 10

4 Kareem 13

5 LeBron Takes His Talents to the Lakers 16

6 The Logo 21

7 At Last 25

8 Flying Under the Radar 27

9 The Announcement 31

10 The Shaq-Kobe Feud 35

11 Born at the Back of the Line 38

12 Going West 43

13 The Zen Master 45

14 The Torch Is Passed 48

15 The Family Feud Erupts 52

16 Relevant Again, Like Magic 55

17 Pelinka Adds the Missing Link 59

18 A Magical Night 64

19 From Clark Kent to Superman 67

20 Riles 72

21 Wilt: Nobody Roots for Goliath 75

22 The Fabulous Forum 79

23 Big Trade for the Big Fella 81

100 THINGS LAKERS FANS
SHOULD KNOW & DO BEFORE THEY DIE

Steve Springer

TRIUMPH
BOOKS

The Library of Congress has catalogued the previous edition as follows:
Springer, Steve, 1945–
  100 things Lakers fans should know & do before they die / Steve Springer.
  p. cm.
  ISBN 978-1-60078-649-5
  1. Los Angeles Lakers (Basketball team)—History. 2. Los Angeles Lakers (Basketball team)—Miscellanea. I. Title. II. Title: One hundred things Lakers fans should know and do before they die.
  GV885.52.L67S65 2012
  796.323'640979494—dc23
                                        2012025815

This book is available in quantity at special discounts for your group or organization. For further information, contact:
  Triumph Books LLC
  814 North Franklin Street
  Chicago, Illinois 60610
  (312) 337-0747
  www.triumphbooks.com

Printed in U.S.A.
ISBN: 978-1-62937-901-2
Design by Patricia Frey
Photos courtesy of AP Images unless otherwise indicated

24 The Streak. 85

25 The Shaq/Kobe Gamble 88

26 Field of Nightmares. 94

27 The Junior Junior Skyhook. 101

28 Big Game James 105

29 A Championship Like No Other. 107

30 Kobe Gets His Man 114

31 Rings Half a Century Late. 118

32 The First Lakers Team 121

33 Gems Before Rings 125

34 Rings. 126

35 Why Lakers? 130

36 Return to Carroll. 132

37 The First Trip to L.A.. 133

38 Short Comes Up Short 138

39 Baylor Beats the Bigots 139

40 Lakers vs. the Harlem Globetrotters 142

41 Chick to the Rescue 145

42 Sports Arena: JFK, MLK, UCLA, and NBA. 149

43 The Clown Prince. 153

44 Nice Shot, Baby 156

45 Lakers-Celtics: Game 8? 159

46 Tight-Fisted Lou Mohs. 161

47 The Hawk: Lakers and All That Jazz. 163

48 Fred Schaus and That Damn Cigar. 164

49 A Laker Corpse? 169

50 A Clock in His Head. 170

51 Jim Krebs: His Luck Ran Out 172

52 Lakers-Celtics: Forgetting Those Unforgettable Moments. . . 173

53 Dodgers/Lakers: It Almost Happened 175

54 The Wrath of Cooke. 177

55 The Balloon Game 181

56 Wilt vs. Butch: No Contest. 184

57 Another Streak—3,338 Straight 187

58 Pulling a Willis Reed. 191

59 Nice Guy Finishes First. 194

60 Stumpy 197

61 Redemption at Last 199

62 The Punch 203

63 They Played It for Laughs 206

64 Monopoly as the Game of Life 207

65 Sand Dabs? 212

66 The Dog Days of Jerry West. 214

67 The Architect of Showtime 215

68 The Downfall of Jack McKinney 218

69 The Substitute Teacher 221

70 The Curious Case of Spencer Haywood 224

71 Silk 226

72 Coach Westhead: To Be or Not to Be. 227

73 No More Magic 230

74 Tragic Johnson 235

75 Who Is the Coach? 237

76 Riles' Roots. 238

77 Destiny's Child 242

78 Beat L.A.! 247

79 Out Like Magic. 249

80 West's Spies. 251

81 They Played It for Laughs, Part II 254

82 25 Years, $25 Million 256

83 Coop. 257

84 The Aging Hippie. 259

85 From Cold Shoulder to Hot Touch 262

86 The Guarantee 264

87 Numbers Game. 268

88 0.4. 270

89 Big Shot Rob. 273

90 Panic in the Bathroom 275

91 The Great Voice Is Stilled. 278

92 Phil and Jeanie 281

93 What If... 284

94 Harsh Reality 288

95 Metta World Peace, Man of Many Names and Many Faces . . 291

96 Kobe's 81 294

97 Kobe's Farewell 60 298

98 Revenge Is Sweet. 302

99 Best and Worst 305

100 A True Fan 307

Acknowledgments 309

Bibliography. 313

Foreword

Growing up in Gastonia, North Carolina, I was a huge Magic Johnson fan. So much so that, even though I knew I was going to go to college at North Carolina, I took a recruiting trip to Michigan State just to see him play. A 6-foot-9 point guard? I had never heard of anything like that.

So I was thrilled when I learned I was going from being a Laker fan to being a Laker forward when they selected me with the first pick in the 1982 draft.

Jerry West picked me up at the L.A. airport in a Porsche 944. I wasn't in Gastonia anymore.

He drove me directly to a picnic for Laker employees. When I met Dr. Jerry Buss there, he turned out to be not at all what I had expected. The genius behind Showtime and all the glitz and glamour surrounding it was very soft-spoken, very low key, wearing ragged jeans, a cigarette dangling from his fingers. I instantly related to him because I was a pretty quiet guy myself.

I broke my leg in April of my rookie season and didn't get a chance to play in the postseason, so my first playoff experience was in 1984, ending with a matchup against the Celtics in the Finals. I had a really good postseason with the exception of Game 2 against Boston. After we won Game 1, I made an errant pass with 16 seconds left in regulation time in Game 2. The Celtics' Gerald Henderson stole it, scored, the game went into overtime, and we lost. That was a painful experience for me. As I sit here writing this all these years later, it still stings because we wound up losing the Finals in seven games.

By the end of that series, I knew I would forever bleed Purple and Gold.

The following year, we were able to get revenge for ourselves and so many previous Laker teams by beating the Celtics in the Finals. And we did it on their parquet floor in Boston Garden, that terrible, bleeping gym. I can still remember getting off our bus on trips there and having to walk in with the fans who would loudly give it to us with their nasty comments. There was no heat in there in the winter, no air conditioning in the spring. You could die in that place. There was cold water only in the showers and no individual locker stalls. It was a mess. In our Boston hotel, there were prank calls all the time, even if you told the operator to please hold our calls. I think they were in on it, too.

For a country boy like me, the whole Laker experience was amazing. Coming from Gastonia, I had never seen a star. Never. I wasn't used to the fast pace or the diversity of different cultures. The reality is, coming from where I did, I was just afraid. It took me about three years to come out of my box and learn to love L.A.

For the Lakers, it started in Minneapolis with George Mikan, No. 99, the first dominating big man.

Then there was Elgin Baylor. He was Mr. Laker, Air Baylor. Chick Hearn used to tell us that none of us could do what Baylor did. I remember seeing an article in the *L.A. Times* in which I was listed as the second-best small forward in Laker history. My initial reaction was, "Who's first?" When I saw it was Baylor, I thought, "What a privilege to be second to him."

Next came Jerry West, then Wilt Chamberlain. They won one title, but once the kid from East Lansing—"Buck" as we called Magic—came along to team up with Kareem, that changed everything.

What was the secret of the success of the Showtime Lakers? We certainly had a unique collection of talent, and we were able to mold that talent into a cohesive unit because we were all so close. Man, we loved each other. We loved being around one another. We couldn't wait to get to practice. And we monitored each other, had respect for each other. Magic could look at you when you walked in the door for practice and know if you had had a fight with your wife or girlfriend, or if you had stayed up all night at a club. Seeing where you were at, he would pull you back into the team.

One of my favorite people was Bill Sharman, who coached the Lakers' first world championship team in L.A. and went on to become general manager and then team president. It was he who started to put together the Showtime Lakers, beginning with the hiring of coach Jack McKinney. Sharman was a true gentleman, very wise. A star player for Boston, he broke in with the Washington Capitols in the 1950–51 season, as did as Earl Lloyd, the first African American player to appear in an NBA game. Lloyd once told me that Sharman would pick him up for every home game and then drive him back afterward to make sure he got there safely, this back in a time when Lloyd's mere presence on the team was controversial.

In the late '90s, West put together another Laker dynasty, getting Shaq and Kobe and filling in the necessary pieces around them like Derek Fisher, Brian Shaw, and Robert Horry. And to run the show, the Lakers got Phil Jackson. They won three titles in a row and, I think, if Shaq and Kobe had stayed together, we would have probably surpassed the Celtics' record 17 championships by now.

After Shaq was gone, Mitch Kupchak, who replaced West in the front office, got Pau Gasol. What a great move that was. I don't think there was anybody else out there who could have fit in that well with Kobe. Gasol, a versatile center with great court intelligence, was perfect.

It was yet another example of the Lakers finding the right people to continue their long tradition of excellence. They went from Mikan to Baylor, West, Wilt, Magic, Kareem, Shaq, Kobe, and Pau. More so than any other team, we always seem to land the iconic players of their respective eras.

And find iconic coaches like John Kundla in Minneapolis, Sharman, Pat Riley, and Jackson to lead them.

Now, with the arrival of LeBron, the Laker brand lives on.

—James Worthy
Seven-time All-Star, three-time NBA champion,
1988 Finals MVP, and member of the
NBA's 50ᵗʰ Anniversary All-Time Team

Kobe: Memories of a Player for the Ages

As my wife, Annette, and I drove home from dinner in Agoura in the Conejo Valley to our West San Fernando Valley home late on the last Saturday night in January 2020, I noticed eerie white strands of fog stretching across the 101 Freeway as if a gigantic spider web was unraveling.

I didn't think much of it then, but now, it haunts me, and will for the rest of my life, because by Sunday morning, those strands had grown into a thick wall that caused the Los Angeles County Sheriff's Department and Los Angeles Police Department to ground their helicopters.

But, as we now know all too well, one helicopter kept flying, a Sikorsky S-76 en route from John Wayne Airport in Orange County to Camarillo Airport north of Thousand Oaks. From there, a car would take Kobe Bryant and eight other passengers to the nearby Mamba Sports Academy, where a girls' team coached by Kobe and featuring his 13-year-old daughter, Gianna, was scheduled to play.

At around 9:45 AM, the helicopter crashed into a hillside, all on board perishing.

When I first heard the news flash on that black Sunday saying Kobe had died, I didn't even repeat it to my wife. Just internet BS, I thought. For days, I still believed Kobe was going to suddenly appear, that trademark smile on his face, saying, as he had so many times when faced with a potentially debilitating injury, that everything would be fine because he would just play on through the pain.

This time, the pain belonged to the whole world.

To me, Kobe wasn't just one of the hundreds and hundreds of athletes I covered in my years at the *Los Angeles Times*. He was a friend.

If my old boss, Bill Dwyre, sees this, he won't be happy. Sportswriters aren't supposed to have friends in the sports community. Maybe you've heard, there's no cheering in the press box. But Kobe made it rough to adhere to that tradition. Yes, he could be tough, fierce, antagonistic in the heat of battle. But that was the Black Mamba.

His alter ego, Kobe, was very different. When Linda Heredero, a friend of my wife, asked if Kobe could possibly meet with her 22-year-old son, Joey, who was suffering from terminal cancer, she got her wish.

In doing so, the Laker superstar broke his own rule. It was during the playoffs, a time when Kobe, who normally did a ton of charity work, took a break to concentrate solely on the pursuit of another ring.

The Lakers got tickets for the Heredero family for a playoff game against the Phoenix Suns, and, after giving his last interview around 11:00 PM, Kobe came into a room in the bowels of Staples Center where the family was waiting, spent 20 minutes talking to Joey—who was in a wheelchair after having a leg amputated—as if they were old friends, signed every item Joey had brought for autographs, and took pictures with everybody.

As he walked out, I went to shake Kobe's hand.

Instead, he said, "I don't want you to write about this in the paper. I don't want to see you on TV talking about it. I don't do this for a pat on the back or for publicity. I do it because it's the right thing to do. If you need me for a good cause, come to me privately and I'll do it."

I'm not violating Kobe's request here.

Joey died several weeks after meeting him.

Six years later, when Kobe went on his 2016 farewell tour, I asked him if he would meet with the Herederos, who live in Lake Havasu, on his final trip to Phoenix. Kobe did, giving them a chance to privately thank him again and say goodbye.

And he allowed me to write the story in *USA Today.*

The night before the marriage of my son, Alan, to his fiancée, Lauren, Kobe did a video for the occasion, shown at the rehearsal dinner.

When I wrote Caron Butler's book, *Tuff Juice,* Kobe, a close friend of Butler, wrote the foreword. Producer Mark Wahlberg subsequently announced that he was going to turn the book into a movie. The next time I saw Kobe, he congratulated me on the movie deal and asked if it was going to win an Oscar.

I wasn't ready to go that far.

Kobe was. He always was in every area of life.

"Whatever you do," he told me, that Black Mamba look in his eyes, "you should always aim for the top. If you're on a basketball team, you shoot for a championship. If you make a movie, you shoot for an Oscar."

And, of course, he himself went on to win an Oscar, awarded to *Dear Basketball* for Best Animated Short Film.

When athletes' careers are cut short—think Roberto Clemente, Magic Johnson—the natural inclination is to wonder what might have been.

Kobe's basketball career was far in his rearview mirror when he stepped into that helicopter. He wasn't going to score any more points or win any more championships. But for him, it was still blue skies ahead. His full potential was just being unveiled.

How many documentaries might he have produced, books might he have written? Would his daughter Gianna have become the next great Bryant on the court, a star in college, the WNBA, the Olympics? Would Kobe have become the major force in promoting women's basketball? What other challenges might he have taken on in his still relatively young life?

So many people who have reached out to me have said that they weren't even basketball fans, but they still felt this was a special person and a devastating loss to society.

Butler cried on TV about Kobe's death. Other prominent Lakers, like LeBron James and Shaquille O'Neal, poured their hearts out about his tragic ending. Some far more removed from Kobe said that it was the first time they had ever cried over the death of someone they didn't know personally.

Perhaps the most intense public instance of tears streaming down a face in Kobe's memory came at his memorial service at Staples Center on February 24.

The date, 2/24, was picked because Kobe wore No. 24, Gianna No. 2.

The Lakers received approximately 100,000 requests to attend. They managed to stretch the building to full capacity to accommodate 20,000 people.

I've been to many, many arenas for big events, but never one like this. There were no cheers as I entered with my son, Alan, certainly no yells of "MVP! MVP!" as usually greeted Kobe.

Just dead silence.

His widow, Vanessa, gave a poignant speech. Beyoncé, Alicia Keys, and Christina Aguilera performed.

But the most memorable moment came when Michael Jordan spoke.

From the moment Kobe first put on a uniform, he wanted to be like Mike. Whenever he was around MJ, he peppered him with questions about the game, constantly called him, even in the middle of the night, and emulated him in so many ways.

Jordan admitted it got to be annoying.

But then, he began to appreciate Kobe's dedication, determination, and work ethic. He began to regard Kobe as a "little brother."

He began to love him.

It all came out at Staples Center, tears flowing from Jordan's eyes in an emotional display matched in public only by the shooting death of his own father.

"When Kobe died," Jordan said, "a piece of me died."

Since the tragedy, Kobe has remained firmly lodged in the hearts and minds of the Lakers. They dedicated every victory to him, often wore his signature Nike shoes and the special black jerseys he helped design, and broke every huddle with one word in unison: "Mamba!"

Some players on other teams also continue to bring his name and his memory up at pivotal moments in their own lives. As do athletes in other sports and other walks of life.

It sometimes seems like the whole world knew him, and knows the magnitude of what has been lost.

—Steve Springer
December 2020

1 Showtime

The name came from The Horn, a Santa Monica nightclub.

Starting back in the early 1960s, it would begin its nightly shows, staged in an intimate setting in a room holding about 150 patrons, by dimming the lights. A singer stationed at one of the tables would stand up and sing, "It's Showtime." A second singer would join him and then a third.

It was the kickoff of a full night of entertainment for the wealthy, hip crowd that filled the encircling booths.

One regular in the audience was a young playboy, a rising star in the real-estate market who never forgot the lessons he learned in those enjoyable nights at The Horn about attracting customers, inspiring loyalty among them, and generating energy and involvement.

Jerry Buss applied those lessons when he bought the Lakers nearly two decades later.

Buss didn't invent the synergy between athletes and Hollywood. That went back as far as big-time professional sports in the city.

Bob Hope and Bing Crosby were investors in the Los Angeles Rams football team.

Another pro football club, the Los Angeles Dons of the All-America Football Conference, was named for actor Don Ameche, one of the team's owners.

When the Dodgers came west, Walter O'Malley wasn't looking for investors. But he was in search of star attractions. So he made sure the box seats were filled with recognizable faces, from Cary Grant to Danny Kaye. When Tommy Lasorda was manager, Frank Sinatra was a frequent visitor to his office.

Hollywood Stars Night—a chance for celebrities to put on a Dodgers uniform and live out their baseball fantasies in a pregame exhibition—was one of the team's most popular events.

Doris Day was the most recognizable Lakers fan in the early days at the Sports Arena, the Jack Nicholson of her time.

Owner Bob Short was thrilled to have her, recognizing that she added credibility and class to his operation.

Only Jack Kent Cooke—among L.A. owners—had the nerve to turn his back on Hollywood.

He took Day off the comp list and then trashed the list altogether.

"We didn't need it," Cooke said. "We were *selling* seats."

Nicholson, however, hung in there. He didn't want comps. He was happy to pay his own way and thus avoid any obligation to the team.

But when Buss took control, the Hollywood snub was over. He understood that filling the courtside seats with famous faces would draw in the general public to fill the other seats.

Being in the entertainment capital of the world, Buss knew the value of celebrities and realized before any of his fellow owners that a natural bond existed between entertainment and sports.

What movie star hadn't imagined themselves in a real-life role as a star athlete? And what athlete wouldn't love a screen career when their playing days are over?

Bringing in the stars, however, was only the beginning of Buss' master plan.

Thinking of the cheerleaders he watched at USC football games, he created his own rooting squad, calling them the Laker Girls.

Incorporating his love of music, Buss brought in a live band.

From The Horn, he took the name to describe his unique approach to basketball: *Showtime*.

First Pick

Take Magic Johnson if he's available in the draft? Was there ever a better example of a no-brainer?

In retrospect, no, of course not.

But at the time, there were those in the Lakers organization who had their doubts.

Honestly.

Nobody will fess up to being in that group now. Jerry West, then a Lakers consultant, was supposed to have expressed his support for Sidney Moncrief, though he won't say so now.

Remember, the Lakers already had a good point guard in Norm Nixon, considered one of the league's rising stars.

Remember, the 6'3" Moncrief from the University of Arkansas was the prototypical shooting guard.

Remember, nobody had ever seen a 6'8" player like Johnson at point guard. Yes, he had done some wonderful things in college, but this was the pros, and he didn't have a great outside shot nor impressive jumping ability.

So yes, some—admittedly not the visionaries—questioned the choice.

Although the draft would not be held until after Buss had officially bought the Lakers from Cooke, the latter was still in charge when the team won a coin flip to decide who had the No. 1 choice.

So Cooke made the decision.

"There was some thought among my counselors that Sidney Moncrief might have been the better choice," Cooke said. "Never any question in my mind. I said to my counselors, 'I don't give a damn what you say. It's going to be Magic Johnson.'"

Cooke got no argument from Jerry Buss.

But he knew that the entertainment could not be limited to the sideline. It had to be evident on the court as well.

No plodding players for Buss. No half-court offense. No sleep-inducing style.

He wanted a flash-and-dash team, a fast-breaking, high-energy squad that could not only win, but do so in a crowd-pleasing manner.

Wanting it is one thing, getting it quite another.

Buss would need a maestro to orchestrate his grand scheme, a ringmaster who also possessed the talent to be the consummate player.

Where could he find such a multitalented athlete? He got lucky in that regard.

The Lakers went into the 1979 Draft with the No. 1 pick in hand.

And sitting there at the top of the list was Earvin Johnson, the 6'8" sophomore from Michigan State coming off an NCAA championship game victory over Larry Bird–led Indiana State.

Magic was just what the doctor—Dr. Buss—ordered.

Magic-Bird

Finally.

After Magic Johnson and Larry Bird faced each other in the 1979 NCAA Tournament championship game—Johnson playing for Michigan State and Bird for Indiana State—fans waited with agonizing anticipation for what they hoped would be sequel after sequel at the pro level.

The appeal was obvious, and it explains why—to this day—that 1979 game remains basketball's highest-rated game, college or pro, ever.

As NBA players, Magic and Bird were not only two of the most talented men to ever play the game, but their rivalry also matched Lakers versus Celtics, West versus East, Tinseltown versus Beantown, Black versus White, and extrovert versus introvert.

Magic guarding Bird at the Forum in 1984 during one of their many Finals matchups.

Johnson had come to symbolize the glitter and glamour of L.A. while Bird seemed to represent the blue-collar work ethic of Boston.

It was, of course, an illusion. Johnson was no more a product of Hollywood than Bird was of the tough New England winters. Both men were Midwestern born and raised.

Imagine if the draft had been reversed. If Bird had gone to the Lakers, with his blond hair, fair complexion, and consummate passing skills, he would have been portrayed as a slick surfer in sneakers. If Johnson had gone to Boston, his die-hard attitude and bruising rebounding style would have been viewed as the epitome of hard-hitting East Coast basketball.

But image is a staple of sports, and so Magic and Bird were locked into their public personas.

All that was needed to instill new appeal and interest in a league, sadly deficient in both as the 1980s dawned, was for Magic and Bird to meet in the NBA Finals.

It took a while because the timing was off. The Lakers reached the Finals in 1980. But with Dr. J, Julius Erving, leading the way, Philadelphia had become a powerhouse in the East and knocked off Boston in the Eastern Conference Finals that season.

A year later it was the Celtics who prevailed and the Lakers who stumbled. With Johnson recovering from a knee injury that forced him to miss a huge chunk of the season, L.A. was knocked out in the first round.

The Lakers got back to the Finals in each of the following two seasons, but again it was Philadelphia coming out of the East.

Then, in 1984, the dream matchup occurred. For the first time in 15 years, the Lakers and Celtics would battle for the NBA title.

It figured to be a fierce, competitive Finals and no one, regardless of loyalty, could later argue it had turned out to be anything less.

The series went seven games, each one a mini classic.

Game 1: The Migraine

Kareem Abdul-Jabbar, prone to such headaches, was stricken by one on the eve of the first game.

He missed the team bus to the arena and the pregame meeting. But Abdul-Jabbar calmed Pat Riley's fears that he'd miss the game as well, telling his coach by phone, "I'll be there. Just give me a couple of hours to rest in a quiet place."

That cleared Abdul-Jabbar's head enough to allow him to take the court. And once he did, it was the Celtics who had the headache as Abdul-Jabbar got 32 points in 35 minutes along with eight rebounds, five assists, two blocked shots and two steals to lead the Lakers to a 115–109 victory.

Game 2: The Lost Pass

It came with 18 seconds to play and the Lakers leading by two.

It was thrown by James Worthy under the Celtics' basket and intended for Byron Scott.

Instead, it was intercepted by Gerald Henderson, who softly laid the ball into the hoop to tie the game. When Magic Johnson was late passing the ball to Bob McAdoo in the closing seconds, the game went into overtime where Boston clinched a 124–121 victory.

Game 3: The Sissies

The Lakers in general and Johnson in particular took out their frustration about fumbling away Game 2 by blasting Boston 137–104 in Game 3. Johnson recorded a triple double with 14 points, 21 assists, and 11 rebounds.

When it was over, Bird referred to his teammates as "sissies."

The *Los Angeles Herald-Examiner* crowned Worthy the Finals MVP a bit prematurely.

Now, it was the Celtics' turn to be angry.

"You guys have already written us off," Boston's Dennis Johnson told the L.A. media. "Why even bother going on with the series?"

Game 4: The Clothesline

There was no such thing as a flagrant foul back then, but if there was, this would have been Exhibit A.

With the Lakers' Kurt Rambis on the end of a fast break, the Celtics' Kevin McHale, running at full speed, wrapped one arm around Rambis' neck and threw him to the hardwood.

The foul was so dramatic that, over three decades later, it is still a favorite film clip for highlight reels and arena big-screens.

Riley called McHale's takedown "thuggery."

But rather than becoming inspired by the play, the Lakers again collapsed at the end. They blew a five-point lead with less than a minute to play, Johnson had the ball knocked away near the finish of regulation time, and he and Worthy each missed two free throws in overtime. The Celtics won 129–125 to even the series.

Game 5: The Sauna

Warm temperatures and Boston are not usually linked. But they were in nearly every sentence describing this game, with the temperature at 97 degrees inside Boston Garden, an arena without air conditioning, on the night of a rare heat wave in the city.

The Lakers wilted—a bad thing when it didn't refer to Chamberlain—losing 121–103.

Game 6: The Allegation

After the Lakers forced a seventh game by winning 119–108 at the Forum, the ugliness on the court in previous games turned into ugly words and accusations.

"[Commissioner] David Stern told one of the fans, a man in an elevator, that the league needed a seventh game because the NBA needs the money," Bird said. "Well, he got his wish."

Was Bird saying the alleged statement by Stern, which was never proven, affected the outcome of the game?

"You never know," Bird said.

He also angered the Lakers by warning them to bring hard hats to Boston Garden for Game 7 because Celtics fans might pose a physical threat.

Game 7: Same Old Lakers Heartbreak

Once again, in their eighth try, they came tantalizingly, agonizingly close to beating Boston for the championship.

Once again it slipped away—not because of leprechauns, or curses, or dead spots in the green parquet floor—but because of the Lakers' ineptness.

The Celtics were leading by eight with just under two minutes to play, but the Lakers cut it to three with 1:15 to go.

Then once again, the magic disappeared. Johnson twice lost the ball in those final ticks of the clock, and the Lakers lost the game 111–102, and with it the series.

Afterward, Johnson spent more than 50 minutes in the shower, but it would take a lot more than that to wash away the sting of this defeat.

3 The Shaq/Kobe Dynasty

As the calendar turned to July 1996 and the gates opened for the stampede of free agents, Shaquille O'Neal didn't budge. Orlando, he insisted, was still his "first option."

Lakers vice president Jerry West is a nervous wreck in the best of circumstances. In this case, sitting in his Forum office with a big hole in the middle—having traded his only quality center, Vlade Divac, to the Hornets for Kobe Bryant—the man who once earned a living making baskets had been reduced to a basket case.

The Lakers offered O'Neal $98 million over seven years. Orlando—able to go as high as it wanted because O'Neal was still its player—merely matched the offer. West shed more bodies, gained more cap space, and upped the potential deal to $121 million. The Magic countered at $115 million. That offer was actually better than the Lakers' because Florida doesn't have a state income tax.

West flew to Atlanta to get O'Neal's answer. While waiting for him in a hotel room, West joked that he would jump out the window if O'Neal said no.

That was a joke, right?

Not to worry. O'Neal said yes.

West had earned the nickname "Mr. Clutch" all over again.

He found less flattering words whispered about him in the wake of the signing such as "tampering." Some found it hard to believe West would have traded away Divac without being assured by the O'Neal camp that he was coming west.

West said the comments were "very, very distasteful," and took "a horrible toll" on him.

As for Buss, he had lived up to his reputation as a superb poker player, throwing away a good hand that included Divac only to pull a pair of kings: Shaq and Kobe.

The reaction by some other teams to the big money being tossed around in the summer of 1996 was less than euphoric.

"Anyone who thinks all of this is good for the NBA," Pistons coach Doug Collins said, "has to have a screw loose."

But anyone who thought the Lakers had an instant dynasty was simply wrong. The coronation took awhile. Four years to be exact. The Lakers made it as far as the second round in the 1997 playoffs—the first for O'Neal and Bryant in tandem—before being eliminated. They were swept out in the third round by Utah in 1998 and by San Antonio in the second round in 1999.

It was sometimes a rough learning curve for Bryant, who was still only 18 when he played his first game in Purple and Gold.

Not that he was easily discouraged. Or ever discouraged, for that matter.

Bryant ignored the criticism, smiled at the pressure, and continued to exude confidence— at least on the surface—despite some early struggles on the court.

The biggest criticism was that he refused to share the ball. "There are times he still likes to go one on five," teammate Nick Van Exel said.

O'Neal didn't have to say anything. He just stood in the middle and glared when Bryant refused to pass him the ball.

The most blatant example of Bryant's perceived selfishness came in the elimination game against the Jazz in the 1997 playoffs.

In the closing seconds of regulation play and then on three occasions in the overtime period, Bryant fired up shots from beyond the three-point arc.

All four were airballs.

In Year Four of Shaq/Kobe, it appeared the Lakers were going to fall short again, even though they were playing their first season under Phil Jackson. Facing Portland in the Western Conference finals, the Lakers found themselves down by 15, trailing 75–60 in the fourth quarter of Game 7 at the Staples Center.

And then, they shot the lights out, turning out the lights on the Trail Blazers' season.

The Lakers outscored Portland 15–0 in just over 10 minutes to tie the game and went on to win 89–84.

The most memorable image from that comeback, the biggest ever in a Game 7, was of O'Neal. After he dunked Bryant's lob pass to give the Lakers an 85–79 lead with 40 seconds left, he opened his eyes and his mouth as wide as if he'd just seen a ghost, raising the index finger on each hand high in the air as he lumbered down the court like a 325-pound child.

Portland, on the other hand, couldn't find the basket. After shooting 50 percent from the floor through the first three quarters, the Trail Blazers hit just 5-of-23 (22 percent) in the final period.

Said Bryant after the final buzzer: "This is what makes champions."

It sure made champions of the Lakers. Not only did they go on to beat Indiana in six games in the NBA Finals, but they also subsequently defeated the 76ers in five games the season after, and swept the Nets the season after that to complete a three-peat.

Could anyone stop Shaq and Kobe?

Only two players could do that.

Shaq and Kobe.

Kareem

In the eyes of so many, Michael Jordan is the greatest basketball player who ever lived. His six championships validate that claim.

Never mind the fact that the Celtics' Bill Russell nearly doubled that total with 11 championships, including an incredible eight in a row and was player/coach for the final two titles.

The passage of 40 years since Russell's last championship seems to have dimmed the memories and curtailed the enthusiasm for calling him the greatest ever.

But what about Kareem Abdul-Jabbar? He, too, won six NBA championships, five with the Lakers and one with the Bucks.

Plus, thanks to the skyhook—the greatest offensive weapon ever unleashed on the NBA—he is the league's all-time leading scorer with 38,387 points.

Yet his six titles are rarely mentioned along with Jordan's, almost as if they never happened.

Adding the collegiate record of the two players gives Abdul-Jabbar a decided edge.

While Jordan won only one NCAA championship at North Carolina during his three seasons there, Abdul-Jabbar, then Lew Alcindor, won titles all three years he was eligible to do so at UCLA. Undoubtedly, he would have won a fourth championship if freshmen had been eligible to play for the varsity back then.

In Alcindor's years as a Bruin, UCLA was 88–2.

He was such a dominating college player that dunking was briefly outlawed because of him.

Surely one of the reasons Abdul-Jabbar does not have more supporters is his personality. Aloof, sometimes surly in public, and

Kareem raises up to sink another of his patented skyhooks.

often uncommunicative with reporters, he was known to be down-right hostile at times when asked for an autograph.

Expected by the league to be available for interviews in the locker room after games, Abdul-Jabbar would sometimes pull out a book and read it at his stall while his teammates were granting interviews, sending the message that he didn't want to be bothered.

Yet when he did speak, he came across as both analytical and articulate, a man equally comfortable discussing Black history and jazz as he was talking basketball.

That's not surprising considering Abdul-Jabbar is the author of 15 books, several of them bestsellers, and produced a feature-length documentary from his book, *On the Shoulders of Giants: My Journey Through the Harlem Renaissance*.

He could even pull off a good one-liner on occasion.

During the 1988 playoffs, a reporter asked Abdul-Jabbar if his defending champion Lakers could repeat. Replied Abdul-Jabbar, "We're the only ones who can."

His image was softened by his appearance in the 1980 comedy *Airplane!* in which he played himself.

But in person, he remained shy and distant.

Abdul-Jabbar even had his ups and downs with teammates. He was generally liked and admired, forever the team captain, but in the early '80s, the always-ready-to-run Showtime Lakers sometimes resented the idea of often shifting to a half-court game to take advantage of Abdul-Jabbar's dominating presence in the middle.

Several players even carried matchbooks with the words "Trade Kareem" on them.

When he was diagnosed with chronic myeloid leukemia in 2009, Abdul-Jabbar received a genuine outpouring of sympathy and support from the Lakers organization and the L.A. fans he had entertained for so long.

But as always seemed to be case, he squandered some of that goodwill in 2011 when he publicly complained about not having a statue at Staples Center that would immortalize him beside Magic Johnson, Jerry West, and Chick Hearn.

His statue, depicting him about to release his legendary skyhook, was erected a year later. More than any of the personal aspects of his life, that is his lasting image—a man who could reasonably be called the best ever about to launch his signature shot, that was, without a doubt, the greatest ever.

5 LeBron Takes His Talents to the Lakers

If free agency is the Wild West, then the commissioner, Adam Silver, is the sheriff, bringing law and order to the proceedings, turning chaos into conformity.

He is following the example of his predecessor, David Stern, who, in the frantic days prior to Shaquille O'Neal's entry into the free-agent market, announced that any public comment by any member of any front office on O'Neal prior to the start of the negotiating period would result in a $1 million fine levied against his team.

No contact is allowed between a team and the player or his representatives, no calls, no texts, no emails, no third-party interventions before a set day and time.

As that time approaches, general managers sometimes act like power forwards boxing out under the rim, getting ready for the ball to drop while making sure that no one gets ahead of them.

In the looming battle for free agents, that's not really necessary because the available big-name players, along with their lawyers, agents, and advisors, already know which team or teams they are interested in, who has the most attractive roster, the required cap space, the best coach, the most lucrative endorsement opportunities, and is located in one of the most appealing cities.

In the summer of 2018, Magic Johnson knew that the player at the top of his most-wanted list had placed his Lakers at or near the top of his own most-wanted list.

LeBron James and the Lakers seemed like a natural fit. The team's brand was steeped in tradition, glamour, and a spotlight befitting the best player in the game. There were also other factors that added to the apparent inevitability of his choice. He and his wife, Savannah, had bought a home in Brentwood. He had set up his production company, SpringHill Entertainment, in West L.A. and was already churning out shows, and he wanted his oldest son, 13-year-old LeBron Jr., or Bronny, to play his high school ball in the L.A. area.

Despite all these encouraging signs, Johnson wasn't taking any chances. He was determined to be first in line.

Yet when the free-agency period officially began at 9:00 PM Pacific time on June 30 with Laker general manager Rob Pelinka and other members of the front office gathered to start making phone calls to players and agents, Johnson was a no-show.

Had he forgotten? Was he overconfident? Decided his staff could handle it?

None of the above. Instead, Johnson had decided to do what had always worked best for him as a player, going one-on-one in pursuit of his goal. Living close to James, Johnson simply got in his car and drove to James' house, arriving an hour before the magic moment when the free-agency gates would swing open.

So Johnson sat in his car and waited. He wasn't about to jump the gun. He had already learned the penalty for that on several occasions. The Lakers had been fined $500,000 by the league after Pelinka had a conversation with free-agent-to-be Paul George's agent following Johnson's appearance on the late-night show *Jimmy Kimmel Live!*, during which he kidded that he would wink at

October 18, 2018: In his first game as a Laker, LeBron James rises up for an uncontested dunk against the Portland Trail Blazers in the first half at Moda Center. (Jaime Valdez/USA TODAY Sports)

George if he ran into him, as if to say, we got a deal, right? And the Lakers had subsequently been fined $50,000 when Johnson publicly praised the talent of Milwaukee's Giannis Antetokounmpo.

Finally, a few minutes before 9:00, Johnson got out of his car and slowly made his way to James' $23 million home.

When the basketball superstar opened the door, the smiles were mutual and the dialogue was easy and natural. This wasn't a case of an executive trying to woo a player. It was two transplanted Midwesterners swapping stories on the sport they love.

In his new role, Johnson liked to call himself "the closer," but in this case, he didn't have to make his case or wave a big check. James had done his homework. He knew the strengths and weaknesses of every player on the Laker roster and seemed ready to sign even if the team couldn't fortify the club with two former Southern California guys who might be available and willing to come, George and Kawhi Leonard.

Sure enough, 24 hours later, despite the fact that George had announced the night before that he was staying with the Thunder, Pelinka got a text from Rich Paul, James' agent, that read "Congrats," and was accompanied by an emoji of balloons.

The 33-year-old James had agreed to a four-year, $153.3 million contract with the Lakers.

This time, rather than burning their LeBron jerseys, most Cavalier fans hung on to them, a keepsake from a brief but glorious time in their city's history. Sure, they would have loved for James to stay, but he had come back, which few thought he would, and won a championship, which many doubted he could.

And in departing, he left an inspirational farewell gift: the I Promise School (IPS), a public elementary school in his hometown of Akron, Ohio, which is an institution whose mission is to help at-risk children succeed. I Promise's top donor is the LeBron James Family Foundation. Partnering with Akron Public Schools, the foundation has already put $2 million into I Promise. After making good on his promise to end Cleveland's long championship drought, James, through this school, has made good on a promise to enrich the area's future.

The switch to Purple and Gold was the third time he had changed uniforms as a pro. James joined the NBA straight out of St. Vincent–St. Mary High School, located in Akron. He didn't have very far to go since the Cleveland Cavaliers, the only NBA team in his state, had the first pick in the draft.

This 6'8", 250-pound man-child quickly proved equal to many of the established stars in the league, giving the Cavaliers something they have never had before: credibility.

But even though the team was vastly improved with James on the court, reaching the playoffs for five straight seasons, including a trip to the NBA Finals, he ached to win a championship. When he saw his chance to do so by partnering with Dwyane Wade and Chris Bosh in Miami, he took the leap, leaving behind angry fans who publicly burned LeBron jerseys.

After winning two titles with the Heat, James stunned the basketball world by returning to Cleveland and promising its fans a championship, something the city hadn't celebrated in any sport in more than a half century. He made good on his promise, beating a Warriors team that had won a record 73 regular-season games in the 2016 NBA Finals and doing so by coming back from a three-games-to-one deficit.

In L.A., he faced a new challenge. When George elected to stay in Oklahoma City and Leonard got his wish to get out of San Antonio, but was traded to Toronto, James knew he would get no star power to help him from the outside.

But he's got his family around him in an exciting city with endless opportunities, his burgeoning entertainment company right down the freeway, and is playing for a storied franchise in the perfect place for a man with one foot in the NBA and the other in Hollywood.

As for recruiting reinforcements in order to continue leading a championship contender, James knows that he has made L.A. a prime destination for future free agents. After all, when they come calling, they will now be greeted by two closers, Magic and LeBron, who have 18 NBA Finals appearances and eight championships between them.

Who would walk away from that?

6 The Logo

All you need to know about Jerry West is that he is the figure on the NBA logo.

There could be no greater tribute.

It's been over four decades since he hung up his uniform. Yet despite the subsequent heroics of Magic, MJ, and Kobe, West's name is still in the conversation about the greatest guard to ever play the game.

A brilliant scorer, ferocious defender, and one of the greatest clutch shooters ever, West could do everything on a basketball court.

Need someone to drive from 35 feet out to the basket in less than three seconds to win an NBA Finals game?

West did that against the Celtics in 1962.

Need someone to make a 55-foot shot in the final seconds to tie up another Finals game?

West did that too, against the Knicks in 1970.

Yet typical of his career, West's team lost both of those series.

If he had taken that 55-foot shot after the creation of the three-point rule in 1979, it would have won the game.

Instead, New York earned the victory in overtime.

That was West. He could pile up enough numbers to become a legend, but he was never able to pile up championships.

Not as a player.

In his years in a Lakers uniform, the team reached the NBA Finals nine times, but won only once, in 1972 against the Knicks.

West piled up plenty of championships later, as the architect of one Lakers dynasty and the general manager and co-architect of another—along with Bill Sharman.

But as a player, he was stuck on teams that always came up short against Boston. Until Wilt Chamberlain arrived, West suffered from the absence of a big man to rival the Celtics' Bill Russell.

Even with Chamberlain as a teammate in his last Finals showdown against Boston in 1969, West lost when the big center went out with an injury during the closing minutes of Game 7.

Imagine if West had been fortunate enough to play with Kareem Abdul-Jabbar, Shaquille O'Neal, Pau Gasol, or LeBron James. West could have matched Magic, Kareem, or Kobe, ring for ring.

Unyielding even in the face of defeat, West was named NBA Finals MVP in that 1969 series, still the only player to ever win that award despite being on the losing side.

What drove West—even when the odds were against him—was an insatiable quest for perfection.

The Statue

Logos are sewed on uniforms or plastered on products. But for Lakers fans, there is a unique opportunity to see and touch a bigger-than-life logo frozen in time outside Staples Center. The Jerry West statue, 14 feet tall and weighing 1,500 pounds, was unveiled in 2011, taking its place along those of Magic Johnson and Chick Hearn; hockey immortal Wayne Gretzky; and boxing champion Oscar De La Hoya.

That quest was never realized, not in his mind, not even in the best of times.

In one game he had a quadruple double (44 points, 12 rebounds, 12 assists, and 10 blocked shots), getting his points by going 16–17 from the field and 12–12 from the free-throw line.

Perfection at last? Not a chance.

"Defensively, from a team standpoint, I didn't feel I played very well," West told *The National.* "Very rarely was I satisfied with how I played."

In the view of others, what more could you ask for?

You want numbers?

In his 14 seasons in the league, West scored 25, 192 career points, which was third all-time when he left the game. He averaged 27 points, 6.7 assists, and 5.8 rebounds. He shot 47.4 percent from the floor and 81.4 percent from the free-throw line.

They didn't keep track of steals and blocked shots in the NBA until West's last season, but observers at the time estimated that he was in double figures in steals in some games.

He earned the nickname "Mr. Clutch" by being at his best when the stakes were the highest. He averaged 29.1 points during the postseason, including 46.3 points during a six-game playoff series against the Baltimore Bullets in 1965, still the record for a postseason series.

You want defense?

"Players were told," former teammate "Hot Rod" Hundley said, "that if they were coming down the court with the ball in the middle on a three-on-one and West was the one [defender], the guy with the ball should shoot it. Because if he tried to pass it, West would get it and be going back the other way."

Columnist Jim Murray once said of West: "He had such great peripheral vision that he could see his own ears."

You want durability?

West played through injury after injury without hesitation. He broke his nose nine times during his career.

You want accomplishments?

West won a gold medal with the 1960 U.S. Olympic team as a co-captain of the squad and was named to the All-Star team in all 14 seasons he played.

Raised in Chelyan, West Virginia, West won a state title with East Bank High School then went on to West Virginia University where he was a two-time All-American. But he also experienced a crushing conclusion to his collegiate career that would prove to be a painful foreshadowing of his life in the pros.

During the 1959 NCAA Tournament, West averaged 32 points in leading the Mountaineers to the championship game only to lose to California by a single point, 71–70.

At age 12, West was devastated by the death of his brother, David, in the Korean War. Perhaps that was the root of the torment he always seemed to carry with him on the court and beyond.

In 1985, with West as general manager, the Lakers finally defeated the hated Celtics in the NBA Finals.

When the Lakers' parade was staged several days later, West chose not to be in it.

Asked why, West, on what should have been one of the happiest days of his professional life, said, "If I was in that parade, the fans would all be cheering me. And if in the draft coming up in the next few days I make a pick that is unpopular, they will all be booing me.

"I don't need the cheers. I don't need the boos."

If he had been listening, West would have discovered that the cheers far and away drowned out the boos during his illustrious career.

7 At Last

In West Virginia, former Lakers coach and general manager Fred Schaus was doing yard work.

In Los Angeles, Tommy Hawkins was in his living room in his Lakers uniform 16 years after he had retired.

The two men had drastically different reactions to the fact that their team was in Boston Garden on the verge of exorcising the demons that had long haunted the Purple and Gold by finally beating the Celtics in the NBA Finals on the club's ninth try.

Too tense to watch, Schaus was outside his home pulling up weeds, his wife coming out again and again with score updates.

And all the while, Schaus kept yanking up those weeds, perhaps imagining one with the head of Red Auerbach and another with that of Bill Russell.

In L.A., when the game had reached the fourth quarter, Hawkins had pulled that old No. 33 out of his closet and not only put it on, but also added the shoes and socks.

And then, he sat down on his couch, all alone, and waited for a moment he had thought might never come.

Certainly no one thought it would come 14 days earlier when the Celtics shellacked the Lakers 148–114 in Game 1; Boston's point total still stands as an NBA Finals record.

But prior to Game 2, Lakers coach Pat Riley, known for his locker room histrionics, came up with a virtuoso performance, evoking the fighting words of his late father, Lee, in their last conversation before Lee's death.

Whether or not his Knute Rockne impersonation was the key factor, Pat got the results he had sought: L.A. winning four of the next five games to clinch the title.

With Kareem Abdul-Jabbar getting 29 points, James Worthy adding 28, and Magic Johnson piling up a triple double (14 points, 14 assists, 10 rebounds), the Lakers beat the Celtics 111–100 in Game 6 for the championship, as sweet a victory as there ever was for the franchise.

Not only did the Lakers accomplish what so many of their predecessors had painfully failed to do, but they also did it on the green parquet floor, the first and only time an opposing team has celebrated clinching an NBA title on Boston's home court.

A year earlier, Celtics fans had rushed onto that same Boston Garden floor upon the conclusion of their team's victory against the Lakers in Game 7, deliriously screaming to the rafters. This time, they marched out of the arena as if they were leaving a funeral.

They would get no sympathy from Riley who had been extremely bitter after the loss to Boston in the 1984 Finals, especially after Red Auerbach—longtime Celtics coach, general manager, and Laker tormentor—had chortled, "What ever happened to that Laker dynasty I've been hearing so much about?"

In response, Riley pointed to the Celtics' "total lack of respect...for us as a team, not just that year, but every year. You would think that, somewhere along the line, we could have walked away with some dignity. But they wouldn't let us. They called us chokers.... You should let the defeated just lie there and wallow in their wounds by themselves.

"They are a proud team, but pride can be defined in different ways. One way is humility and being proud of your accomplishments, but not puffing yourself up and thinking you're better than everybody else. I think they are a proud team to the point of being arrogant and cocky, letting everybody know about it, and I think that's something that rubs every team in this league wrong. I think every team in this league gets more pleasure out of beating them than [beating] any other team...to me, they have no class at all."

In West Virginia when Game 6 ended, Schaus finally put down his rake to acknowledge a moment he never got to enjoy as a member of the organization.

"I enjoyed watching Red [Auerbach] walk out without that lit cigar," he said.

Jerry West, then the team's general manager, also watched at his home, studying his old nemesis as had Schaus.

"I loved the look on [Red's] face when he walked off," West said. "And I loved his comments afterward [that the best team had not won]. That was typical."

Hawkins was enjoying his own celebration.

"The past weighed heavily on me," he said. "There was a monkey on my back, just as there was with everyone else who ever played on the Lakers in that losing tradition…. When the Lakers walked out of Boston Garden with a victory, we were free at last, free at last."

Flying Under the Radar

He was Dr. J before Dr. J, MJ before MJ.

He was soaring above the hoop in an era when nearly everybody else still had their Converses planted firmly on the hardwood.

While others would settle for a set shot, Elgin Baylor would leave them in his wake, taking advantage of his ability to leap, hang, and maneuver around the hoop.

Add to that his sure-handed shooting touch, powerful rebounding skill, and brilliant passing ability, and the result was the consummate superstar, a man able to dominate a game and a league.

Before Wilt Chamberlain, it was Baylor who held the league's single-game scoring record with 71 points.

Baylor still holds the league's single-game scoring record for the NBA Finals with 61 points.

If he played today, he would be a multimillionaire and have a recurring role on *SportsCenter*, his every move glorified, highlighted, and emulated.

Everybody would "want to be like E.B."

"Elgin certainly didn't jump as high as Michael Jordan," teammate Tommy Hawkins told the *San Francisco Examiner*. "But he had the greatest variety of shots of anyone. He would take it in and hang and shoot from all these angles. Put spin on the ball. Elgin had incredible strength. He could post up Bill Russell. He could pass like Magic [Johnson] and dribble with the best guards in the league."

The New York Knicks' Dave DeBusschere called him "a marvel of the ages."

Unfortunately for Baylor, he came along in an age when the NBA was still a second-tier sport, lost in the shadow of Major-League Baseball and the NFL.

True aficionados of the game marveled at his athleticism, but there just weren't enough of them.

On the night Baylor scored his then-record 61 points—Game 5 of the 1962 NBA Finals against the Celtics at Boston Garden—the Celtics' Tom "Satch" Sanders was assigned the unenviable task of guarding Baylor.

"He was such an exceptional passer," Sanders said, "that we couldn't really double team him. Before the game, they'd tell me, 'Satch, you're on your own.' Which, to tell you the truth, did not exactly inspire me.

"Elgin did develop a left hand. People talk about his fabulous right hand, but, in one playoff game, two times in a row, he went

Zeke from Cabin Creek

While Baylor was pure entertainment on the court, he could also be quite entertaining to his teammates off the court.

Possessed with a great sense of humor, Baylor made it his mission to give each of his teammates a colorful nickname.

His most enduring was the moniker he slapped on Jerry West after seeing the rookie with deep rural roots arrive from West Virginia. Baylor tabbed him "Zeke from Cabin Creek."

West hated the name. And besides, he pointed out he wasn't really from Cabin Creek.

It didn't matter. Zeke from Cabin Creek was what Baylor decided on, and Zeke from Cabin Creek it would always be.

to his left. The party was over after that. You didn't know where to play him."

Or how to stop him. Baylor averaged 27.4 points (totaling 23,149) and 13.5 rebounds (11,463 in his career and most in team history). Despite standing only 6'5", he led the club in rebounding for seven straight seasons in a Hall of Fame career that stretched more than 14 years. He was an All-Star in 11 of those seasons, standing out from the beginning by winning the Rookie of the Year Award for the 1958–59 season.

When the NBA named its 50 greatest players in 1996–97, the league's 50th anniversary season, Baylor's name was on that list.

Baylor—whose father named him for his prized possession, an Elgin watch—played his college ball at Seattle University.

He was selected No. 1 overall in the 1958 NBA Draft by the Minneapolis Lakers, even though he had only completed his junior year.

"If he had turned me down then," Lakers owner Bob Short said, "I would have been out of business. The club would have gone bankrupt."

Despite all his talent and having Jerry West as a teammate, Baylor never realized the ultimate goal of every player: winning a championship.

Always foiled by the dominating figure of Celtics center Bill Russell, Baylor was forever a bridesmaid.

And perhaps most painful of all was that Baylor—hobbled by weak knees, slowed by age, and disheartened by his inability to play at the unprecedented level he was accustomed to—retired nine games into the season of which he had always dreamed.

On November 5, 1971, the 37-year-old trendsetter announced he was leaving the game that had been his life.

That day, the Lakers beat the Baltimore Bullets 110–106. It was the first victory of their all-time record 33-game winning streak.

That 1971–72 team, without Baylor, would go on to win the championship he had long hungered for.

Technically, he was a member of that team. But in reality, he was long gone by the time the celebration had begun.

After a stint as an assistant coach, Baylor served as head coach of the New Orleans Jazz for nearly three seasons and then the general manager of the L.A. Clippers for 22 years.

He had little success in either position, leaving a new generation unaware of the brilliance that he once brought to the NBA.

But for those who were fortunate enough to see him play, Air Baylor will always be remembered as soaring as high as Air Jordan or any of the other aerial shows who came later. Elgin Baylor was a true pioneer in the evolution of the game.

9 The Announcement

It began as a routine medical test and ended as the greatest test of courage and resolve faced by one of the greatest players ever.

Magic Johnson was sitting in a Salt Lake City hotel room prior to a preseason game against the Jazz on October 25, 1991, when he learned via a phone call that he had a medical problem.

That alone didn't set off any alarms. After all, he had undergone major knee surgery a decade earlier and had collected all of the normal bumps and bruises that go along with a sport he had been playing nearly as long as he had been walking.

But Johnson was puzzled by the call, which came from team physician, Dr. Michael Mellman. Having looked at the results of a blood test Johnson had taken as part of a life-insurance physical tied to his new contract, Mellman was insisting Johnson return to L.A.

Immediately. Forget the game. Come home and come to my office *now.*

As he recalled in his book, *My Life,* some crazy ideas about all sorts of diseases flowed through Johnson's head as he gazed outside the window on the flight home.

Still, he wasn't prepared for what heard from Mellman a few hours later while sitting across from the doctor in his office, Johnson's agent, Lon Rosen, by his side.

Referring to the test results, Mellman, speaking in a somber but steady voice, told Johnson, "You tested positive for HIV, the virus that causes AIDS."

AIDS? The word sent Johnson into shock. Back then, the disease was relatively new to the general public, its existence identified in the U.S. only about a decade earlier. Most people thought it just affected homosexual men.

Most also thought HIV always led to AIDS (acquired immune deficiency syndrome).

That's what Johnson thought.

After hearing the stunning diagnosis, he thought first of his wife, Cookie, who was pregnant. Could she have contracted the disease? What about their unborn child? What about his career?

Mellman had no answers for him until additional tests were run.

In the meantime, Johnson faced what he said was the hardest thing he ever had to do: tell Cookie.

When he did, he started to say that he would understand if she wanted to leave him.

Before Johnson could even finish uttering the words, Cookie slapped him across the face. She didn't even want to discuss that option. She had waited to marry him since their undergraduate days at Michigan State, and they had finally taken the vows just over a month earlier.

Tests showed that neither Cookie nor the fetus had been affected by the HIV virus.

As for Johnson, he was told by Dr. David Ho, director of the Aaron Diamond AIDS Research Center in New York, that although Johnson had no AIDS-related diseases at that time, he shouldn't play basketball for at least the upcoming season.

"It's a judgment call," Ho said, "and my judgment is that you don't play."

Johnson decided to retire from the Lakers at age 32, the number he had worn on his jersey for so many years.

The press conference, announcing the end of his career, was held on November 7, 1991, at the Forum, the scene of so many moments of joy for Johnson.

Although the others around him wore looks of anguish and depression, Johnson remained upbeat as he spoke about his future beyond the Lakers.

"I plan on going on living for a long time, bugging you guys like I always have," Johnson told the hastily assembled media as his words carried across the nation and around the world. "So you'll see me around. I plan on being with the Lakers and the league and going on with my life.... I'm going to be a happy man.

"Sometimes we think only gay people can get it, or it's not going to happen to me. Here I am saying it can happen to everybody. Even me, Magic Johnson."

It was the only press conference in memory where reporters left with moist eyes, their professional obligations clashing with their emotions.

Back in a hallway connecting the Forum offices, Lakers owner Jerry Buss and retired center Kareem Abdul-Jabbar hugged in their mutual grief.

Johnson had spoken about beating HIV as if it were just another opponent, as if this disease came clothed in Celtics green.

Many around him felt he was in denial. They were convinced they would have to endure the pain of watching this man die in public.

If he could beat AIDS, he was truly a magic man.

Beat it Johnson did, although the disease remains in his blood to this day. But given cutting-edge medication and taking advantage of an ever-widening body of knowledge about HIV and methods of treatment, he has been able to live a full and fruitful life, becoming a highly successful businessman worth hundreds of millions of dollars.

Even Johnson's days of basketball glory were not over. In 1992 he enjoyed some of his most satisfying moments on the court, first by playing in the 1992 All-Star Game, which turned into a tribute to him. Johnson played 29 minutes, had a game-high 25 points, hit all three of his three-point shots, handed out nine assists, won the game's MVP Award, and was embraced by both his teammates and the players on the opposing East team.

As exhilarating as that day was, an even greater high awaited him later in the year. What Johnson refers to as "winnin' time" has always been his most significant time. Having already won at the high school, college, and pro levels, he won at yet another level in 1992. The Dream Team member added an Olympic gold medal to his already overflowing treasure chest.

Still, the fact that he had not been able to retire from the NBA on his own terms tormented Johnson.

He attempted two comebacks with the Lakers. Following the Olympics, the first one was quickly aborted when a cut on his arm during a preseason game elicited obvious alarm from those around him.

Karl Malone, a teammate on the 1992 Olympic squad, publicly expressed fears about playing against Johnson.

"Maybe I shouldn't have said that," Malone later conceded, "but I meant what I said. You're young, [and] you don't know a lot of information on it."

"Magic can score anytime he wants," a player's wife had said sarcastically when Johnson attempted his comeback. "All he has to do is cut his wrist before driving down the lane, and no one will dare touch him."

After it was definitively established by doctors that the disease could not be spread through the open air, Johnson came back again at age 36. But by then, he had been gone for too long, and his body no longer allowed him to make his trademark magical moves.

He played in 32 (there's that number again) regular-season games in 1996 and the first round of playoffs that ended with the Lakers' early elimination. When the season was done, so was he.

But an even more important role—that of being a visible symbol of hope for others diagnosed HIV positive, of being living proof that life does go on—continues for Johnson to this day.

Nearly three decades after many wondered if they'd ever see him again, it's hard to miss him. After basketball, Johnson created a new cable network, bought a piece of the L.A. Dodgers, maintained his role as an ESPN basketball analyst, stayed involved in the business community, and, in 2017, was named president of basketball operations for the Lakers by team president Jeanie Buss. Johnson has also continued to be the most visible spokesman for those battling, researching, treating, or trying to prevent HIV/AIDS.

Johnson says he's both a blessing and a curse in the HIV/AIDS community. He's a blessing because the fact that the disease is barely detectable in his blood and he can live a full life gives other sufferers hope they can do the same. But he feels he's also a curse because others see him and figure they too can have a risky lifestyle and survive.

10 The Shaq-Kobe Feud

Magic Johnson and Kareem Abdul-Jabbar weren't always on the same page.

On the court, Johnson, one of the great point guards of all time, wanted to run, run, run, fast-breaking his way to title after title. Abdul-Jabbar, possessor of the skyhook—the greatest offensive weapon ever—was better served unleashing it in a half-court game.

With his bubbly personality, wide smile, and ingratiating charm, Johnson was embraced by Lakers fans. Abdul-Jabbar? Not so much. His shy and aloof nature caused him to often keep the public at arm's length.

With these glaring differences, it would have been understandable for Johnson and Abdul-Jabbar to feud. But they were smart enough to understand they needed each other. Together, they could make basketball history, while going their separate ways would shatter a dynasty.

Shaquille O'Neal and Kobe Bryant also had glaring differences. O'Neal thought Bryant was selfish, unwilling to share the ball, and more interested in putting up shots than pulling in teammates.

Bryant thought O'Neal was selfish in his own way, unwilling to put in the time and effort to stay in shape so that he could be his best.

Ultimately, they let their feelings overwhelm common sense.

With Jerry West—someone to whom both men would have listened—gone from the organization, it was up to coach Phil Jackson and the players to try to keep the lid on the feud.

Rick Fox tried. At one point, he told O'Neal and Bryant, "I love you both, but you are tearing us apart, tearing down everything we have built. Don't you see what you are doing?"

Things got even uglier after Bryant was charged with sexual assault in Colorado, a charge that was later dismissed.

When Bryant missed the beginning of training camp prior to the 2003–04 season, O'Neal responded by saying, "The full team is here."

Later in that exhibition season, when O'Neal suggested Bryant pass the ball more, Bryant reacted by saying, "I know how to play my guard spot. He can worry about the low post."

O'Neal responded by saying: "Just ask Karl [Malone] and Gary [Payton] why they came here. One person. Not two. One. Period. So he's right. I'm not telling him how to play his position. I'm telling him how to play team ball."

Bryant wasn't the only one with whom O'Neal was having issues. While he wasn't openly feuding with owner Jerry Buss, O'Neal was certainly simmering over the issue of a contract extension.

His feelings came out during an exhibition game against the Warriors in Honolulu. With Buss courtside, O'Neal scored on a rim-rattling dunk, then exclaimed loud enough for the Lakers owner to hear him, "Now you gonna pay me?"

Not what O'Neal wanted.

After originally signing a seven-year, $121-million contract with the Lakers in 1996, he was given a three-year, $88.5-million extension to 2006.

Since O'Neal would make $30 million in the final year of that contract, that's how much he wanted from Buss annually for two additional years, taking him to 2008.

Buss countered at $22 million per season.

Impasse.

On Super Bowl Sunday of 2004, Buss went to Bryant's home, presumably for more than just chips and salsa.

When Buss subsequently decided to get rid of both O'Neal and Jackson after the Lakers lost to the Pistons in the NBA Finals in five games, Bryant got blamed for it. Supposedly, Bryant, who was a free agent at season's end, had demanded Buss get rid of O'Neal and Jackson before he would agree to stay.

In reality, what weighed most heavily on Buss were O'Neal's weight and his financial demands. More than 50 pounds overweight at somewhere above 375 pounds, O'Neal would be 36 in the final year of the extension he was demanding.

"Shaq is the most dominant player in the game," Buss said. "There's no question about that. The question is, if I wait until he isn't the most dominant player, will I get adequate return on him? Maybe I'm trading him too soon. Maybe I'm trading him too late. I don't know."

Buss rolled the dice after the 2004 Finals, sending O'Neal to the Miami Heat for Lamar Odom, Caron Butler, Brian Grant, and two draft picks.

Buss had doubts whether his coach would be as effective now that the Lakers were in a rebuilding mode, so he cut Jackson loose as well.

Bryant seriously flirted with leaving the Lakers to go down the hall at Staples Center to the Clippers, but ultimately, he stayed.

Still, for the last man standing, the road back to the top was fraught with uncertainty.

11 Born at the Back of the Line

The history of America is filled with inspirational stories of men and women who clawed their way to fame and fortune from humble beginnings.

But few have ever had a steeper climb than Jerry Hatten Buss.

At the age of four, his concept of success was a hot meal, a roaring fire, and a roof over his head.

Living with his single mom, Jessie, in Evanston, Wyoming, during the latter stages of the Great Depression, Buss would stand in a bread line at mealtime, waiting for his gunnysack to be filled with nourishment.

When he became older, Buss would scrounge the neighborhood for material—from old newspapers to telephone books—to burn to provide warmth for him and his mother.

Buss' spirit wasn't diminished by his circumstances. It was the only life he had ever known.

"Standing in line with a gunnysack to get canned food doesn't sound like you were living the life of luxury," he said, "but at the time, it doesn't necessarily hit you that way."

Still, Buss' horizons were widened considerably at the age of nine when Jesse, in search of better employment opportunities, took him to Los Angeles where she got a job as an accountant at a greeting-card company.

The bleak life of Evanston had been replaced with sun and surf.

It didn't last. With a chance to remarry, Jessie returned with Jerry to Wyoming three years later.

But Jerry had seen paradise and he was determined to return.

This time, he and his mother settled in Kemmerer, Wyoming, where Jessie's new husband, Cecil Brown, opened a plumbing business.

By the time Jerry was a teenager, Brown decided his stepson—along with his own son—needed to contribute to the household by helping out in his business.

Brown's idea of helping out was getting up at 4:30 AM—even in the frigid winter when the temperatures often dropped well below zero—to dig ditches where Brown had pipes to lay.

"After three or four hours of this," Buss said, "we were supposed to go to school."

That motivated him to look for other forms of income. Quickly.

He got a job at the Kemmerer Hotel, where his titles included bell boy, shoeshine boy, and janitor. Salary: $2 a day.

He also started a mail-order business, buying and selling stamps. Profit: might be $2 a month.

Finally, Buss had enough. He left his home, school, job, stamps, and bid a less-than-fond farewell to those backbreaking ditches. At age 15 after his junior year, he went to work as a gandy dancer.

That's not as glamorous as it might sound. Not even close.

A gandy dancer is a railroad worker whose job might entail laying, stabilizing, or performing maintenance on the tracks. It's tough work just getting to the site because the gandy dancer has to use small handcars driven by pumping a metal lever up and down.

Buss found himself working for "Mile-A-Day" Mike McGuire, whose goal was just that: laying a mile of track a day.

That could mean a 14-hour shift. In comparison, dawn in those ditches back home didn't seem so tough.

"After three months," Buss remembered, "I said, 'Wait. W-a-a-i-i-t a minute. This is not the right life. Go back and finish your education.'"

And that's what he did, putting miles between himself and Mile-A-Day Mike.

But while Buss was happy to be back in school for his senior year, he wasn't about to put himself back under the thumb of his stepfather. So he worked out an arrangement to not only get his old job back at the Kemmerer Hotel, but also a room there as part of the deal.

It was a bad deal as far as Kemmerer High School science teacher Walt Garrett was concerned. He saw potential in young Buss, college potential, but knew it would only be realized through classroom discipline and good study habits.

So Garrett convinced Buss to move in with him, even though all Garrett could offer was a cot to sleep on.

"I still had no idea what I wanted to do with my life," Buss said. "All I really wanted was to get out of my house, have my own house, my car, and lead my own life."

Garrett knew Buss loved card games, so he would play with his student for hours in his apartment, always steering the conversation back to chemistry.

Buss became so knowledgeable that Garrett turned one of his classes over to his young roommate and let Buss become the teacher of his fellow students.

Still, he wasn't sold on college until spotting a job notice in the post office. The government was looking for chemists, but one year of college was required.

"I thought, 'Well, hell, one year can't be much,'" Buss said.

With Garrett's enthusiastic support, Buss earned a scholarship to the University of Wyoming in Laramie.

One year turned into two. By then, Buss had found a good reason to stick around: JoAnn Mueller.

The two met in Buss' sophomore year and married before Buss' graduation.

He hadn't, however, forgotten his first love: L.A. He packed up their belongings after finishing college and headed west with his new bride soon to follow.

They would be starting a new life with few worldly possessions.

And those few possessions would be dramatically reduced to zero before they even started. On Buss' trip to Los Angeles, someone broke into his car—parked in front of a relative's house—and stole everything inside.

This time, he wasn't even left with a gunnysack.

But Buss still had his sharp mind, was still well schooled in science, and still possessed an aptitude for crunching numbers.

With a wife, and kids soon to follow, Buss didn't need Walt Garrett to motivate him to fulfill his potential. Buss enrolled at USC, earned a PhD in physical chemistry, and wound up doing aerospace work at the Douglas Aircraft Company.

It was there that he met Frank Mariani, and the two forged a plan to increase their income (Buss was making $700 a month, Mariani $500).

Buss set aside $83.33 a month with the goal of amassing $1,000 in a year. Mariani did the same. A few other investors were rounded up, and, after a year of saving, the group bought their first piece of property in 1959, a 14-unit apartment building in West Los Angeles for $105,000.

They had formed a no-frills company called Cal-Ven, Inc. No frills meant no maintenance men. Buss and Mariani did all the necessary repairs themselves.

In a way, Buss was back to gandy dancing. Except instead of dealing with spikes and rails, he was working on plumbing and air conditioning.

One night, he and Mariani were doing repairs in one of their units when they found a big hole in the wall.

Neither man knew what to plug it with, but exhausted after a long day of aerospace engineering, they weren't interested in spending much time looking for a conventional solution.

So Buss took off his T-shirt, rolled it into a ball, and stuffed it into the hole which they then plastered and painted over.

Such problems didn't last long. As Buss and Mariani bought and sold properties, expanding their holdings and growing their assets, they soon found themselves on the cusp of a great real-estate boom.

By then, Buss could afford to buy the best shirts in the best stores in Beverly Hills and hire top-notch contractors and subcontractors.

By 1967, at the age of 33, he had made his first million.

By 1979, he and Mariani had a real-estate empire that stretched over three states—California, Nevada, and Arizona—and was worth approximately $350 million.

It was wealth beyond his dreams, but Jerry Buss also had other dreams.

12 Going West

Having decided to head for the West Coast, the Lakers decided to take along the pride of West Virginia, a sharpshooter named Jerry West.

After the Cincinnati Royals made Oscar Robertson the No. 1 pick in the 1960 Draft, the Lakers used the second pick to take West, who averaged 24.8 points in college, and was also the Most Outstanding Player in the 1959 NCAA Tournament.

The Lakers signed West to a two-year contract worth an estimated $24,000. Despite his credentials, that was a lot of money in those days for an untested rookie.

"I am sure that Jerry would have been in a position after his first year of pro basketball," Lakers general manager Lou Mohs told the *Los Angeles Times,* "to do a pretty good job of dickering with us for his second-year salary. That's why we've signed him to a two-year contract."

West's transition from college to the pros was eased by the fact his college coach came along with him.

The team hired Fred Schaus to be the first coach of the *Los Angeles* Lakers, but Schaus later revealed it wasn't a slam dunk that he was going to accept the position even with his prize pupil on the roster.

"Had I known the real financial condition of the franchise," Schaus later said, "I'm not sure I would have taken the job. It was nearly bankrupt."

Nor was there a pot of gold waiting for the team in its new home. While the Dodgers got a downtown parade upon their arrival from Brooklyn and drew record crowds in their temporary home, the Los Angeles Memorial Coliseum, the Lakers came in largely under the radar.

Attracting fans in Los Angeles proved to be no easier than it had been in Minneapolis.

Much like in their former city, the Lakers lacked a permanent home court for their first season in L.A., and that didn't help.

The Lakers were supposed to play in the Los Angeles Sports Arena where the seating capacity for basketball at that time was 14,500. It was a gleaming new edifice that hosted the 1960 Democratic National Convention a few months earlier. John F. Kennedy had won his party's presidential nomination on the floor of that arena.

But the popular Sports Arena had already committed to other events before the Lakers' arrival. As a result, the team couldn't play all of their regular-season home games there.

So, the Lakers also played in the L.A. State (now California State University, Los Angeles) gym (capacity 5,200) and on the stage of the Shrine Auditorium for a *playoff* game against the Detroit Pistons in front of a capacity crowd of 3,705.

That game nearly resulted in a disaster when the Pistons' Walter Dukes, chasing a loose ball, fell off the stage into the orchestra pit. Fortunately, he wasn't seriously hurt.

The Lakers even played a preseason game against the Boston Celtics at Anaheim High School.

Morgantown Lakers

It was common in the NBA in those days to play neutral-site games. Taking advantage of their unique position as the NBA's only West Coast team, the Lakers tried other markets.

They played two games in San Francisco and two in Portland.

With both Schaus and West as attractions, the Lakers also played one game in Morgantown, West Virginia.

Lakers and Celtics in a high school gym? Well, it was only the preseason, one might say. But fans didn't exactly rush to see the two teams once the regular season began. For one game at the Sports Arena, Lakers vs. Celtics drew a crowd of 9,224.

Mohs and several players had come out in the summertime to drum up interest for Los Angeles' newest team, but obviously it was a drumbeat to which few paid attention.

The Lakers' first-ever regular-season game in Los Angeles—against the New York Knicks—on October 24, 1960, drew 4,008.

The next night, the two teams played again and the attendance dropped to 3,375.

The Lakers wound up with a total regular-season attendance for that first season of 151,344, averaging 5,045 for 30 games.

It was Minneapolis all over again.

13 The Zen Master

Born and raised in sparsely populated areas often buffeted by harsh weather, he came from a spartan background. But Phil Jackson found success in the three largest cities in the country: New York, Chicago, and Los Angeles—the epitome of cosmopolitan living.

Because of his father, a Pentecostal minister, and his mother, an evangelist, Jackson was denied popular forms of entertainment such as TV or movies while growing up. Yet he wound up in L.A.—the entertainment capital of the world—living with Jeanie Buss, who combined business acumen with a glamorous persona that once included a spread in *Playboy*.

Although he was a tough, intense, intelligent power forward, Jackson never made it into the starting lineup after being drafted by the Knicks. Yet he went on to become one of the biggest names in NBA history as a coach with a record 11 championships, including a trio of three-peats.

Becoming a coach, he entered a field where the rules and practices had been standardized over decades of trial and error. But he brought his own unique approach: part Eastern philosophy, which earned him the nickname "Zen Master"; part Native American spiritualism, gleaned from his early surroundings; and part old-school innovation.

The latter came from Tex Winter, master of the triangle offense, a system that emphasizes teamwork over individual play. It's a refreshing approach in an age when, too often, the goal is making *SportsCenter*'s Top 10 plays.

If there is a knock on Jackson—hard to justify with a man owning as many championship rings as he does—it is that he has always had the talent to win. In Chicago, it was Michael Jordan and Scottie Pippen; in L.A., Shaquille O'Neal, Kobe Bryant, and Pau Gasol.

The counterargument is that coaching big egos requires a special touch possessed by only a few. Getting a great star to also be a good teammate can be the ultimate coaching challenge.

Some coaches are best at building dynasties, and some are best at rebuilding disasters.

"I would probably have no capability of absorbing a 60-defeat season as a coach," Jackson said. "It would be a foreign experience. My whole career, even as a player, has been on winning basketball clubs, and it just seems to have been a part of the makeup of what's been given me…. Some people can make fun of it, or some people can have a good time with it, or some people can resent it. It's just what it is."

Jackson played in the NBA for a dozen years—10 of those with the Knicks, averaging 6.7 points and 4.3 rebounds.

The hardest season for Jackson was 1969–70 because he didn't play that year, sitting out due to a back injury. What made it especially painful was that the Knicks won the title that season.

He couldn't have appreciated it at the time, but it was the best thing that could have happened to Jackson. Knicks coach Red Holzman—determined not to lose Jackson mentally as well as physically—asked him to work with team photographer George Kalinsky on a photo journal of the season and also to take notes on every game for the coaching staff.

Analyzing the action from the sideline rather than on the court gave Jackson a new perspective of the game. That brought back memories of his high school and college days when he coached youth baseball. But just because he started thinking like a coach again didn't mean he was ready to seriously consider it as an option once his playing days were done. That would come later. But at least the idea had been planted in his head.

What he had lost in the 1969–70 season, he made up for three years later when the Knicks won the title with Jackson back in uniform.

What he had gained in 1969–70 in terms of a coaching experience, he expanded when he joined the Nets, serving as a dual player/assistant coach in the first of his two seasons with New Jersey.

Jackson retired after the 1979–80 season. Was his basketball life over? At one point, he had imagined that was the way it was going to be.

"When we were playing together," former Knicks guard Mike Riordan told the *Los Angeles Times,* "Phil said to me, 'Mike, you're the type of guy who can't live without basketball. When you're finished [playing] basketball, you're such a junkie, you'll have to be coaching in basketball the rest of your life…that's not for me.'"

But it was.

After Jackson retired, he stayed on one more season as strictly an assistant with the Nets.

He coached in Puerto Rico in a summer league and in the Continental Basketball Association, where he spent five seasons with the Albany Patroons and won a championship.

In 1987, Jackson joined the Bulls as an assistant and became head coach two years later when Doug Collins was fired.

Winning six NBA titles in Chicago over a stretch of eight seasons, he was already a legend when he came to L.A.

14 The Torch Is Passed

The Lakers have spent much of the last four decades as championship contenders. They won titles, experienced droughts, then reinvented themselves. From Magic and Kareem to Kobe and Shaq to Kobe and Pau, there was always a new force for the league to reckon with.

And it wasn't just players. As general manager, Bill Sharman assembled the linchpins of the first dynasty before handing off to Jerry West, who eventually handed off to Mitch Kupchak. Paul Westhead coached the team that won the first championship of the Showtime era, followed by Pat Riley, who coached four championship teams before Phil Jackson added five more titles.

But always, there was one constant in this cavalcade of excellence, Jerry Buss.

The winningest owner in sports history with 10 titles, he still wasn't satisfied. He wanted the championship parades to continue under the Buss banner even after he was gone. So, he trained his kids—Jeanie, Jim, Johnny, Janie, Jesse, and Joey—to take over the family business when the time came.

That time was 2013. Jerry died of cancer in February, leaving in place a chain of command. Jeanie, a member of the league's Board of Governors, would serve as president and run the business side; Jim would handle the basketball operation; Janie, the charity wing of the organization; Johnny, corporate development; Jesse, scouting; and Joey, the D-Fenders, the team's entry in the NBA Development League.

Putting a strain on this chain was tension at the top between Jeanie and Jim. It first erupted a few months before Jerry's death.

In his first season replacing Jackson, Mike Brown had coached the Lakers to a 41–25 record and into the second round of the playoffs, where they were eliminated in five games by the Thunder. When the Lakers started out the following season 1–4, Jim abruptly pulled the plug, firing Brown, the man he himself had hired.

Did Jim panic? It seemed so to many. Jackson, observing from the comfort of retirement, told Jeanie that it was not fair to any coach to be given the hook that quickly, before his team had a chance to jell. But there was a feeling in the organization that Jerry didn't have much time left, so there was an urgency to speed up the rebuilding process.

Jeanie figured there was no way Jackson would be included in that process because her father and her brother seemed committed to resurrecting the fast-breaking Showtime style that had proven so successful in the Magic era,

So Jeanie was surprised when Jim came to her office only hours after the Brown firing, told her he felt bad he had made the mistake of hiring Brown in the first place and expressed guilt for needlessly costing the organization money by signing the coach to a contract the club was going to have to honor.

Then Jim shocked Jeanie by asking if she thought he and Jackson could work well together if the Lakers were to hire him back. Jim and Jackson had had an arms-length relationship in the past.

Jeanie replied that it was a discussion Jim needed to have with Jackson himself. But Jeanie did say that, following knee replacement surgery, Jackson had his energy and focus back.

When Jim called Jackson the next day, a Saturday, the former Laker coach invited Jim to come to his house to talk.

When Jim arrived, Kupchak was with him. To both Jackson and Jeanie, that was a sign the meeting was the result of genuine interest in hiring Jackson rather than just a PR stunt designed to satisfy Laker fans that the organization had reached out to the former coach before picking someone else.

To Jackson, it seemed the meeting went well. He told Jim and Kupchak that he wanted to speak to his doctors and his family before seriously considering the possibility of a return. They said they would also be talking to two other candidates, Mike D'Antoni and former Laker coach Mike Dunleavy. Jackson, Jim, and Kupchak agreed on a follow-up call Monday morning.

As the weekend wore on, Jackson warmed more and more to the idea of resuming the role that had made him a dominant figure in the game for over two decades. He met with his longtime assistant coach, Kurt Rambis, to plot a game plan for the Lakers moving forward. Jackson also called his agent, Todd Musburger, in Chicago and told him to fly to L.A. for a Monday morning meeting with the Lakers.

When Jackson sat down to dinner Sunday night in the house he shared with Jeanie, he was wearing his Laker Hawaiian shirt, an item he'd saved from the years the team held its preseason training camp on the islands. When he was still coaching, Jackson often wore it around the house.

Jeanie smiled. She knew that, mentally, he was already back at work.

Until the house phone rang at 11:30 that night with Jackson and Jeanie already in bed asleep. When Jackson picked it up,

Kupchak was on the line with a stunning message. The Lakers had just hired D'Antoni.

"They came to you," said an outraged Jeanie after Jackson hung up. "You were not looking for the job. I cannot believe this."

She was numb as her cellphone started ringing nonstop and constant media speculation began to buzz around her head the next morning from all sorts of outlets.

Two days after Kupchak's call, Jeanie was working out at her gym when the emotional dam burst. She suddenly began crying hysterically. Her reaction was so jarring that she was advised to go home.

In her book, *Laker Girl,* she wrote, "The sequence of events—Phil almost coming back and then being told somebody else was better for the job—practically destroyed me.... It felt like I had been stabbed in the back. It was a betrayal. I felt that I got played. I was devastated."

Jeanie said that any progress she and her brother had made in their relationship "evaporated" with that call.

Jeanie didn't dwell on the situation for long, however, because all her attention soon went back to her father as his condition worsened.

When he died, Jeanie and her siblings were faced with the harsh reality of taking over a team that had less potential than any of those overseen by her father. Like Jackson, many of the Lakers' established players were gone, leaving a youthful core lacking in experience, and a battle-worn Kobe Bryant whose expiration date was on the horizon.

At first, Jeanie expressed full confidence that her generation would be able to successfully carry on her father's legacy. While her personal relationship with Jim seemed permanently shattered, she was determined to make their professional relationship work. "This is the way my father wanted us to run the team," she said, "and I would never go against his wishes."

But her father's first wish was for a return to the dominating days of old, and that possibility was nowhere in sight.

15 The Family Feud Erupts

In the first full season after Jerry Buss passed away, the Lakers won only 27 games, the club's lowest total since the 1959–60 season, the team's last in Minneapolis. And it went downhill from there with 21 and then 17 wins in the following two seasons.

The pressure was on Jim who, along with Kupchak, was running the basketball side. Anxious to buy himself some time, Jim, at an organizational meeting in early 2014, made a promise that came back to haunt him.

"If this doesn't work in three or four years," he said, reiterating his remarks to the *L.A. Times*, "if we're not back on top—and the definition of top means contending for the Western Conference [title], contending for a championship—then I will step down because that means I have failed."

Jeanie held Jim to his promise. Three years after his announcement, Jeanie removed Jim from his position and fired Kupchak.

It wasn't just the seemingly endless losing and an absence from the playoffs—once almost as automatic for the Lakers as the regular season—that was about to stretch to four seasons. In their entire history going back to 1949, the team had never missed the playoffs for more than two consecutive seasons and that had happened only once.

What also frustrated Jeanie was the team's inability to sign major free agents, or, in some cases, to even get them to listen to an offer.

The Lakers couldn't convince Carmelo Anthony or LaMarcus Aldridge to put on the Purple and Gold, Aldridge after two visits to meet with team officials. They couldn't even get an audience with Kevin Durant to make a presentation.

When they did sign free agents, they paid amounts that raised eyebrows all over the league for lesser talent. Forward Luol Deng and center Timofey Mozgov both got four-year contracts, Deng for $72 million, Mozgov for $64 million. The Mozgov deal was named the fourth-worst signing over the previous five years by Bleacher Report.

Jeanie said at the time that she questioned the thought process of her front office.

Still trying to respect the wishes of her father, she made one last-ditch attempt to keep her brother in his front-office position by reaching out to an old familiar face, Magic Johnson. In February of 2017, she brought him on board as an advisor.

But it soon became obvious that wasn't going to accomplish anything because Jim ignored Johnson, keeping him out of the loop when possible transactions were being explored.

It was only then that Jeanie brought down the ax, removing Jim and replacing him with Johnson.

The brothers Buss did not go quietly. Three days after Jim was relieved of his duties, Johnny called a meeting of the Lakers shareholders. On the agenda was a list of four proposed members for the team's board of directors moving forward—Jim; Johnny; Dan Beckerman, the president and CEO of Anschutz Entertainment; and Romie Chaudhari, a property investor.

Two names were noticeably absent: Jeanie, a member of the NBA's Board of Governors, and Joey Buss, the Lakers' alternate governor. According to the team's corporate bylaws, the organization's controlling owner must be on the board of directors. It was a not-so-subtle way of trying to kick Jeanie out.

She wasn't the only one protesting the takeover bid. Beckerman issued a statement saying he fully supported Jeanie. Chaudhari said he never agreed to be on the board and had no desire to get involved in a family feud.

Jeanie responded by having her attorney file a motion in L.A. County Superior Court for a temporary restraining order. Jeanie didn't hold back in a declaration that was filed along with the motion.

"Jim has already proven," she wrote, "to be completely unfit even in an executive vice president of basketball operations role… I could not allow the damage being done to the franchise over the past few years to continue."

She added that leaving Jim in his role would have caused "irreversible damage to the Lakers team and brand."

A hearing was scheduled, but the brothers surrendered the night before, postponing the shareholders meeting. Subsequently, they signed an agreement that made Jeanie a permanent member of the board and controlling owner for life.

It was a long, ugly, painful battle, but ultimately Jerry Buss got the outcome he wanted. His oldest daughter, whom he had first introduced into the family business when she was just 19 and a student at USC by making her the general manager of the Los Angeles Strings of World Team Tennis, was going to run the show. And by her side would be Magic Johnson, the "son" Jerry always trusted most back to the time when he, too, was 19 and poised to run the show on the court, the most entertaining show basketball had ever known.

16 Relevant Again, Like Magic

When the bell rang in Jerry Buss' Bel Air home in the summer of 1979, his 17-year-old daughter, Jeanie, ran to answer it. When she swung the door open, she found herself bathed in the glowing smile radiating from the face of another teenager, 19-year-old Earvin Johnson, better known as "Magic."

Jeanie broke into a smile as well. She was happy to greet the hottest young star in the basketball galaxy, the player who had led his Michigan State team to the NCAA championship only a few months earlier, beating Larry Bird and his Indiana State squad in front of the largest TV audience to ever watch a basketball game.

But now, Johnson was exchanging his Spartan Green and White for the Purple and Gold of the Lakers, the team Jeanie's father had just purchased. It was Jack Kent Cooke who had drafted Johnson and signed him to a contract, but Jerry Buss, as the new owner, would now control Johnson's career.

He had been brought to the house, along with his agent, Dr. Charles Tucker, by Lakers general manager Bill Sharman to meet Buss. When he heard the bell ring, Buss, upstairs getting dressed, told Jeanie to welcome the group and supply them with drinks.

Johnson opted for a "soda pop."

Jeanie told Johnson how excited she was that he would be joining the Lakers. Johnson's answer caused the smile to quickly fade from her face. He said he was only planning on staying for the length of his contract because, having been raised in East Lansing, Michigan, he was a lifelong fan of the Pistons and had always dreamed of playing for them.

Jeanie excused herself and ran up the stairs to tell her father the shocking news.

Jerry just smiled and said, "The first time he plays at the Forum, he is never going to want to leave."

Jerry was, of course, right. So right that, 38 years later, Johnson was still in town, still devoted to the Lakers, and willing to take over as president of basketball operations after Jeanie had relieved her brother of his duties.

While her decision to make the switch was almost universally cheered in and around the organization, there were understandable doubts about Johnson's ability to make the massive changes necessary to return the Lakers to greatness.

While he was a master at orchestrating the personnel on the court in his years as the team's point guard—arguably the best ever in league history at that position—orchestrating in a suit and tie had not been anywhere near as successful for Johnson.

Admittedly, there wasn't much of a body of work to judge him by. At the end of the 1993–94 season, with the Lakers 10 games under .500, head coach Randy Pfund was fired. Assistant coach Bill Bertka filled in for two games while Buss convinced a reluctant Johnson to finish out the season as coach. His heart wasn't in it, but he couldn't turn down Buss, who was like a second father to him. So Johnson coached the last 16 games, going 5–11.

Del Harris was brought in for the following season.

Johnson went from the bench back to his courtside seat, where he remained the team's No. 1 fan.

He cut his financial ties to the Lakers when he sold his 4.5 percent ownership stake in the club in 2010. Two years later, when Guggenheim Partners purchased another L.A. team, the Dodgers, from Frank McCourt for $2.1 billion, Johnson contributed $50 million for a new ownership stake.

But he never lost interest in his old club, publicly cheering for the Lakers while never hesitant to publicly criticize Jim Buss after Jerry Buss died when he felt the younger Buss was making moves that were prolonging the team's dismal performances season after season.

"Jim is trying to do it himself and trying to prove to everybody that this was the right decision that [his] dad gave [him] the reins," said Johnson on ESPN. "He's not consulting anybody that can help him achieve his goals and dreams to win an NBA championship."

December 18, 2017: The new Lakers leadership, Magic Johnson, Jeanie Buss, and Rob Pelinka, pose with Kobe Bryant during a halftime ceremony retiring Bryant's uniform numbers at Staples Center. (Robert Hanashiro/USA TODAY Sports)

In a tweet, Johnson wrote, "If I was Jim Buss, I would travel [with the Lakers]. Jim needs to find out what the issues are with the team. He can't do that from an office."

Before his death, Jerry Buss had wistfully spoken of bypassing his son and bringing in Johnson to run the club with Jeanie, knowing Johnson was more qualified to attract and sign talent, but Jerry just could not bring himself to pull the trigger and do that to his son.

But Jeanie could and did, calling on the man who had been a loyal friend and supporter since their teen years, Johnson had to show he was up to the challenge. It wasn't just going to be a matter of flashing his smile, picking out a few superstars, giving them his signature hug, and assuring them that he'd take care of them. There were agents to deal with, salary caps to analyze, trades to consider, and the draft to deal with.

Jeanie had also wanted to bring Kobe Bryant on board in some capacity, but he wasn't willing to give up his new endeavor as a film producer. Still, the Lakers got some of his input secondhand by hiring his agent, Rob Pelinka, to replace Mitch Kupchak as general manager.

With Pelinka on board, the Lakers began to slash their salaries to create space under the cap, getting rid of Timofey Mozgov, D'Angelo Russell, Jordan Clarkson, and Larry Nance Jr.

They wanted Paul George and hoped there was some way to get Kawhi Leonard, who wanted out of San Antonio.

But most of all, the Lakers were zeroing in on their prime target: LeBron.

What if it didn't work out? What if, despite Johnson's reputation, his confidence, and his charisma, ultimately, there was no magic there?

He told reporters the outcome was assured. He said that, having battled Larry Bird, won an NCAA championship, and played in nine NBA Finals, he wasn't worried about his ability to oversee the rebuilding of a faded franchise.

"I'm Magic Johnson," he declared.

And then he went a step further, taking the same precarious path that had doomed his predecessor, Jim Buss. If after two years, Johnson said, he had not signed any superstar free agents, he would resign.

Not a chance. Nearly four decades after he first announced he'd be leaving for Detroit, nearly three decades after being told he might have a fatal illness, nearly a decade after severing his financial ties to the team, Magic was back.

Here to stay, in control, in command, wheeling and dealing like it was the 1980s all over again.

17 Pelinka Adds the Missing Link

Jeanie Buss needed to draft two new Laker teammates. And she had her eye on two of the greatest to ever wear the Purple and Gold.

Those two had been legends on the court, but she wanted them in the front office, signing the next generation of legends.

The year was 2017. Frustrated after her team had failed to qualify for the postseason for the previous three seasons, a Laker record for futility, Buss took drastic action, removing her brother Jim from his position of executive vice president, basketball operations, and replacing him with Magic Johnson.

But Buss still had a second position to fill, having also fired Mitch Kupchak, the team's general manager.

Buss would have loved to replace him with Kobe Bryant.

Bryant, however, having already launched the next phase of his life by getting involved in producing animated films and children's books, as well as promoting women's basketball at all levels, wasn't interested in returning to his old franchise.

So Buss decided to settle for the next best thing. She hired Rob Pelinka to be the general manager. Although he had no front-office experience, Pelinka was, as Bryant's longtime agent, very familiar with the process of attracting free agents, signing players, and balancing cap space.

Pelinka himself had played at the highest level of college basketball as a member of Michigan's 1989 NCAA national championship squad. He was also a member of two other Wolverine

General manager Rob Pelinka (left) and head coach Frank Vogel (right) introduce superstar Anthony Davis as the newest Laker on Saturday, July 13, 2019. (AP Images/Damian Dovarganes)

teams that reached the Final Four and became known as the Fab Five.

Through Pelinka, Jeanie would be able to hear Bryant's opinions on the state of the Lakers.

Johnson and Pelinka didn't know each very well, but it soon became obvious that their approach to their new positions would be very different. Johnson is not a nine-to-five guy. He has far-flung business investments, is a minority owner of the Dodgers, and travels extensively, while also carving out time to interact with present and former NBA players. Tying him to a desk would require a pair of handcuffs.

To Pelinka, however, an office is central to his job. It was in his agent days and is now with the Lakers. Hunched over a screen, his cellphone an extension of his hand, he is in his element.

Those divergent lifestyles soon became a point of contention between the two men.

It was Johnson who closed the deal to get LeBron James in the summer of 2018. But he and others in the organization knew that James, then 34, could not bring the Lakers back to contention by himself. While George Mikan was the dominating force in the creation of the first Laker dynasty, back in Minneapolis, he had four Hall of Famers playing alongside him. Wilt Chamberlain teamed with Jerry West to lead the Lakers to their first championship in L.A. Johnson partnered with Kareem Abdul-Jabbar to lead the Showtime Lakers. Kobe and Shaq had each other for the next championship run.

Who could serve as James' second in command? It seemed like he definitely needed help after a groin injury limited him to only 55 games in his first season in Purple and Gold, the fewest in his 17 NBA seasons.

James knew just who he wanted: Anthony Davis.

But before that could happen, Johnson jumped ship.

It happened suddenly and totally unexpectedly, just before the Lakers' last game of the 2018–19 season, James' first in L.A.

The cheers and excitement that had greeted him when he arrived in town were long gone. Nothing had changed. The Lakers again exited before the postseason had begun, extending the team's playoff drought to a franchise-record six seasons. Johnson and Pelinka had been running the show together for two-and-a-half of those seasons.

Johnson's resignation came out of nowhere, with no hint about what was about to happen.

As the normal pregame meeting between coach Luke Walton and the media broke up and Walton headed back into his locker room, Johnson, standing off to the side, stepped forward. Some media members had already shut off their recorders and closed their notebooks, about to depart for a quick meal in the media dining room when Johnson started talking.

His first words brought everybody scurrying back.

He was quitting.

"I want to go back to having fun," said Johnson, seeming to fight back tears. "I want to go back to being who I was before taking on this job. We're halfway there with LeBron… I think this [coming] summer, with that other star coming in, whoever is going to bring him in, I think this team is really going to be in position to contend for a championship."

It was hard to begrudge him for wanting to ease off on his heavy workload, as he was about to turn 60. The criticism came from the fact that he didn't inform Buss—whom he has known since both were teens—about his decision in advance, and that she learned about it only after he went public.

Especially since Johnson had met with Buss the day before in her office for a three-hour planning session about possible moves to make in the off-season.

Johnson said he didn't know he would decide to resign until that morning.

"Somebody is going to have to tell my boss," he said in his farewell remarks, "because I know she's going to be sick. But I knew I couldn't face her face-to-face and tell her."

When she learned what had happened, Buss' response came by tweet: "Earvin, I loved working side by side with you. You've brought us a long way. We will continue the journey. We love you."

The direction of the journey was certain. Making sure it ended with Davis in a Laker uniform was now in the hands of Pelinka alone. The training wheels had long since been removed. It would be his job, and his alone, to get the last big piece of the puzzle.

Just 25 at the time, Davis definitely qualified as the missing link. A 6'10", 253-pounder out of Kentucky, he had spent all seven of his NBA seasons in New Orleans, where he averaged a double-double (23.7 points, 10.5 rebounds) along with 2.4 blocks per game. He was a big man with a soft touch, able to score either inside the key or outside the arc.

All he was missing was a ring, and he wasn't willing to wait until the Pelicans put enough talent around him to make his championship dream a reality.

So, in January 2019, he requested a trade. His desired landing spot seemed obvious, especially since he and James have the same agent, Rich Paul.

Pelicans general manager Dell Demps wasn't ready to grant Davis his wish. Before Johnson left, he reached out to Demps, but the Pelican official never entered into serious negotiations with him. Demps wouldn't even discuss a deal with Pelinka.

The impasse was finally broken when Demps was fired, replaced by David Griffin, the former GM of the Cleveland Cavaliers.

The Lakers knew that they would have to pay a steep price in terms of both players and draft choices in order to get Davis. But they were determined to hang on to Kyle Kuzma, the two-year veteran envisioned as the third scoring alternative on a team featuring James and Davis.

Ultimately, the Pelicans agreed, settling on three players (guard Lonzo Ball, forward Brandon Ingram, and swingman Josh Hart) and three first-round draft choices, including the No. 4 pick in the 2019 draft, along with the option of swapping picks with the Lakers in a future draft.

It was validation for both Pelinka and Buss that hiring him to be the general manager was the right choice.

When Johnson walked out, he pointed a finger at Pelinka as a main cause of his departure. But, undeterred by the criticism, not even content to kick back and bask in the glory of the championship that resulted from the acquisition of Davis, Pelinka kept his foot on the gas, wheeling and dealing into the off-season to strengthen his team for a title defense. Pelinka signed Montrezl Harrell and Wes Matthews, and traded for Dennis Schroder.

At that point, even before Pelinka subsequently resigned Kentavious Caldwell-Pope and signed Marc Gasol, Johnson tweeted, "Can we say Executive of the Year?"

Kobe would be proud.

18 A Magical Night

The 1980 NBA Finals may have been won at LAX.

At least psychologically.

When the Lakers arrived at the airport to board a plane bound for Philadelphia for Game 6, they were not a happy group despite the fact they were leading the series 3–2.

Imprinted in their minds was the sight from the previous night of center Kareem Abdul-Jabbar limping so badly that he had to be supported by trainer Jack Curran as he left the Forum court.

Abdul-Jabbar had severely sprained his left ankle and was out of Game 6, and perhaps, if it was necessary, Game 7 as well.

In their front court, the 76ers had Darryl "Chocolate Thunder" Dawkins at center, Caldwell Jones at power forward, and at the other forward spot, some guy named Dr. J. On the bench was forward Bobby Jones, a shutdown defender.

Who could fill the middle for the Lakers, playing center against that imposing group?

In those days before teams used charters, the Lakers would routinely buy out all—or at least whatever was available—in first class on commercial flights, giving them some semblance of privacy.

Each had their favorite seats on those flights, and Abdul-Jabbar's was the first aisle seat on the left side facing the bulkhead.

When the Lakers boarded the plane that day, Earvin Johnson confidently marched down the aisle and took the seat of the missing captain.

"Never fear," he said to his teammates, "E.J. is here."

What the players would soon learn was that coach Paul Westhead had asked Johnson to start at center in Game 6.

Johnson's reaction? "I'd love to. I played some center in high school."

Dose of reality: this wasn't high school.

He may have been called Magic, but he was still a 20-year-old kid in his first trip to the NBA Finals, trying to make an unlikely leap from the backcourt to the frontcourt in the national spotlight on 24 hours notice.

In Philadelphia many believed Abdul-Jabbar would show up. There was a feeling the Lakers were going to pull the same Willis Reed emotional move that had sunk them a decade earlier—Abdul-Jabbar limping onto the court at game time.

Prime Time

Nothing better illustrates how far the NBA has come than that night in Philadelphia. Anyone outside of L.A. or Philly wishing to watch that Game 6—one of the most entertaining Finals games ever—had to wait until 11:30 PM to see a tape-delayed version on CBS.

In those days, network executives wouldn't dare preempt prime-time television to show a "minor sport" like basketball.

It was Johnson and archrival Larry Bird who soon proved that the NBA was indeed ready for prime time.

There were reports of Kareem sightings at the Philly airport all day.

But when it came time for tip-off at the Spectrum, out came Johnson to match up against Dawkins.

"Philadelphia thinks this game is already over," Johnson told his teammates in the locker room before the game, "but we can use that to our advantage. We can beat them because they'll have a problem matching up against us. But only if we go into this game believing we can win."

Johnson didn't really play center that night. He played everywhere. As he had predicted, the 76ers, used to dealing with an Abdul-Jabbar type in the frontcourt, were ill-prepared for a player like Johnson, who provided a movable feast for himself and his teammates.

"We moved around so fast," Johnson said, "they didn't have a chance to react."

Need someone to whip no-look passes to teammates? Bang the boards? Provide scoring? Be inspirational?

Johnson did it all in leading the Lakers to a series-clinching 123–107 victory.

He certainly didn't do it alone. Forward Jamaal Wilkes scored 37 points, including 16 in the third quarter. Michael Cooper was suffocating on defense. Norm Nixon had nine assists despite playing with a dislocated left ring finger. Jim Chones took over the center position on defense, holding Dawkins to 14 points while also pulling down 10 rebounds.

But it was Johnson's stats that stood out above all the rest—42 points (14–23 from the field and 14–14 from the free-throw line), 15 rebounds and seven assists.

With champagne dripping from his hair in the locker room afterward, Jerry Buss, in his first year of ownership, said, "You don't know how long I've waited for this moment."

On the flight home, a reporter said to Johnson, "You played center, you played forward, you played guard. Do you want to write our stories for us, too?"

Johnson, flashing his trademark ear-to-ear grin, replied, "I know I could do that."

And who could doubt him? He was right. Never fear. E.J. was there.

19 From Clark Kent to Superman

When the Minneapolis Lakers arrived to play the New York Knicks one night at Madison Square Garden, the Lakers couldn't help but notice the huge marquee out front.

It read "Geo. Mikan vs. New York Knicks."

None of the players seemed to pay the sign much attention.

In the locker room, George Mikan, intent on getting ready, stripped off his clothes and began to put on his uniform. It was then that he noticed all of his teammates still sitting around in their street clothes.

He wanted to know what was going on.

"It's your name on the marquee," guard Slater Martin said. "It says you are playing the Knicks. So go out and play them."

After a good laugh, his teammates joined him, but the message was clear. In post–World War II America—where baseball was king, pro football was in the shadow of college football, and college basketball was also very popular—pro basketball was just a blip on sports' radar screen.

It seemed that only Mikan could grab the public's interest.

He did it by creating a role that would be emulated by one giant after another over the ensuing decades. He was basketball's first big man and the first in a line of centers who would lead the Lakers to title after title.

Before Shaq, before Kareem, before Wilt, there was George.

With glasses and his mild manner, he looked more like Clark Kent than Superman. But once it was tip-off time, he became a superstar.

Mikan combined the skills of many of his successors. He was agile for a big man, had elbows that he wielded like weapons, and possessed a deadly hook shot.

Mild-mannered?

"His brother, Ed, played for the Chicago Stags," Martin said. "In one game, George had blackened his brother's eye, scraped him up pretty good.

"We went out to dinner with his whole family afterward, and George's mother [Minnie] said to him, 'Why do you have to beat your little brother up so bad?'

"George told her, 'Momma, if you'd have been out there, I would have beaten you up, too.'"

Born in Joliet, Illinois, Mikan loved to play basketball as a kid but never thought of it as a career. Few did in an era when there were no multimillion dollar salaries on the horizon. Pro basketball players in those days needed another job, at least in the off-season, to survive.

Mikan didn't take off the glasses when he became Superman.

Besides, Mikan had loftier goals than hooking a basketball through a hoop. While attending Quigley Preparatory Seminary, he thought about becoming a priest.

Mikan soon came to realize, however, that his temperament was better suited to the ferocity on the court than the serenity of the church.

That didn't necessarily mean basketball was ready for him. Considered too awkward to be effective, Mikan was rejected by Notre Dame.

DePaul University coach Ray Meyer decided to take a chance on the kid. His approach was certainly unorthodox. He treated Mikan more like a boxer preparing for a big fight than a basketball player getting ready to step on the court. Meyer had Mikan shadowbox, skip rope, and even dance with a female student to become more graceful.

It all worked. Combining his fancy new footwork with an aggressive style, Mikan became so effective at swatting the ball away from the rim that the NCAA passed a goaltending rule to blunt his defense.

Nothing, however, could blunt Mikan's rise to become the most dominant player at every level he competed. He led the Blue Demons to an NIT championship and led his first pro team, the Chicago Gears of the National Basketball League (NBL), to the league title.

Mikan went on to play for the Minneapolis Lakers, leading them to an NBL title, a championship in the Basketball Association of America (BAA), and then four more titles after the BAA became the NBA in 1949.

Mikan won seven championships in his first eight seasons of pro basketball, spanning three leagues.

"Nobody ever had better offensive moves under the basket," said Larry Foust, a frequent Mikan opponent. "When George played, he owned that lane."

Road Trip

For Lakers fans, Mikan and the Minneapolis era are nothing more than old, grainy black-and-white film and dusty history books.

But there is one way to get a better feel for those memorable years. Literally.

Travel to Minneapolis and go to Target Center, home of the Timberwolves.

There in the lobby leading to the court stands a life-size statue of Mikan—frozen in time, one leg off the ground, ball in his left hand, poised to launch his famous hook shot.

What better way to get in touch with the period that launched the franchise?

Mikan led the NBA in scoring three times and once in rebounding and was the Most Valuable Player of the 1953 NBA All-Star Game. His career average was 22.6 points over nine seasons, even though he played all but 37 games before the advent of the 24-second clock.

"He made me a great coach," said John Kundla, at the helm for five Lakers championships, "and made Minneapolis a big-league city."

Mikan retired after the 1953–54 season, sat out a year, and then briefly returned for 37 games the following season before hanging up his uniform for good.

After retirement, Mikan agreed to come back for the 1957–58 season to coach the Lakers but quit after the team lost 30 of its first 39 games.

He returned to the game he loved one more time, becoming the first commissioner of the American Basketball Association in 1967. He served two and a half years before devoting himself fully to his second career as a lawyer.

Inducted into the Basketball Hall of Fame in 1959, Mikan died in 2005 at the age of 80.

"He lifted us out of the doldrums and made the league respectable," Hall of Fame guard Bob Cousy said.

"He showed us how to do it," Kareem Abdul-Jabbar said. "I certainly would not have had a hook shot that went in if it wasn't for the fundamentals I learned from George Mikan's game."

Or, as Shaq said, "Without George Mikan, there'd be no me."

20 Riles

It may be hard to fathom today that Jerry Buss or anybody else in basketball would feel trepidation about putting Pat Riley in charge of a team.

But back in 1981 on the day head coach Paul Westhead was fired, it wasn't so easy to picture Riley as his successor.

Riley himself wasn't even sure about assuming the role of assistant coach when Westhead—who took over after head coach Jack McKinney was injured in a 1979 bicycle accident—offered Riley that position.

Riley was very comfortable serving as announcer Chick Hearn's analyst and was hesitant about going down on the sidelines.

For many years people thought of Riley solely as an athlete. He was a good one, good enough to be drafted by both the NBA's Rockets—then playing in San Diego—and the NFL's Dallas Cowboys.

Any temptation to go the football route was squelched when Riley, who had played quarterback in high school, was told the Cowboys envisioned him as a defensive back.

A 6'4", 205-pound swingman, Riley spent three seasons with Rockets before being taken by Portland in the 1970 expansion draft.

Hating the idea of playing for a new team with little chance of success, Riley reached out to the man who would twice put him on the right path at a crossroads moment in his career.

That man was Chick Hearn.

After an exhibition game between the Trail Blazers and the Lakers, Riley waited in a dreary downpour near the Lakers' team bus outside Portland's Memorial Coliseum.

When the Lakers announcer emerged, Riley told him, desperation in his voice, "You've got to get me out of here."

Hearn had a lot of influence in the front office in those days under owner Jack Kent Cooke. Hearn put Riley's name in Cooke's head, and nine days before the season opener, the Lakers purchased Riley's contract.

It was an amazing leap forward for a journeyman, going from an expansion club to one of the best teams in the NBA.

And one season later, Riley found himself on one of the best teams in NBA history, the 1971–72 Lakers, a squad that won a then-record 69 regular-season games, including a record 33 in a row, and finished up with the team's first championship in L.A.

Riley spent five full seasons with the Lakers, then was traded two games into the 1975–76 season to Phoenix. It turned out to be his final year. He retired at age 31 because of a bad knee.

Life after basketball wasn't pretty.

He inquired about coaching positions, but nothing materialized. So Riley spent his time playing volleyball on the beach and remodeling his home, taking out his frustration with a hammer and a drill.

The low point came one night at the Forum when, after watching a game as a spectator, he attempted to get into the press lounge where he had spent so many enjoyable nights.

"Sorry," a security guard told him after looking at the championship ring on Riley's finger, "no ex-players."

Once again, it was Chick to the rescue.

With the departure of broadcast partner Lynn Shackelford, Hearn offered Riley the opportunity to put down his hammer and pick up a microphone.

He agreed to become Hearn's new on-the-air sidekick and soon reveled in the task of producing the halftime features.

When Westhead asked Riley to be his assistant, it was assumed McKinney would soon be back. Riley wondered where that would leave him.

Hearn promised Riley his old job would still be open. So Riley went down on the sideline, never to return.

Bill Bertka

The night in Utah when Magic Johnson demanded to be traded, most people connected to the team knew what was about to happen.

Westhead was going to get fired.

Also fired, presumably, would be his assistant coach, Pat Riley. New coaches usually bring in their own people.

In the bar atop the Lakers' Salt Lake City hotel, Riley sat, staring into his drink and bemoaning his fate. He had grown to love his coaching gig and now he figured he was going to lose it.

"Things have really changed," he said bitterly to a couple of reporters. "In the old days, a player just worried about playing and never tried to get involved in coaching decisions, at least not publicly."

As Riley sat there, a coaching buddy came over, put his arm on Riley's shoulder and said, "Don't worry, Pat, you never know how things are going to turn out."

That buddy was Bill Bertka, director of player personnel and an assistant coach for the Jazz.

When Riley became head coach and Jerry West retreated back up to the front office, Bertka was the first man Riley called to be his assistant.

Now nearly 40 years later, Riley is long gone, but Bertka is still in the Lakers organization, working on a part-time basis.

21 Wilt: Nobody Roots for Goliath

He was unquestionably the most dominating offensive player the game has ever known.

A 7'1", 275-pounder, Wilt Chamberlain put up gargantuan numbers that will probably never be equaled, such as 100 points in a single game, 55 rebounds in a game, and averages of 50.4 points and 48.5 minutes for an entire season.

He is also the NBA's all-time leading rebounder with 23,924, and the only man to score more than 4,000 points in one season.

One year, Chamberlain decided to show that he was about more than just muscle, so he set out to lead the league in assists.

And did so, with 702.

Nobody could argue with the numbers the man piled up. Except for one number, that is. In his second autobiography, *A View from Above*, Chamberlain claimed to have slept with 20,000 different women. Short of producing a stat sheet with names and places, he wasn't going to convince many people of that.

But there was no doubt he often looked like a man among boys on the court, even though those boys were other NBA players.

Chamberlain was a powerful force on defense as well as offense.

Can a dunk be blocked? Chamberlain did so against Walt Bellamy, swatting away a ball that seemed as if it was already in the hoop.

The line that best describes the futility defenders felt in trying to stop Chamberlain came from Darrall Imhoff, a former Laker who was part of the monumental trade that brought Chamberlain to L.A. from Philadelphia. When Imhoff retired, he said, "It was a privilege to have spent 12 years in [Wilt's] armpits."

Was Chamberlain the greatest player in NBA history? Asked that question, Oscar Robertson, whose own name is often brought up in that conversation, said in the *Philadelphia Daily News,* "The record books don't lie."

Chamberlain was such an overwhelming presence that he not only left his name all over the record books, but also caused changes in the rule book as well. Because of him the lane was widened and goaltending became a penalty.

Yet despite all his individual accomplishments, Chamberlain could never escape the criticism that he wasn't a winner, that all his mind-blowing numbers didn't translate into enough championships.

He won two—with the Philadelphia 76ers in 1967 and with the Lakers in 1972.

Never one to shy away from critics, Chamberlain said that people who claimed he wasn't a winner "were stupid."

On many occasions he was foiled by his nemesis, the Celtics' Bill Russell.

Although Russell was three inches shorter and considerably less muscular than Chamberlain, he usually won the one-on-one battles because he was the best defensive player ever and arguably the greatest player of all time.

Those who point to Michael Jordan's six championships to bolster the claim that he is the best ever seem to forget Russell won 11 championships in 13 seasons, including an unbelievable eight in a row, and captured his last two titles while serving as player/coach.

While with the Warriors, Chamberlain once scored 62 points against Russell's Celtics, but—summing up their whole rivalry in 48 minutes—Boston won the game.

When they first met in the playoffs during the spring of 1960, Chamberlain outscored Russell by 81 points, but Chamberlain's team lost the series in six games.

A Free Lunch

Had it not been for a generous restaurant owner, the 1971–72 season might have turned out very differently for the Lakers.

Taking over the club that season, Bill Sharman had an idea that was radical for the NBA: a shootaround.

Now it is commonplace. Prior to a night game, coaches require their players to show up at the arena or the practice site around noon to stretch their legs, shoot some baskets, and generally awaken their muscles—especially on the road where players are often still sleeping at noon.

Sharman had made shootarounds mandatory when he coached in both the American Basketball League and the American Basketball Association, and they proved successful if not popular.

But Sharman knew, for it to work in the NBA with the Lakers, the idea would have to have the approval of the big fella, Wilt Chamberlain.

Not one to be up and about early, Chamberlain might well reject the plan. And if he balked, it would be a tougher sell to his teammates.

So Sharman decided to take Chamberlain out to lunch to make his case.

To his horror, Sharman, while at the table eating, realized as he ran his hand over his back pocket that he had somehow forgotten his wallet.

"Great," he thought. "This will go over real big. I'm about to squander my goodwill and I haven't even brought up the shootaround yet."

Sharman didn't even want to think about Chamberlain's reaction when he learned that his luncheon invitation from the coach would end with the big center getting stuck with the bill.

Much to Sharman's relief, that bill never arrived. Instead the owner came over, announced how delighted he was to have such celebrities in his establishment, and said he didn't want them to even think about paying.

Deciding to strike before some other problem arose, Sharman brought up the subject of the shootaround.

Chamberlain thought about it before answering.

"I don't sleep well at night," he finally said, "so I like to sleep in the mornings. But let's try it and see what happens."

What happened was one of the greatest seasons in NBA history.

The shootaround was here to stay.

Russell and Chamberlain faced each other in eight postseason series. Russell's Celtics won seven of those.

"My friends," Chamberlain recalled, "would say, 'Hey man, you should throw Russell in the basket, too.'"

Despite his success, Russell never showed a lack of respect for Chamberlain.

"Every time I went out on the court," Russell said, "that guy seemed to grow a little taller."

When the Lakers obtained Chamberlain from the Philadelphia 76ers in 1968 in exchange for Darrall Imhoff, Archie Clark, and Jerry Chambers, it appeared L.A. had the first dream team. Chamberlain with Jerry West and Elgin Baylor? Who could stop them?

Well for one, Chamberlain himself. When he removed himself in the closing minutes of Game 7 of the 1969 NBA Finals against Boston after injuring a knee and the Lakers lost. Critics questioned whether the team was any better with him in the lineup than it had been with the long string of average centers it had employed since George Mikan had departed over a decade earlier, half a continent away.

Although the Lakers had put together a triumvirate of power, much as the Miami Heat have done with LeBron James, Dwyane Wade, and Chris Bosh, it ironically was only after Baylor retired that the Lakers were able to take advantage of Chamberlain's presence to at last win a title.

Finally, Chamberlain had a season to remember in terms of leadership, teamwork, and devotion to a common cause.

The 1971–72 Lakers with Bill Sharman as head coach won an all-time record 33 straight games and finished the regular season with a then-record 69-13 won-lost mark (Chamberlain's 76ers were 68–13 the first time he won a title). L.A. went 12–3 in the playoffs that year, beating the Knicks in five games in the NBA Finals.

There was, however, no dynasty ahead. Chamberlain retired a year later at 36, going on to write a few books, make a movie, briefly coach, play some volleyball, and flirt with the idea of an NBA comeback into his fifties.

He often said that "nobody roots for Goliath," but, when he died in 1999 at 63, Chamberlain left behind at least one staunch supporter.

"He and I," Russell said, "will be friends through eternity."

22 The Fabulous Forum

It didn't have luxury suites, a scoreboard with all of today's bells and whistles, or even a prime location.

When Lakers owner Jack Kent Cooke announced he was going to build a new arena in Inglewood, he was met with laughter. And when he revealed it would be modeled after the Roman Forum, complete with togas for the ushers, the laughter turned to ridicule.

The building would be oval in shape with 80 concrete columns, giving it the look of ancient Rome.

The cost: $16 million.

No one was laughing after the Forum opened its doors in the round on December 30, 1967, and quickly became L.A.'s new hot spot.

Not only did the Lakers play there, but also Cooke's expansion hockey team, the Kings.

So did performers from every corner of the music world. Elvis was there—before he left the building. The sounds of artists as diverse as Barbra Streisand, Prince, Neil Diamond, and the Grateful Dead filled the arena.

Jackpot

On the day the Forum opened, Cooke took one last tour of the premises to make sure everything was running properly.

Spotting a vending machine, he pulled a coin out of his pocket and inserted it into the slot.

Down came a soft drink along with about $10 in change, sounding like Cooke had just hit the jackpot on a Vegas slot machine.

With a big grin, Cooke scooped up the coins and stuffed them in his pocket while commenting, "Story of my life."

Muhammad Ali fought there, as did other stars of the ring. Forum boxing eventually turned into a regularly scheduled event.

After Jerry Buss purchased the building from Cooke along with the Lakers and the Kings, he added other sports—from the Lazers indoor soccer team to the Blades roller hockey club—to fill the empty nights.

The Forum hosted the gold medal–winning men's and women's basketball teams in the 1984 Olympics.

The arena became a place not only to see events but to be seen. Stars from every facet of the entertainment world packed the Forum Club, which soon became tougher to get into than the best clubs on the Sunset Strip.

More movie deals may have been consummated in Forum courtside seats than in the high rises of Century City.

In all, more than 66 million fans had paid their way into the building by the time the Lakers and Kings abandoned the Forum for their new arena, the Staples Center, in 1999.

For Lakers fans who have only seen their team play at Staples Center, a stop in Inglewood has to be on the to-do list. The arena is still used for concerts. Attend one and get a feel for the building where all sorts of sports history was made.

Lakers teams reached the NBA Finals 14 times in the Forum era and won six of those.

It was at the Forum that Cooke hung balloons for a Lakers championship celebration that never happened, where Jerry West launched his 55-foot NBA Finals buzzer beater, and where the Lakers clinched their first title in Los Angeles.

It was also where the Kings staged the Miracle on Manchester, coming back from a five-goal deficit in the third period to beat the Edmonton Oilers in overtime in a 1982 postseason game.

So many of the greats of that era—from Wayne Gretzky to Magic Johnson and Kareem Abdul-Jabbar to Kobe Bryant and Shaquille O'Neal—played there.

The arena became the first to sell naming rights. In 1988, Great Western Bank paid Jerry Buss to turn the building Cooke called "The Fabulous Forum" into the Great Western Forum.

"You want it to stand for something," Lakers executive Jeanie Buss said. "For us, it worked out great. It was the Great Western Forum. It fit better than it probably would have…if we were the Clorox Forum."

Fabulous or great, it was a sports landmark in its time, and tangible proof that no one ever got rich underestimating Jack Kent Cooke.

23 Big Trade for the Big Fella

It was owner Jack Kent Cooke's finest hour.

Nothing he did before or after was as beneficial to the Lakers as the move he made in 1975, trading Elmore Smith, Brian Winters, Dave Meyers, and Junior Bridgeman to the Milwaukee Bucks for Walt Wesley and a center named Kareem Abdul-Jabbar.

Cooke had been frustrated by the Lakers' failure to repeat their championship season of 1972 or to even remain contenders for long. In the season following the championship, the team finished the regular season 60–22, made it back to the Finals, and faced the Knicks in a rematch of 1972. But this time it was the Lakers losing in five games.

Then Wilt Chamberlain retired and nobody proved capable of filling the gaping hole in the middle.

In the first year of Chamberlain's absence, the Lakers finished 47–35 and were knocked out of the playoffs in the first round by Abdul-Jabbar's Bucks. The Lakers wound up a dismal 30–52 the next season and missed the playoffs for the first time in 17 years and for the first time since they had arrived in L.A.

That was more than Cooke—not exactly a patient man in the best of times—could bear.

Abdul-Jabbar was a logical replacement for Chamberlain. No one in Los Angeles needed to be convinced of Abdul-Jabbar's greatness. The 7'2" center had attended UCLA—back when he was still Lew Alcindor—and dominated college basketball.

He made his presence felt right from the start. In those days freshmen were not allowed to play on the varsity team. So Alcindor was relegated to the frosh squad. When it played the Bruins varsity at the start of the season, Alcindor scored 31 points, had 21 rebounds, and blocked seven shots, and his team, known as the Brubabes, won 75–60.

Impressive?

Even more impressive considering the squad the freshmen faced was coming off back-to-back national championships and was ranked No. 1 in the nation.

In an era before star players were one-and-done with college basketball, Alcindor played for the Bruins varsity for the three seasons and UCLA won the national championship all three years.

Overreacting to Alcindor's dominance, the NCAA banned the dunk prior to the 1967–68 season, his second as a varsity member. Dumb move.

For one thing the rule handcuffed some of the game's great stars and took away some of the sport's most explosive moments.

For another, it didn't slow Alcindor down. In his arsenal, he also had the skyhook, arguably the most accurate, unstoppable shot ever released on the court.

The NCAA finally rescinded the no-dunk rule nearly a decade later. By then, Alcindor was long gone, dominating the NBA as he had the NCAA.

Drafted by Milwaukee, he won a title there in 1971, sharing the spotlight with another future Hall of Famer, Oscar Robertson.

When the Lakers' 33-game-winning streak ended in 1972, Abdul-Jabbar was the opposing center.

Off the court, life wasn't as pleasing for him. Born and raised in New York and intellectually stimulated by his undergraduate days in L.A., Abdul-Jabbar was a big-city guy. The predominately Caucasian, small-town environment of the Midwest left him cold.

Figuratively as well as literally.

"Live in Milwaukee? No, I guess you could say I *exist* in Milwaukee," Abdul-Jabbar said at the time. "I am a soldier hired for service and I will perform that service well. Basketball has given me a good life, but this town has nothing to do with my roots. There's no common ground."

In his first book, *Giant Steps*, Abdul-Jabbar said of Milwaukee, "This Midwestern town had none of the excitement that I had assumed was always in the air like oxygen.

"For instance, I expected my friends to be the guys in the slick suits and shades because those were the people I was used to seeing in Harlem and Westwood. In my new home, I was dealing with at best very square business suits. Other than that it was the polyester set, which I just could not relate to, or farmers. Farmers!"

Having already converted to Islam but not revealed it publicly, Abdul-Jabbar said that his time in Milwaukee made him feel like he was from "an alien urban culture."

Abdul-Jabbar wrote, "My religion wouldn't permit me to gamble or to drink, but I didn't tell [teammates] the reason. I just didn't go out for a beer. And in Milwaukee, that's mainly what you did for entertainment. In fact, that's all you did.

"There wasn't the Vanguard or Five Spot to hang in and hear some music. There were polka joints. Serious culture shock.

"Milwaukee was a beer town. People socialized in bars.... Purist that I was, I wanted no part of it. Looked to me like a whole lot of rednecked farmers getting drunk."

Abdul-Jabbar told the Bucks he wanted out but agreed to keep his wishes quiet to allow management to maintain at least a modicum of leverage in shopping him around.

Abdul-Jabbar's first choice was his hometown, New York. But when that didn't work out, he was happy to learn an acceptable deal was on the table with the Lakers.

He gave the okay and headed west.

"It was strange though. By the time I was about to leave Milwaukee, I had finally developed an appreciation of its people," Abdul-Jabbar wrote. "The team owners treated me with respect, and paid me well, and the fans turned out to be great. They are the salt of the earth. They show up when you're winning, they show up when you're losing. They come early, stay late…they were a different kind of people than any I'd met before, but I came to know them as generous and good."

24 The Streak

It began on one of the saddest days in Lakers history.

At 37, his knees aching and his trademark leap reduced to a hop, Elgin Baylor, one of the greatest players in NBA history, announced his retirement.

It was November 5, 1971, just nine games into the season.

Twenty-three year-old forward Jim McMillian had heard about Baylor's decision a day earlier.

"We had a game the next day, but nobody said a thing," McMillian later recalled. "Nobody called me. Nobody said, 'Okay, Jim, get ready. You're going to be starting. Nothing.

"We get there [the next day]. We get dressed, and in the team meeting, finally, the coach [Bill Sharman] says, 'Jim, you're going to be starting and you're going to be guarding so-and-so."

Prepared or not, McMillian did all right. The Lakers won that night, beating the Baltimore Bullets 110–106.

And they won the next game and the next and the next. McMillian became the first and only player in NBA history to go 33–0 at the start of his career.

He had come along at just the right time: the start of the greatest winning streak of any professional team in American sports history.

With Wilt Chamberlain in the middle fulfilling the potential the Lakers had seen in him when they traded for him three years earlier; with two future Hall of Fame guards—Jerry West and Gail Goodrich—in the backcourt; and with a solid power forward in Happy Hairston, the Lakers ran the table for the rest of November, all of December, and into January.

Although he stood only 6'7", the 225-pound Hairston was an effective rebounder who had a career season in 1971–72. He averaged 13.1 rebounds per game, 15 over the second half of the season, even though he was sharing the front court with Chamberlain.

Hairston, as it turned out, was just warming up. He went on to career rebounding highs in each of the ensuing two seasons as well, with 13.2 in 1972–73 and 13.5 the following season.

Teammates chuckled because at the end of every quarter, if a last-second shot was attempted, Hairston would race down the court in case the ball missed its mark. The more of a desperation throw it was, the faster he ran.

After all, he figured if he could get every one of those missed shots, that would be four more rebounds per game.

Among the bench players on that 1971–72 squad was a 26-year-old swingman named Pat Riley, who played just under 14 minutes a game.

The four-point win against the Bullets was the smallest margin of victory during the entire streak. On December 10, the Lakers beat the Suns 126–117 in overtime for their 20th straight win, enabling them to tie the previous NBA-record winning streak set by the Bucks a year earlier.

Covering the Streak

It may be hard to imagine in this current era when the Lakers own Los Angeles, but back in those days, they were held in such little regard that the media rarely traveled with them.

When it became obvious, however, that the winning streak was headed for historic proportions, Mal Florence of the *Los Angeles Times* began covering all of the team's road games.

On the morning after the streak-ending loss to the Bucks, Sharman saw Florence in the lobby of the team's hotel, bag in hand.

"Where are you going, Mal?" Sharman said.

"We don't cover losers," Florence replied with a twinkle in his eyes.

Twenty-four times during the Lakers' streak, they won by 10 points or more.

"It was a situation," McMillian told the *Los Angeles Times*, "where when you walked onto the court, you knew you were going to win and the other team knew it, too."

"We just played with a great deal of swagger," said Goodrich.

And why not?

When the Lakers passed another milestone, the Bullets were again the victims. On December 22 in Baltimore, the Lakers won 127–120 for their 27th straight victory. That broke the previous winning-streak record for any professional American team, the 26 in a row by the New York Giants baseball team in 1916 (and that streak included a tie).

The end for the Lakers after 33 straight wins came in no small part, ironically, because of a future Laker great, Kareem Abdul-Jabbar,

On January 9, 1972, Abdul-Jabbar, Milwaukee's center, led the way as the Bucks pounded out a 120–104 victory against the Lakers in Milwaukee.

Abdul-Jabbar beat Chamberlain that day in every meaningful category, outscoring him 39–15, outrebounding him 20–12, and outdoing him in blocked shots 10–6.

But neither Chamberlain nor his teammates had anything to be ashamed of. They had set a standard that has stood for nearly seven decades and may well stand forever.

"I always believe records are made to be broken," Goodrich said "but I'm not sure ours is going to get broken."

"We knew it had to end sometime," Sharman said, "but I would trade all the records for a championship."

Such a trade was not necessary. Nothing could diminish one of the great accomplishments in NBA and sports history, and Sharman also got his ultimate goal at the end of the season.

The Lakers set another all-time league record by finishing the regular season 69–13, a mark later broken by the Bulls (72–10 in the 1995–96 season) and then the Warriors (73-9 in 2015-16).

The Lakers got revenge on the Bucks by beating them in six games in the Western Conference Finals.

And the Lakers culminated a season to remember by beating the Knicks in five games in the NBA Finals for their first title in Los Angeles.

"The 33 games were just icing on the cake," Goodrich said. "I don't think it really hit us until it was all over."

25 The Shaq/Kobe Gamble

When Chick Hearn picked up the phone, he heard Jerry West on the other end, but he had never heard West quite like this. The Lakers vice president sounded out of breath.

"Have you been running?" Hearn said.

"No," West said, "I just came back from watching the best 17-year-old player I've ever seen."

Thus, Kobe Bryant got on West's radar screen. Getting him on the Lakers, however, was going to prove a far more difficult task.

The son of former NBA player Joe "Jellybean" Bryant, Kobe spent some of his formative years in Italy when Joe moved there to continue his basketball career.

From the age of six on, Kobe found himself constantly pulled away from his first love—basketball—to the soccer field.

"After school I would be the only guy on the basketball court, working on my moves," he told SI.com, "and then kids would start showing up with their soccer ball. It was either go home or be the goalkeeper."

But Bryant wasn't about to give up his love of basketball, the NBA in general, and the Lakers in particular. As he entered his teens, the family moved back to Pennsylvania, where he found plenty of competition on the court.

Beginning with his father.

As Kobe's skills blossomed, his one-on-one games against Joe grew more serious, more physical, more cutthroat.

Or at least, more cut *lip*.

Kobe recalls getting elbows in the face from his father as he became more aggressive and more competitive, despite the fact he was still in his early teens and Joe was an NBA veteran.

As Kobe's talent grew, so did his confidence. When a camp counselor warned him that only one in a million make it to the NBA, Bryant responded, "I'm going to be that one in a million.

In high school, Bryant led his team, Lower Merion, to a state championship and finished his prep career with 2,883 points, breaking the Southern Pennsylvania mark of 2,359 set by Wilt Chamberlain.

"[Kobe] not only wanted to win every game," said Lower Marion assistant coach Mike Egan, "but every drill, every practice. He wanted to win scrimmages 11–0…He had such a killer instinct, he wanted to rip your heart out every time down the court."

Bryant was recruited by Duke and could have had his choice of colleges, but he decided his dream was not to be denied—or even delayed.

He was going to the NBA right out of high school.

Hearn wasn't the only one West called after seeing Bryant. He also phoned Arn Tellem, Bryant's agent, telling him, "We've got to figure out a way to get him here."

West also had his eyes on a bigger prize. At least bigger physically.

He didn't need a workout to convince him that 7'1", 325-pound Shaquille O'Neal could carry a team on his huge shoulders. He could be the next Lakers big man at the center of a dynasty, carrying on a tradition of dominance in the middle that had stretched from George Mikan to Chamberlain to Kareem Abdul-Jabbar.

After O'Neal's mother, Lucille, and father, Joe Toney, split up, she married an army sergeant named Phillip Harrison. O'Neal thus became an army brat, spending part of his youth in Germany. Attending high school there on the base in Wildflecken, he had grown to 6'8" by the time he was a sophomore.

When O'Neal attended a coaching clinic in the area, the man running the session, LSU coach Dale Brown, did a double take.

Who knew the next big thing in basketball was to be found in Wildflecken. Kind of like the moment Kevin Bacon's character discovers Saleh in the movie *The Air Up There.*

Except this wasn't reel life, but real life. And this kid would go on to become a movie star in his own right. Not to mention a charismatic celebrity, rap star, TV personality, and the most dominating basketball player of his era.

All Brown knew was that he wanted the kid. He wanted him even more when he learned O'Neal was only 16 and might still be in the growing stage.

How frightening was that?

O'Neal and his family moved to San Antonio where he transferred to Cole High School.

By the time Brown got his man, O'Neal, enrolling at LSU, had grown to 6'11" and 265 pounds.

Seeing O'Neal as a freshman, Golden State coach Don Nelson said he was "in love."

O'Neal entered the NBA Draft after his junior year, arriving on stage to shake commissioner David Stern's hand with the burden of great expectations and incessant comparisons to Wilt Chamberlain.

What's in a Name?

Bryant's parents, Joe and Pam, got the idea for his name from the Kobe Japanese Steak House in Valley Forge, Pennsylvania. Joe was playing for Philadelphia at the time.

In 2001, when the Lakers were facing the 76ers in the NBA Finals, the restaurant management showed loyalty to the home team by temporarily putting a thick red line through the word "Kobe" on their sign and replacing it with "The Answer," the nickname of 76ers star Allen Iverson.

Both men, surprisingly agile for their size, could move well around the basket. But while Chamberlain seemed interested in showing he was more than just a big man, whether it was with finger rolls or leading the league in assists one season, O'Neal seemed more inclined to demonstrate his overwhelming physicality. He could effectively pass or throw up a hook shot, but often he would just plant his gargantuan body in the low post and go for the stuff, even if he had one, two, or three defenders on his back.

A foul could have been called—and often was—every time O'Neal struggled with defenders. And every foul, it seemed, could have gone either way.

Of course, with O'Neal, opposing coaches just wanted to hear the whistle, even if the call went against them. With O'Neal shooting 52.7 percent from the foul line over a 19-year career, the odds weren't much better than even money that he'd be successful when he went to the free-throw line.

Drafted by the Magic, O'Neal reached the NBA Finals just once in his four years in Orlando, only to be swept by the Rockets in that 1995 series.

Nevertheless, when O'Neal became a free agent, the line formed at his door, led by West.

O'Neal was conflicted about staying with the Magic. His relationship with the organization had soured over, among other

Kobe hugs the Larry O'Brien Trophy as Shaq holds the Bill Russell Finals MVP Trophy after the duo led the Lakers to the NBA championship, defeating the Indiana Pacers in the 2000 Finals. (Getty Images)

things, the death of his grandmother, Odessa. The Magic supplied him with a private jet to attend the funeral, several team officials accompanied him, and he was told to stay with his family as long as he felt was necessary.

But when front-office executives hadn't heard from him for five days—a period that included two Magic games—and an Orlando paper wrote that he had been seen in a nightclub, controversy ensued.

"I just wish people would stick up for me more," O'Neal said. "Where in the hell did they think I was? They saw me at the funeral. Did they think I was out waterskiing with Cedric Ceballos?"

Ceballos was a Lakers forward who took off in the middle of the 1995–96 season to go waterskiing at Arizona's Lake Havasu without informing the team.

O'Neal also questioned the loyalty of his teammates.

"They never stood up for me," he said. "I got fouled a lot, and they never said anything."

As free agency opened, Orlando owner Rich DeVos raised the stakes, making it clear that a big offer from him would require a big contribution from O'Neal as well.

"I want your heart, not just your body," he told his center.

Jerry Buss was an ardent card player who had been in the World Series of Poker and had been known to frequent L.A. poker parlors in the middle of the week just to get a game. But in the summer of 1996, he and Jerry West played a high-stakes game with the Lakers that far exceeded anything he'd ever attempted on a felt table.

The Lakers traded Vlade Divac, their only quality center, to Charlotte in exchange for the 13th selection—once West knew that pick was Kobe Bryant—in the 1996 Draft. That enabled West to free up $4.5 million in cap space and secure the 17-year-old phenom.

Now, West would have the other leg of his budding dynasty if he could sign O'Neal.

A big if.

Without Divac to play center, nothing more than the future of the franchise was on the line.

26 Field of Nightmares

It seemed like just another road trip, just another game on a visiting court, just another flight home.

But when the Minneapolis Lakers boarded their two-propeller DC-3 on the night of July 17, 1960, in St. Louis for the trip back to Minneapolis after losing to the Hawks in Kiel Auditorium, they found themselves on a journey unlike any other ever experienced by an American professional sports team.

Some players plopped into their seats in search of a good nap while the regular card players in the group pulled open their specially designed table, made to fit in the narrow aisle, and opened a much-worn deck.

None of them, however, were in a particularly good mood after losing to St. Louis 135–119 to drop to a dismal 13–30 on the season. It was the Lakers' fourth straight loss and seventh in nine games.

Their leading scorer, as was usually the case, had been Elgin Baylor with 36 points.

In his second year with the team, Baylor was clearly the star of the club. A brilliant scorer and ferocious rebounder, Baylor would go on to lead the Lakers in both categories that season. His 29.6 scoring average would be more than double the 13.7 posted by runner-up Rudy LaRusso. Baylor's team-leading rebound average would be 16.4, with LaRusso again second at 9.6.

But in a few minutes, neither man would be concerned with being team leaders at the end of the season. They would be concerned, instead, with just surviving to the end of the season.

Not to mention the end of the night.

There was sleet falling when the team bus arrived at St. Louis' Lambert Field. The flight was delayed for two hours because of the weather.

The team was scheduled to leave from Gate 13. No one attached any significance to that.

"When you lose as often as we did," coach Jim Pollard later said, "you get over being superstitious."

When the decision was finally made to take off, the sleet was still falling, but the forecast was for better conditions ahead.

And so off they went, pilot Vern Ullman, co-pilot Harold Gifford, and trainee Jim Holznagel—as the third man in the cockpit—along with 19 passengers, including players, wives, and several children.

About 10 minutes into the flight, there was suddenly more to worry about than bad weather. The lights grew brighter, dimmed and then went out altogether. So did the heat.

Most alarming to those in the cockpit was the fact that the instruments had gone out as well.

It was later determined that the left generator had malfunctioned, putting the full load on the right generator. That proved too much of a burden and it blew out as well.

For the first time ever, the players' never-ending card game ceased.

As the temperature dropped, an even bigger chill went through the passengers as they peered up the aisle to the cockpit. The door was open, and they could see the crew trying to function with flashlights.

As if all that wasn't bad enough, the prediction of better weather was proving to be false. Instead, the storm continued unabated, leaving the pilots to deal with yet another serious problem.

They couldn't land at a big-city airport. Without a radio, they could not receive clearance from the control tower to fly into potentially crowded airspace.

Not that they could even find a big-city airport. As the tense minutes stretched into harrowing hours, the flight crew wasn't even sure where they were.

They had five flashlights, but those gave out, one after another, as the flight neared the five-hour mark. All the crew was left with for illumination was a tiny light on the end of a ballpoint pen.

Trying to get above the storm, the plane had climbed from 10,000 to 17,000 feet. But with no heat, the bitter cold soon became unbearable.

Frost formed on the windows, including those in the cockpit. But, there was no power to run the windshield wipers.

The pilots were forced to dive back into the storm with the hope they would at least shake off a bit of the cold at a lower altitude.

The frost, however didn't melt. Down to a few hundred feet, Ullman and Gifford slid back their side windows and, equipped with goggles, they stretched their necks out into the driving storm, trying to assess the terrain.

What they found was a winter wonderland with snow as far as the eye could see—broken by a thin black line.

That dark line was their first ray of hope. It was a freshly cleared highway.

Follow the road, they figured it would surely lead to a town.

It had better do so. The pilots didn't need a gauge to know that they had to be running out of fuel.

That's when they spotted a water tower, a common Midwestern landmark indicating a town was nearby.

Sure enough, there it was, surrounded by farms, the buildings and homes on its snowy streets mostly dark at 1:30 AM.

All Gifford could see on the snow-covered tower were two letters: LL.

"We're flying into hell," he joked to Ullman. As they would soon learn, it was Carroll, Iowa, population 8,000, located about 100 miles northwest of Des Moines.

"I could see there were people down there staying alive," Gifford said. "That's what I wanted to do, too."

Minutes later, his chances of staying alive nearly slipped away.

Assured that they were in a populated area, Ullman and Gifford, after buzzing over the town, decided to continue following what they would later learn was Highway 71 to see if there was a more favorable landing site.

Instead, they lost the highway. Looking down, all they suddenly saw was white. Unbeknownst to them, the highway had swung left at a perpendicular angle.

Both Ullman and Gifford looked out their respective windows trying to relocate the comforting strip of black.

"Have you got it?" Ullman asked, meaning control of the plane.

"Yeah," replied Gifford, thinking Ullman meant a view of the highway.

With no one at the controls, the plane dipped dangerously. It was Holznagel who realized what was happening.

Just as he screamed that neither man in front of him had a hand on the instruments, the plane tilted so low that one wing nearly brushed the top of a grove of trees.

Gifford reacted instantly, regaining command of the aircraft.

He and Ullman decided they had gone far enough. No sense testing their luck any further. It was time to turn the plane back in the direction they had come. It would be Carroll or nothing.

As they swooped back toward town, Ullman suggested they try to set the DC-3 down on the highway.

Gifford had a better idea. As the plane circled and circled Carroll, nine times in all, he spotted a cornfield, Emma Steffes' cornfield. Gifford figured there would be no boulders or even rocks in that small stretch of land since it had been cleared for the crop, and the combination of the cornstalks and the snow would cushion their landing.

Wheels up or down?

"We wanted them down," Gifford later said. "Coming in with the wheels up would be considered a crash landing. And then we'd have all that paperwork to fill out."

Besides, neither Gifford nor Ullman figured that what they were about to do was crash.

Both pilots had flown in the military and equated what they were going to attempt with landing on an aircraft carrier.

Calculating that the field was a couple of hundred yards long, they were determined to touch down as close to where it began as possible to give themselves as much room as possible to come to a stop.

Back in the passenger cabin, there was deadly silence. The usual wisecracking and sarcasm characteristic of the team was long gone.

"There was a lot of praying and bargaining with God going on," Baylor said.

Athletes like to refer to game-ending shots as do or die, but this was the real thing.

Down came the plane, its wheels enveloped by the cornstalks close to where the field began; so close, the pilots would later learn, that the plane's tail end hooked into the fence bordering the property and dragged it along.

As it turned out, that was a good thing because pulling the extra weight slowed the aircraft down.

Inside the cabin, the passengers could hear the sounds of cornstalks beating against the windows.

The plane came in without a bounce, the landing amazingly smooth. The DC-3 went slower, ever slower until it finally creaked to a stop at 1:40 AM.

The plane had traveled about 200 feet through the cornfield, leaving only about 100 more before it ran out of room.

For a few seconds, there was still absolute silence inside the aircraft. Nobody dared believe their horrifying journey had ended without a scratch.

And then the cabin exploded in joy, the noise much louder than any victory cry.

The crew later learned that they had only enough fuel to keep them airborne for another 15 minutes.

Anxious to get out of the cabin before anything else happened, the players piled out the door into the snow.

Some began picking up snowballs and throwing them at each other.

Joe Twit, the town ambulance driver/mortician, was one of the first townspeople to greet these famous passengers that had just dropped out of the sky.

"Thought I was going to have some business tonight, boys," he said.

Jim Harzog, a local resident, had heard the plane roaring over his house. As he pulled his coat on, his wife asked him where he was going.

"I don't exactly know," he said, "but I know those people are in trouble."

When he reached the cornfield, Harzog jumped out of his car and trudged through the snow only to stop in amazement at the tall passengers heading his way.

Instead of autographs, he had to settle for carrying a few players' bags.

With more cars arriving, its drivers getting out of warm beds to help the unexpected visitors on that cold night, everybody was soon transported to the nearby Burke Hotel.

"The worst ordeal in our lives was over," Gifford said. "God must have been my co-pilot."

In the modern era of instant communication, if the Lakers' plane were to disappear off a radar screen, the entire world would know about it in minutes. But back then, nobody outside Carroll was aware the Lakers were even in trouble.

Bob Short, the team's owner, was first alerted when he was awakened at home by a call from the Civil Air Patrol.

"Are you the owner of the Minneapolis Lakers?" the caller asked.

"Yes," Short said.

"Your plane is missing," he was told.

At the hotel, the players lined up in the lobby to call their families.

When center Larry Foust, who was known to take a drink now and then, got a hold of his wife, he said, "Honey, I want you to know I'm all right, but we just crashed in an Iowa cornfield."

There was a pause, and then she replied, "That's great. When you sober up, call me back."

As it turned out, it was a good thing he didn't call her back.

Bob "Slick" Leonard, a guard on the team, recalled there was a liquor cabinet in the lobby.

"They had a padlock on [it]," he said, "and old Larry…went over there and twisted that sonavubitch right off of there. He got himself a fifth of VO [Canadian whiskey] and poured himself a big glass."

The next day, the players were bussed back to Minneapolis, passing by the plane sitting in the cornfield, on their way out of town."

"Everything was back to normal," center/forward Jim Krebs said. "God had answered our prayers. We had broken our losing streak."

The Junior Junior Skyhook

It began on the stairs leading to the second floor in the Lansing, Michigan, house where Magic Johnson grew up, living with his parents and six siblings.

He was just Earvin then, a young kid, so like many others, dreaming of hoops and glory.

He would place a laundry basket at the top of the stairs, fold pairs of socks into balls, scoot down to the bottom of the stairs and proceed to shoot the sock balls in a high arc toward the basket.

As he did so, he would add some play-by-play: "Five seconds... four...three...two...one...Earvin Johnson shoots and scores at the buzzer!"

Everybody in his neighborhood knew that Johnson was obsessed with basketball. It wasn't hard to tell. If his mother sent him to the market, he would dribble a ball all the way there and back, alternating hands at each new block.

He'd be up at dawn before the school playground was open, dribbling down Middle Street, pretending the parked cars were defenders, annoying neighbors who were awakened by the sound of ball on asphalt.

As Johnson grew and grew, reaching a height of 6'8", his fascination with the game grew as well.

He continued to recreate those clutch shots he had made on the stairs even as the socks became a real ball, the laundry basket a true hoop, and the stakes higher and higher.

He won a state title at Everett High, an NCAA championship with Michigan State, and NBA titles with the Lakers.

And along the way, Johnson left a trail of frustrated defenders, fired-up teammates, and fascinated fans.

Against the Suns in his very first NBA postseason series, he made a play that offered a preview of the magic he would weave through game after game over the years.

With two minutes to play and the Lakers clinging to a three-point lead in Game 3 in Phoenix, the Suns' Paul Westphal got a steal, and the ball wound up in the hands of teammate Walter Davis. Westphal then sprinted down the court and caught a long pass from Davis while in full stride within a few steps of the basket.

Thinking he was all alone and envisioning a soft layup to bring his team to within one, Westphal slowed down like a wide receiver about to glide into the end zone.

Bad move.

Seemingly out of nowhere, Johnson appeared.

From behind, he batted the ball from Westphal's grasp and fired it all the way back up the court to Kareem Abdul-Jabbar, who converted at the other end.

The Suns never recovered, losing that game to put themselves in a 3–0 hole, ultimately losing the series in five games.

Sometimes Johnson's play was so mystical, he not only fooled opponents, but also himself.

One night in New York, he pulled down a rebound after a Knick missed a shot. Seeing his teammate had control of the ball, Norm Nixon sprinted down the floor.

While still staring straight ahead at the backboard, Johnson flung the ball over his head with enough force to send it all the way downcourt. It bounced within easy reach of Nixon, who grabbed it and laid it in.

Johnson was asked after the game how he knew Nixon had taken off for the opposite end of the court.

"I saw him go," Johnson said.

"No, you didn't," he was told by a reporter. "You never looked behind you."

Johnson was genuinely puzzled.

"I thought I did," he said.

If he indeed saw Nixon, he must have eyes in the back of his head.

With all the amazing plays Johnson pulled off in his 13-year career, none is as well remembered as the Junior Skyhook, the shot he himself calls "the biggest basket of my life."

The Birth of Magic

It was the kind of performance Magic Johnson would produce over and over throughout his Lakers career.

But this wasn't the NBA or even the NCAA. It was Everett High School, and he was still Earvin Johnson Jr. of Lansing, Michigan. So when he scored 36 points, pulled down 18 rebounds, and handed out 16 assists, he left a lot of jaws hanging.

Among those amazed by Johnson's performance was Fred Stabley Jr. a sportswriter for the *Lansing State Journal*.

Coming into the locker room after the game, Stabley told Johnson, "I think you should have a nickname. I was thinking of calling you Dr. J, but that's taken. And so is Big E—Elvin Hayes. How about if I call you Magic?"

Embarrassed, Johnson sheepishly agreed, but it was a heavy burden to put on the shoulders of a 15-year-old.

Stabley's editor thought so, too. When the sportswriter came back to the office and announced he'd branded Johnson with a new name, his editor said, "Don't call him Magic. The kid is off to a great start, but it'll never last."

In his book, *My Life,* Johnson recalled that his parents didn't like the nickname either. His father, Earvin Sr., thought it put too much pressure on his son and would needlessly fire up opponents. Johnson's mother, Christine, a deeply religious person, felt putting a magical aura around her son's accomplishments downplayed the fact his talent came from God.

So, she refused to call him Magic, sticking to Earvin or Junior. His Lakers teammates would call him Buck or Earv.

But to the basketball world, he would always be Magic.

It came in Game 4 of the 1987 NBA Finals between the Lakers and Celtics at Boston Garden.

Five seconds remained. Boston had the lead by one. The Lakers had the ball on an in-bounds play.

It went to Johnson, who later admitted the thought of the two games he let slip away in the Garden in the 1984 Finals flashed across his mind.

But not for long.

He had bigger problems at that instant. As he came across the middle, the entire All-Star front line of the Celtics—Larry Bird, Kevin McHale, and Robert Parish—loomed in front of him.

That left Kareem Abdul-Jabbar open, but Johnson didn't see him.

Instead he decided on Abdul-Jabbar's signature shot, the skyhook. Except with the 6'8" Johnson instead of the 7'2" Abdul-Jabbar, it was a junior skyhook.

No matter. With perhaps an inch to spare, Johnson got it over the grasp of the straining McHale and Parish and through the hoop. Johnson labeled the shot as the 'junior junior skyhook."

Bird missed a three-pointer at the buzzer, and the Lakers escaped with a 107–106 victory en route to another NBA title at Boston's expense.

"You expect to lose on a skyhook," Bird said. "You just don't expect it to be from Magic."

28 Big Game James

Chick Hearn bestowed the nickname.

But it was earned by James Worthy, never more so than in Game 7 of the 1988 NBA Finals, matching the Lakers against the Pistons.

He picked basketball's biggest game to have his own biggest game, getting the first triple double of his Hall of Fame career. Worthy had 36 points, 16 rebounds, and 10 assists in leading the Lakers to the NBA title via a 108–105 victory.

Born and raised in North Carolina and bolstered by an unshakable confidence that never lapsed into arrogance, Worthy always seemed old beyond his years.

"What I remember most clearly," Ervin Worthy, James' father, told the *Washington Post*, "was sitting at the dining room table one night and looking at all my bills. James…came in and said to me, 'Daddy, when I go to college, you won't have to worry about having to pay for me because I'm going to get a scholarship.'"

That he did at—where else?—the University of North Carolina where he learned the fundamentals of the game under a pretty good teacher by the name of Dean Smith.

In the 1982 NBA Draft, the Lakers had the first pick, and Worthy was available. He was coming off a national championship season for the Tar Heels and the honor of being selected the Most Outstanding Player of the NCAA tournament.

Slam dunk choice? Yeah, of course.

But back then, it wasn't so simple. Georgia's Dominique Wilkins, a player with so much athletic ability that he became known as "the Human Highlight Film," and Terry Cummings,

Worthy lays in an easy two in a playoff game against the Mavericks.

a DePaul power forward who would also flex his muscles impressively in the NBA, were also available.

But fortunately for the Lakers, Jerry West was the man making the decision for them and he was astute enough to select Worthy.

That West had made the right choice soon became obvious. As Worthy's career played out over 12 years, it also became obvious that he deserved to be called "Big Game James." During the regular season over his career, he averaged 17.6 points, 5.1 rebounds, three assists, and shot 52.1 percent from the floor. In the postseason, those numbers grew to 21.1 points, 5.2 rebounds, 3.2 assists, and 54.4 percent.

Big Game James, indeed.

29 A Championship Like No Other

No team in any sport has ever faced a tougher journey on the road to a championship, a road filled with unimaginable, unacceptable, unruly obstacles.

In a dark and desperate period for the entire world, the 2019–20 Lakers were faced with confrontation, crushed by grief, stopped by disease, depressed by isolation, but fueled by anger.

And that doesn't even count the challenges they faced on the court, which were easy in comparison.

The Confrontation

Their travails began at the start of a season whose biggest question mark was thought to be: Can Anthony Davis be the partner LeBron James needed to bring the Lakers back to championship contention after a decade of irrelevance?

It would start with a seemingly easy first step, an exhibition-season trip to China where the Lakers were the NBA's most popular team, thanks to a long love affair between the Chinese people and Kobe Bryant.

Upon arrival, the Lakers, scheduled to play two games against the Brooklyn Nets, discovered there was no longer any love lost between themselves and the Chinese government.

After traveling 15 hours to get to Shanghai, the Lakers found out they had landed in a hornets' nest. A day earlier, Houston Rockets general manager Daryl Morey had tweeted: "Fight for freedom. Stand with Hong Kong," in support of pro-democracy protesters in the semi-autonomous region.

Chinese officials responded by going after the two U.S. teams temporarily on their soil, refusing to broadcast their two games, tearing down promotional ads, killing sponsorship deals, and cancelling several other scheduled events involving the NBA.

The Chinese government, having registered its outrage, soon backed off and both exhibition games went on as scheduled.

The Lakers left China without incident, the uproar no more than a blip on their radar screen.

If only the same could be said for what lay ahead.

The Grief

On January 25, playing against the 76ers in Philadelphia, James scored his 33,644th career point, passing Bryant for third place on the all-time scoring list.

In response, Bryant sent James a tweet: "Continuing to move the game forward. Much respect, my brother."

The two briefly spoke the following morning. Then, hours later, on board the Lakers' charter on the flight home, James learned of Bryant's passing.

"I promise you I'll continue your legacy, man," James wrote the next day. "Watch over me!"

The Lakers had been scheduled to return to the court in two days to face the Clippers, but they were too grief-stricken to do so. Anthony Davis was particularly hard hit by the tragedy, because Bryant had been a mentor to him.

When the postponed game was finally played, James addressed the crowd, saying, "In the words of Kobe Bryant, 'Mamba out.' But in the words of us, 'Not forgotten.' Live on, brother."

The Pandemic

When word of a potentially fatal coronavirus first spread across the world, many athletes figured they wouldn't be affected. Being young, healthy, supremely fit, and sheltered from the dangers that the general public often encounters, they assumed they were bulletproof.

Those illusions were shattered on March 11, when Utah Jazz center Rudy Gobert tested positive for the virus, causing the entire NBA to shut down.

A day later, the NCAA cancelled its men's and women's basketball tournaments for the first time in its history. March Madness had been turned into March Sadness.

The Bubble

Had the Lakers finally run into an immovable obstacle?

Would their dream of ending their decade-long championship drought not be denied by a team of rival players, but by a team of doctors?

An uncertain future stretched from early March to the middle of summer. How do you require teams to travel around the country, interact on a small court, and yet prevent the spread of a deadly disease?

After intense deliberations, the NBA came up with a plan that proved far more successful than those of either the NFL or Major League Baseball. Twenty-two of the league's 30 teams were invited to continue the season. They played eight games each at a neutral site, the ESPN Wide World of Sports Complex at the Walt Disney World Resort near Orlando, to determine the 16 postseason participants. The top eight clubs in each conference when play was halted were included, along with the six teams that were within six games of the eighth seeds.

Players were housed in the luxury hotels on the premises, one to a room. They had their meals in secure ballrooms, could hang out at a bar, listen to a DJ, and take advantage of all sorts of recreational diversions, ranging from video and arcade games to ping pong and even fishing in a pond on the site stocked with fish. At their disposal, the players had the services of doctors, trainers, and chefs, along with six barbers and three manicurists.

Their workday consisted of either playing on one of the three courts designated for games, complete with piped-in music and a PA announcer, along with virtual fans, or walking onto one of the seven courts reserved for practice on off days.

Leaving the complex would result in a mandated quarantine period before a player could return.

It was comfortable, their every reasonable wish satisfied. But after a while, boredom and loneliness set in. How many fish can you catch? These are guys used to an active social life, traveling to exotic locations all over the world, treated like royalty wherever they went, hanging with celebrities from all walks of life.

And suddenly, they were confined to a minimum-security prison—a luxury prison without bars except for drinking to be sure, but still in confinement.

The Dilemma: To Play or Not to Play

The debate began in the days following May 25, when George Floyd, a Black man, was taken into police custody on suspicion of trying to use a counterfeit $20 bill in a Minneapolis store. He died when an officer put his knee on Floyd's neck while he lay in the street and kept it there for over eight minutes.

The outrage over his death, captured on a bystander's phone, triggered massive demonstrations in cities across the nation.

NBA players joined the chorus of loud, angry voices demanding justice, but, ultimately, went back to work when the games resumed.

But they did not come back quietly. When faced with media questions about shot selection or offensive rebounds, they answered with condemnation of police brutality and demands for social justice. The words "Black Lives Matter" were displayed on arena floors and players wore uniforms that included words like "Power to the People" and "Equality."

But then came another blow to the cause in late August. In Kenosha, Wisconsin, an unarmed Black man named Jacob Blake was shot seven times in the back by a policeman.

The Milwaukee Bucks, whose arena is less than an hour's drive from the shooting, refused to take the court for their playoff game that day. Soon, the entire league boycotted that day's games.

Then what? Again, the question arose, do we play?

Both the Lakers and the Clippers voted to end the postseason immediately and go home, even though one of them figured to be in the Finals.

Other squads, however, were reluctant to stage a mass walkout, taking into consideration the money they would lose and the long period of isolation they had already endured in order to pursue a championship.

Ultimately, the remainder of the postseason was salvaged when NBA officials agreed to support player demands for initiatives aimed at reforming police departments and shining a light on systemic racism. Also, arenas controlled by team owners would be transformed into voting sites for the upcoming presidential election.

STEVE SPRINGER

Finally, the NBA Finals

With all the obstacles removed at last, three favorites for the title
stood tall: the Lakers, the No. 1 seed in the Western Conference;
the Clippers, the team down the hall at Staples Center; and the
Milwaukee Bucks, the top Eastern Conference seed. The Heat, the
fifth seed in the East, wasn't mentioned as a serious contender by
too many outside of Miami.

The Lakers lived up to the hype as the playoffs moved along,
beating the Trail Blazers, Rockets, and Nuggets, each in five games
in the best-of-seven series.

The Clippers season ended in disaster as they failed to even
reach the conference finals for a much-anticipated Battle of L.A.
Instead, they collapsed in the second round, losing to the Nuggets
after taking a three-games-to-one lead.

The Heat shut out the Pacers, upset the Bucks in five games,
and beat the Celtics in six.

In the Finals, the Heat began with a huge handicap because
injuries to two starters, center Bam Adebayo and guard Goran
Dragic, limited their playing time and effectiveness.

But Miami's Jimmy Butler raised his game to the superstar
level and inspired his teammates with his grit, determination, and
energy, making it a tough series for the Lakers anyway. Butler
had triple-doubles in Miami's victories in Game 3 (40 points, 11
rebounds, and 13 assists) and Game 5 (35 points, 12 rebounds,
and 11 assists).

With a three-games-to-one lead, the champagne on ice, and
the Larry O'Brien championship trophy polished and ready, the
Lakers, wearing their Kobe Bryant–designed snakeskin jerseys—in
which they had been undefeated—were ready to party, party,
party, popping the bubbly booze and then popping the bubble
after what would wind up being 95 days of isolation.

Game 5 came down to the final 7.1 seconds. The Lakers
Danny Green, standing behind the arc, had a wide-open, possible

112

series-clinching three-pointer, but clanked it off the front of the rim. Teammate Markieff Morris got the rebound, but his subsequent pass went out of bounds, enabling the Heat to win, 111–108.

And so, the longest season in NBA history went on.

But finally, in Game 6 in AdventHealth Arena, it was mission accomplished. Led by James, the Lakers won 106–93, giving the team 17 NBA championships to tie the Celtics for the most in league history.

James had a triple-double (28 points, 14 rebounds, and 10 assists) and was named Finals MVP, becoming the first player to win that award with three franchises (the Heat and the Cavaliers previously).

LeBron and AD celebrate after defeating the Heat in six games to capture the 2020 championship. (AP Images/Mark J. Terrill)

It was a night of vindication for:

- James, who failed to even get the Lakers into the postseason in his first year in L.A.
- Anthony Davis, who finally got a ring to go along with his phenomenal stats.
- Jeanie Buss, who ousted her brother Jim and fired general manager Mitch Kupchak, hoping to restore the team to the glory years it had enjoyed under her father's leadership.
- Rob Pelinka, who proved he could make the leap from agent to successful general manager.
- Frank Vogel, the Lakers' third choice to be the team's head coach.

It was also a night for the man who wasn't there, Kobe Bryant, whose memory inspired his teammates and added to the legacy of a team that always had a prominent place in his heart.

30 Kobe Gets His Man

Kobe Bryant was unhappy—unhappy enough to ask for a trade.

Shades of Magic Johnson a quarter century earlier? Not exactly. Johnson had wanted out because he didn't want to play for his coach, Paul Westhead.

Bryant wanted out because he didn't want to play for a team he felt lacked the talent to win a championship.

Bryant's outburst came at the end of the 2006–07 season, three years after dominating center Shaquille O'Neal had been traded because of contract issues.

Even after O'Neal's departure left a gaping hole in the middle, the Lakers reached the playoffs twice in the following three seasons, but they were eliminated in the first round both times by Phoenix. The first time, in 2006, the Lakers blew a three games to one lead.

Over those years, the frontcourt was manned by players like Chris Mihm, Kwame Brown, Brian Grant, Brian Cook, Slava Medvedenko, Vladimir Radmanovic, Andrew Bynum, and Vlade Divac. Having been drafted at 17, Bynum was then too young, and Divac was too old when he joined the Lakers for his second stint at age 36.

The Lakers had featured the best big men in the league for much of their previous 55 years. But watching this display of mediocrity around the basket caused Bryant to lose patience. He wanted to contend for a title again while he was still young enough to be a force. The breaking point occurred after the Suns eliminated the Lakers in five games in 2007.

"I would like to be traded, yeah," Bryant, who would be 29 before the start of the following season, told *ESPN Radio*. "As tough as it is to come to that conclusion, there's no other alternative. They obviously want to move in a different direction as far as rebuilding.

"I just want them to do the right thing…at this point, I'll go play on Pluto."

The futility was personified by Brown, known for his inability to hang on to the ball.

When Brown was accused of grabbing a birthday cake from a man on the street and throwing it at him in a late-night escapade, Phil Jackson told reporters Brown was innocent.

With a grin, Jackson said, "If it had been Kwame, he would have dropped the cake."

Bryant eventually calmed down and stuck it out with the Lakers and, on February 1, 2008, he was thrilled that he had.

In a blockbuster deal—the most significant trade by the Lakers since they had obtained Kobe Bryant a dozen years earlier—they sent Brown, Javaris Crittenton, Aaron McKie, the draft rights to Marc Gasol, and two future first-round draft picks to the Grizzlies for a future second-rounder and Marc's older brother, Pau.

It was a deal that caught the basketball world by surprise. Coach Phil Jackson didn't even know it was coming down, according to Jeanie Buss.

Kobe and Pau celebrate a win over the Mavericks in 2011. (Getty Images)

ESPN called it a "grand theft."

Bryant, the smile back on his face, said he took "his hat off" to Lakers management.

"It really does advance our cause quite a bit," Jackson said.

You think?

That's certainly what Spurs coach Gregg Popovich thought.

"What they did in Memphis is beyond comprehension," he told SI.com. "There should be a trade committee that can scratch all trades that make no sense."

No sense for San Antonio, that is.

Whenever a Lakers deal is made, the first question is: how will the newcomer work with Bryant?

In this case, the answer came in the first 10 minutes of their first game together. It seemed as if Gasol and Bryant had been playing together for 10 years.

Gone was Bryant's dissatisfaction. Gone was the longing of Laker fans for the sight of O'Neal in the middle.

Back was the Lakers' ability to be effective in the half-court game and maintain a smoothly running triangle offense.

An international star while playing for his native Spain, Gasol, at 7'0" and 250 pounds, was more Kareem than Shaq, a big man with finesse. With an excellent mid-range jumper, a sharp and consistent passing game, great court awareness, and an effective if not dominating defensive presence, Gasol became a key cog for the team.

The knock on him was that he was soft on defense, a charge he was labeled with when the Celtics outmuscled the Lakers to win the 2008 NBA Finals.

But those charges were muted when the Lakers, reaching the Finals three seasons in a row with Gasol on the floor, came back to win NBA titles in 2009 and 2010, the latter against Boston.

In the subsequent two seasons, he struggled in the postseason, especially with the emergence of Bynum. Gasol was even briefly traded before the start of the 2011–12 season until NBA commissioner David Stern blocked the deal.

In the final quarter of the Lakers' final game in 2012, Bryant and Gasol openly yelled at each other as the Oklahoma City Thunder finished the Lakers off in the fifth game of their second-round series.

A free agent after the 2013-14 season, Gasol opted to sign with the Bulls.

But none of that can take away what Gasol had brought to the team four years earlier.

He just might have kept Kobe Bryant in Purple and Gold. That alone should guarantee Gasol a place of honor in team history.

31 Rings Half a Century Late

While the championships won in Los Angeles were honored with banners that covered the walls of the Forum and then Staples Center, there was no evidence of the five titles won by the team back in Minneapolis.

That bothered the superstar of those Minneapolis clubs, George Mikan.

"We were also Lakers," he said in a 2001 interview. "How do you separate Minneapolis? We are proud of the Lakers, proud to be a part of the organization's history. The only thing that separates us is miles.

"The young people today have benefitted from what we did. Are they trying to live us down in Los Angeles? We were there first."

Were they ever.

After winning the championship of the National Basketball League (NBL) in the 1947–48 season by defeating the Rochester Royals, the Lakers moved to the BAA (Basketball Association of America) the following season and won another championship.

Since the BAA would become the NBA a year later, that counted as their first NBA title. The name of the league may have changed for the 1949–50 season, but the name of its champion remained the same: Lakers.

The two-time champs fell short the following year, but Minneapolis then came back to three-peat before Byron Scott, originator of the term, was even born. The Lakers won the NBA Finals in 1952, '53, and '54.

While Mikan was clearly the league's dominant player, he had plenty of help from his teammates in establishing a Lakers dynasty. Jim Pollard, Slater Martin, Clyde Lovellette, and Vern Mikkelsen all joined Mikan in the Hall of Fame along with their coach, John Kundla.

Soon after the remarks by Mikan, then 77, about a lack of recognition appeared in a story I wrote in the *Los Angeles Times,* Lakers owner Jerry Buss called me to explain that he wasn't sure the media would approve of adding a Minneapolis banner to Staples Center. I assured him that wouldn't be the case.

I added that, if he was considering doing it, the banner should be unveiled before the Lakers, then winners of eight titles in L.A., got close to the Celtics' total, then 16, so that it wouldn't look like Buss was merely trying to pad the Lakers' total to catch the Celtics.

Several weeks Lakers, Buss announced that the Minneapolis stars would be honored at Staples Center.

In 2020, with the Minneapolis Lakers included, the team celebrated a 17th championship, tying the Celtics for the most in league history.

With Jerry's daughter, Jeanie, then the team's executive vice president of business operations, handling the Minneapolis induction ceremony back in April of 2002, the old Lakers received honors beyond anything Mikan could have dreamed of.

Not only was a banner unfurled on the wall of Staples Center—blue to denote the key color of the old Minneapolis franchise—but each of the Hall of Famers received a championship ring as well.

"Rings…have become such a meaningful part of any title in any sport," Jeanie said. "Players don't talk about winning a banner or winning a pennant. They talk about winning a ring. I know what the rings mean to our players. Yet the Minneapolis champions missed out on that. They never had a memento of their own.

"So I decided to give them all rings. That would be only fitting."

The Lakers kept the rings a secret from the former Minneapolis coach and his players until the presentation ceremony.

That only heightened the thrill when they finally put the ultimate symbol of their triumphant run on their fingers.

As a coach, Kundla's top annual salary was $6,000. The ring he received was worth $9,000.

The evening of tribute afforded Kundla yet another bonus. He was flown to L.A. in first class, the first time he had ever sat in that section of a plane.

Mikan died three years later, but there was solace in the fact he had at least lived long enough to be reunited with the team that had defined his life.

32 The First Lakers Team

Could the Twin Cities support pro basketball? That might seem like a silly question now for an area that not only has an NBA team, the Minnesota Timberwolves, but also the NFL's Vikings and MLB's Twins.

But it was no sure thing back in the late 1940s when pro basketball was still considered a poor substitute for college basketball, and the focus in Minneapolis was on the University of Minnesota basketball team.

So before the Detroit Gems were purchased with the idea of moving them to Minneapolis, two other National Basketball League (NBL) teams, the Oshkosh All-Stars and the Sheboygan Redskins, were brought in to play an exhibition game at Minneapolis Auditorium in December 1946.

When more than 5,000 paying customers showed up, Minneapolis' future in the sport was assured.

While Morris Chalfen and Ben Berger were the money men, Sid Hartman, a sportswriter for the *Minneapolis Tribune,* was the driving force behind the arrival of pro basketball in that city.

It was Hartman who first approached Chalfen, and the latter brought in Berger, a business partner.

It was Hartman who insisted that buying the Gems would be a good deal even though no players would be included (they were sent to other NBL clubs).

It was Hartman who negotiated the purchase price.

It was Hartman who met Gems owner Maury Winston at an airport in Detroit and consummated the deal by giving him a check for $15,000.

"I think that was absolutely the right thing at the right time," Berger later said, "though Sid went over and bought a Detroit team that had gone bankrupt in the National League and paid $15,000 for nothing. He could have gotten it for free. Well, you don't know things [at the time]."

While Hartman would continue to play a key role in stocking the new team with players while still keeping his job at the *Tribune*—a glaring conflict of interest that would not be tolerated under today's journalistic standards—a general manager was brought in to handle the business end of the front office. He was Max Winter, who owned a Minneapolis restaurant and had done some sports promotion.

Winter not only took the job, but he also bought a share of the team.

It was Hartman who selected the first Lakers coach, John Kundla, a recognizable local figure who had starred at the University of Minnesota in both basketball and baseball.

Kundla, comfortable coaching at St. Thomas College in St. Paul, was uncomfortable at first with the financial uncertainty then surrounding a pro franchise—especially a new franchise in an untested city. So he rejected Hartman's offer.

When Chalfen and Berger responded to Kundla's doubts by agreeing to pay the coach three years of salary in advance, Kundla changed his mind and agreed to become the first coach of the Lakers.

His three-year deal of $6,000 per season doubled his annual salary at St. Thomas.

One matter still remained: finding players.

Hartman first set his sights on Jim Pollard, a 6'4", 185-pound former All-American at Stanford who was playing AAU ball when Hartman came calling. Others from that era claim Pollard, nicknamed "the Kangaroo Kid" for his jumping ability, was the first player to dunk.

Pollard accepted an offer from Hartman of $10,000 for the 1947–48 season along with a $3,000 signing bonus, a huge package back then for a basketball player.

Pollard was good enough to be the cornerstone of a franchise, but Hartman had an even bigger idea. Big as in Mikan.

A star at DePaul, Mikan had stayed in Chicago to play with the American Gears, another NBL franchise.

After they won the 1946–47 NBL title in Mikan's first season with the team, owner Maurice White pulled the Gears out of the NBL to form his own league, the (PBLA) Professional Basketball League of America.

The PBLA lasted one month before collapsing. The Gears players were scattered among the remaining NBL clubs as had been the case with the Gems when they were disbanded.

The prize acquisition, of course, was Mikan.

As would later be the formula for the NBA Draft, the NBL dispersed the players to teams in reverse order of their finish. That resulted in the No. 1 overall pick going to the newly named Lakers, coming off the Gems' 4–40 mark the previous season.

Which meant Mikan. That was a no-brainer.

Signing him was not so simple.

In negotiations with Hartman and Winter in the Lakers' Minneapolis offices, Mikan rejected the team's best offer after several hours of discussion, saying he was ready to just take his ball and go home.

Home was Illinois, and he insisted his next option was law school.

The talks at a standstill, Mikan asked Hartman and Winter to drive him to the airport.

In the car, Winter could see a disaster at the end of the road. Once Mikan got on that plane, Winter knew the Lakers would never see him again—at least not in their uniform.

Since both Winter and Hartman were Jewish and understood Yiddish, Winter used that language to tell Hartman, who was driving, to pretend he was lost.

Hartman complied, going around in circles until he was sure the last plane had left Minneapolis for the night.

Mikan was stuck in town.

With an extra day to talk, Hartman and Winter convinced Mikan to sign.

"They wore me down," he said.

Mikan would get $15,000 for the upcoming season.

Complementing Mikan and Pollard, the two powerhouses in the front court, were a bunch of former University of Minnesota players. The rights to Tony Jaros and Don "Swede" Carlson were obtained by Hartman from the Chicago Stags of the Basketball Association of America (BBA) for $25,000. Hartman also added former Golden Gophers Don Smith, Ken Exel, and Warren Ajax. And playmaking guard Herm Schaefer came from the Indianapolis Kautskys.

With Mikan leading the way, the Lakers not only won the NBL title, beating the Rochester Royals 3–1 in the best-of-five finals, but also took a break in the middle of the playoffs to win the World Professional Basketball Tournament in Chicago.

Pro basketball's first dynasty was born.

33 Gems Before Rings

The Lakers entered the basketball world far from the glitter and glamour of L.A. Back before the NBA itself had come into existence, they were even removed from the Minnesota lakes that spawned their name.

In a time before owners dared dream of packed arenas, nationally televised broadcasts, and diamond-studded championship rings, the Lakers began as the Detroit Gems in 1946.

It had been a half century since the first professional basketball game had been played at Masonic Hall in Trenton, New Jersey, between two local teams.

Over the years, leagues were formed. There was the National League, the (ABL) American Basketball League, and the (NBL) National Basketball League.

The Gems were formed as an NBL franchise for the 1946–47 season under the ownership of a local jeweler named Maury Winston and his associate, C. King Boring.

Naturally, a team owned by a jeweler would be named the Gems.

It was also the inaugural season for the (BAA) Basketball Association of America. That league had its own team in Detroit that first season, the Falcons, who finished a dismal 20–40.

But as bad as that record was, it still looked good in comparison to the Gems, who were an abysmal 4–40.

Even more dismal than their record was the support the Gems received from the community. The team didn't have a permanent home, moving instead from court to court—whatever was available —around the city.

Dollar Bills
In the 1896 Trenton game, considered by many to be the first ever in which basketball players got paid, the pot couldn't be divided equally.
Admission was charged to offset the cost of renting Masonic Hall. After each player had received $15 from the profits, one dollar was left over. It was decided to give that remaining buck to Fred Cooper, a team captain.
Thus, for at least one day, Cooper—with $16 in his pocket—was the highest paid player in pro basketball.

But the fans, few in number and fewer still in attendance, didn't move with them. Some games would attract only a few dozen spectators.

One game drew only six paying customers. Winston gave each of them a refund.

There would be no second chance for the Gems to grow either on the court or in the eyes of sports fans. At least not in Detroit. Before their second season, they were purchased by Chalfen, an ice-show promoter, and Berger, a Minneapolis theater owner and restaurateur.

In the time it took to write a check for $15,000, the Gems were gone, snatched away to a new city and a new era, one they would dominate.

34 Rings

When fans think of championships in every sport, they think of the gaudy, diamond-studded rings that sometimes look more like paperweights than jewelry.

But in the early days of the NBA, there were no rings. When they finally became the standard symbol of a championship, they were produced by the league in cookie-cutter fashion. Regardless of the title-winning team, the style was the same season after season. Only the names and the year changed.

Until Pat Riley spoke up.

Coach of the Showtime Lakers for most of the 1980s, Riley wanted something unique for his players. After all, they won five championships in that decade, and Riley didn't think the rings should be interchangeable—especially since he had owned the same style ring himself for a decade, having won his first as a player on the 1972 Lakers championship squad.

League officials said that if the Lakers wanted something different they had to pay for it.

And that's what the team did, designing a special ring for each championship. Other teams followed suit, giving the crowning prize of each season a distinctive look.

The only league requirements are that the ring contains diamonds, totaling at least one karat in size, and bearing the NBA logo on it.

The production of these elaborate rings has become a long process that begins soon after a team wins its title. Diagrams are drawn and models are constructed. The only limit to the deliberations is the imperative that the rings be ready for their grand presentation on opening night of the following season.

The Lakers have had to be especially creative because they have had the enviable task of designing ring after ring. And they have been equal to the challenge.

On the side of the diamond-studded band denoting the 2000 championship are the words "Bling, Bling," because that was the expression Shaquille O'Neal kept using as he envisioned his first title ring.

Shortly after the Lakers won in 2002, Chick Hearn, the only Los Angeles play-by-play man the team had ever had at that point, passed away. To honor him the Lakers engraved a microphone on the side of that season's ring along with the words "Slam Dunk," a term invented by Hearn.

Other Lakers rings have included representations of the Forum, Staples Center, and a triangle in tribute to the team's long-running triangle offense.

After the 2009 championship, each player's ring included a laser image of his face.

Since the 2010 championship was the Lakers' 16th in the NBA, those rings have 16 white diamonds along with two championship trophies (signifying the back-to-back titles) made of 16 karat gold. The ring also contains a tiny shred of the ball used in the title-clinching Game 7 against the Celtics. On this ring, the images of the players' faces are three-dimensional.

What's next, virtual reality?

There are also female versions of the ring worn by mothers, wives, and girlfriends.

Some players rarely pull out their glitzy hardware. But when Phil Jackson was coaching, he made it a point to wear one of his many rings at the start of the postseason each year to inspire his players and remind them of the prize they were battling for.

So many rings have their own story. None is as uplifting as the one about the 2010 championship ring of Metta World Peace (Ron Artest). He announced that he would auction it off to raise money for charity.

Some were dubious, knowing how flaky Artest can be.

But not this time. He held a raffle for the ring that raised $500,000.

The winner was Raymond Mikhael, a father of four from Hawthorne, California. The money went to Artest's Xcel University, a program that works with community centers and schools to

Jeanie's Ring

If one of your goals before you die is to wear a Lakers championship ring, try to attend a Jeanie Buss autograph session, either for her memoir, *Laker Girl*, or for another team event.

As fans present her with a book, she allows them to put on her championship ring for photo opportunities or to simply enjoy the feel of it.

At one Staples Center book signing, her ring suddenly disappeared. While others around her panicked that someone had stolen it, Jeanie calmly assured them that it was probably some absentminded Lakers fan who had inadvertently wandered off with the valuable jewelry still on their finger.

Sure enough, an elderly couple soon showed up, embarrassingly holding the ring in their hands.

Yet another memorable story to add to the lore of the Lakers rings.

identify and help high-risk youth. Specifically, the donation will focus on mental health issues.

Artest being Artest, there was one stipulation attached to his auction. He insisted on keeping the box the ring came in. It contained two lights that highlighted the glittering band as it spun around.

Maybe if Xcel needs additional funds, he can auction off the box.

There was nothing uplifting about the fate of one of Jeanie Buss' rings. She was wearing it one morning in the late 1980s as she drove into the parking lot outside her Forum office.

With no game that night, it was quiet at 10:00 AM as she headed for the steps that led down into the building.

It was then that Jeanie noticed a man lurking at the bottom of the stairs. Despite feeling a bit of apprehension, she kept going.

All of a sudden, there was a gun in her face.

The man demanded all her jewelry, including the championship ring.

Steve Springer

After Jeanie turned it over, he said, "Go in the building and don't call the police because I know who you are, I know where you work, and I will come back and kill you."

She picked up her purse and headed toward the glass doors.

It was then that the robber realized he had neglected to take her money.

"Come back," he demanded.

Five feet separated Jeanie from the doors. With the man furiously yelling at her, she decided to keep going.

As she dashed through the doors unharmed, the man disappeared.

And so did her ring, never to be seen again.

One of Hearn's rings wasn't seen in public for the last 30 years of his life. He liked to wear a championship ring to every game, choosing from his vast collection as the mood struck him.

But there was one he never wore. It was the ring from the 1972 championship, the Lakers' first in Los Angeles. Hearn had given it to his only son, Gary, shortly after the Lakers won the title.

Soon after that, Gary died of a drug overdose. He was 29.

"Because Gary has worn it," Chick said, "I can't wear it."

And he never did.

35 Why Lakers?

When the Detroit Gems were moved to Minneapolis for the 1947–48 season, the choice of a team name seemed obvious.

Their name in Detroit had come from one of the owners, Maury Winston, who was a jeweler. But in Minnesota, known as

Lakers' Colors

Winter got his say when it came to the Minneapolis Lakers' colors. He opted for light blue and white because those are the colors of the Swedish flag, and there is a heavy Swedish population in Minnesota.

After the Lakers came to Los Angeles, the colors were changed to purple and gold when Jack Kent Cooke bought the team.

While he loved the color purple, Cooke hated the sound of the word. So instead, the uniform colors—under orders from Cooke— were referred to as "Forum blue and gold."

"the Land of 10,000 Lakes," what could be a more fitting name than *Lakers*?

The first suggestion came from Max Winter, the team's general manager that first season. He wanted the name *Vikings* because of the Scandinavian roots of many in the area.

Winter had even gone so far as to put *Vikings* on the team's stationery.

But that stationery would become a collector's item when a local radio station—with the cooperation of the transplanted Gems—sponsored a contest to name the team. First prize was either season tickets or a $100 savings bond.

A local businessman, Ben Frank, came up with *Lakers*, fitting not only because of the preponderance of lakes in the area, but also because of the distinct boats that plowed the waters of the Great Lakes, carrying ore and other cargo, stopping on the shores of Minnesota and other area states. Those ships were called "lakers."

While Frank may have had an everlasting influence on the team, he wasn't tied to it emotionally. For his prize he chose the savings bond over the season tickets.

When the NFL granted an expansion NFL franchise to the area over a decade later, Winter got his team name immortalized as well. He became part-owner of the Minnesota Vikings.

When the Lakers moved to Los Angeles, they found themselves in an area relatively devoid of lakes. There is MacArthur Park, the lake at Westlake and a few other minor bodies of water spread around. But there are not enough lakes to warrant naming a team after them.

It was a situation similar to the one faced by the New Orleans Jazz when that team moved to Salt Lake City. The sounds of jazz echo all over New Orleans. Salt Lake City? Not so much.

Nevertheless, the team stuck with Jazz.

Bob Short, the Lakers' owner who moved the club to Los Angeles, contemplated a name change to…the Oceaneers.

Honestly.

Fortunately, Short thought better of it.

Actually, he didn't. The reason he stuck with Lakers, he said, was because "we have a lot of trophies with that name on them."

Good thing they won so many championships in Minneapolis.

36 Return to Carroll

Today the cornfield is long gone. A green park now spreads out over the property with homes on either side of the spot where the Lakers' DC-3 made an unscheduled landing.

In the middle of the park is an outdoor basketball court. It is purple and gold, named Laker Court, and paid for by the club. A plaque next to it recounts the events of that unforgettable flight.

Visiting Laker Court is the ultimate road trip for any fan putting together a to-do list.

Lakers vice president Jeanie Buss and former player Tommy Hawkins—one of the passengers on that ill-fated flight—made that trip for the court's dedication in September 2010, a half century after the daring landing.

Buss told the residents who gathered for the occasion that they should take pride in all the team has accomplished in the last 50 years because if the plane had tragically crashed with no survivors, the franchise, struggling financially in those years, might have ceased to exist.

When it was Hawkins' turn to speak, he first dropped to his knees and kissed the ground.

"I've been waiting 50 years," he said, "to do that."

37 The First Trip to L.A.

In today's sports environment, an NBA team that won six titles in less than a decade and could boast of the game's reigning superstar along with four other future Hall of Famers and a future Hall of Fame coach would be embraced by the fans of its city.

Woe to the local politicians who let such a prize get away. And woe as well to the owner who tried to pull off a deed as dastardly as packing up and leaving.

To this day the names of Walter O'Malley (Dodgers), Robert Irsay (Colts), and Art Modell (Browns) elicit shaking fists and four-letter insults in the cities they abandoned.

But there was no such venom directed at Bob Short when he decided to move his Minneapolis Lakers. He remained popular enough in Minnesota to later run for the U.S. Senate, though he didn't win.

The lack of outrage can best be explained by the fact that there were few fans to express that outrage.

Besides, they had been numbed after hearing rumors of a move for several years.

The beginning of the end came in 1957. With Mikan retiring and the glory years in the rearview mirror, owners Morris Chalfen and Ben Berger let it be known that the Lakers were for sale.

A group surfaced that expressed an interest in moving the club to St. Louis. Another group wanted to purchase the team and transplant it to Kansas City.

Short, who made his fortune in the trucking business, headed a group of 100 individuals and corporations that bid for the Lakers, pledging to keep them in Minneapolis. Short had the winning bid: $150,000.

The purchase price was 10 times what Chalfen and Berger had paid for the club.

But Short's arrival didn't alleviate the many problems the Lakers faced.

For one thing they weren't very good. The Lakers had losing seasons in all three years Short owned them in Minneapolis, their cumulative record 77–142, including 25–50 in 1959–60, their last year in Minnesota.

They weren't treated with much respect. Although Minneapolis Auditorium was supposedly their home court, they had to share it with various other events. That meant playing in five other locations as well, including several outside the Twin Cities.

Who wanted to support a nomadic team with a bad record? Fewer and fewer fans as the decade came to an end.

And the new decade figured to be even worse for Short. In 1961, the Vikings, an NFL expansion team, and the Twins, a Major League Baseball team moving from Washington, would begin play, battling Short for the sports dollar.

He looked with envy to the West Coast where Los Angeles was proving to be a paradise for any professional club courageous enough to make the big leap.

The Cleveland Rams had gone there in 1946 and played to huge crowds, surpassing 100,000 on three occasions, in the cavernous Memorial Coliseum.

Then, in 1958, the Dodgers left Brooklyn to also play in the L.A. Coliseum. O'Malley was building a baseball stadium in Chavez Ravine, but, in the meantime, the Dodgers, too, were filling up much of the Coliseum. They drew more than 78,000 for their first game there, more than 92,000 for each of three World Series games in 1959, and 93,103 for an exhibition game that season against the New York Yankees.

Short wasn't looking for crowds that size. Anything in excess of 10,000 in the Los Angeles Sports Arena would be more than adequate for him.

He decided to bring his players west for an exploratory road trip. They would play one game in San Francisco's Cow Palace and one in the L.A. Sports Arena to test the California market.

The trip was scheduled for the end of January, 1960.

The problem was transportation.

Just two weeks earlier, the Lakers' DC-3 had been forced to come down in a Carroll, Iowa cornfield. The landing in 10 to 15 inches of snow had been so incredibly smooth that there had been little damage to the plane.

The only equipment that had to be replaced were the blownout generators that had caused the premature end of the flight.

The cornfield was bulldozed and Vern Ullman, the pilot, stepped back into the cockpit to fly his plane out of Carroll.

"I put it in there," he said. "I'm going to take it out."

And that he did, on a sunny day with more than 1,000 spectators watching.

In the meantime, the Lakers were flying on commercial airliners to their road games.

But one night, Short came into the locker room after a game and said, "Boys, I can't keep flying you commercial. It's too expensive. Especially since I want to take you out to the West Coast for a few games.

"So how many of you will get back on that plane?"

Not a single hand was raised.

"Well then, the hell with you," he said. "You either get on that plane or you can look for another team to play for."

The players weren't happy about it. Their wives weren't happy about it either, but playing pro basketball sure beat a 9-to-5 job. So the Lakers reluctantly stepped back onto the D-3 just 12 days after riding it down into a cornfield and headed for San Francisco.

They played in the Cow Palace on January 31 against the Philadelphia Warriors, a team that would eventually move to the Bay Area and become the San Francisco and later Golden State Warriors.

Philadelphia, behind Wilt Chamberlain's 41 points and 33 rebounds, won 114–104.

The next day, the Lakers headed south to play their first-ever game in Los Angeles.

It was February 1, 1960. Again, the opponent was the Warriors. Again, the Lakers lost despite 36 points from Elgin Baylor. Final score: Warriors 103, Lakers 96.

But the numbers that most interested Short were the attendance figures. A crowd of 10,202 showed up at the Sports Arena.

They were at least partially lured by the offer of seeing two games for the price of one. Buyer beware, it wasn't two NBA games. Before the Lakers and Warriors ran up and down the court, there was a preliminary game between the Los Alamitos Navy and the Vagabonds, a club that called itself "the All-Negro basketball team."

The Lakers came back less than a month later and played two more games in the Sports Arena, both against the St. Louis Hawks.

The crowd was a combined 8,300 for *both* games.

That should not have been a surprise to Short. Both the UCLA and USC basketball teams played in the Sports Arena and their crowds generally averaged around 6,000–6,500.

So was it worth the gamble for Short?

"A gamble?" he said. "Hell, we were broke in Minneapolis. We did have some confidence in L.A., but it wasn't the basketball capital of the world back then."

Short may have had confidence in L.A., but the other NBA owners didn't have any confidence in his bold plan. They voted 7–1 against allowing him to move.

At a time when St. Louis was as far west as the league stretched, the owners didn't want to bear the cost of flying all the way to the West Coast to play one team.

"We've got to move," Short told one owner. "We're going to die in Minneapolis."

"Then that's the way it's going to be," the owner replied.

And that's the way it might have been had it not been for Abe Saperstein.

On the same day the NBA turned Short down, Saperstein— the basketball genius who took over the management of an all-Black basketball team in 1926 and turned it into the Harlem Globetrotters—made an announcement. If the NBA did not grant his request for a franchise, he would form a rival league, the (ABL) American Basketball League.

Suddenly, the West Coast was up for grabs. If Saperstein went through with his threat, whoever got there first would have a huge advantage.

When the NBA owners met again later that day, they took another vote on Short's request.

It went 8–0 in his favor.

The Los Angeles Lakers were born.

38 Short Comes Up Short

But, after winning the bidding, Short soon learned that the $150,000 purchase price was just a down payment on the money required to keep this floundering team from sinking out of sight.

After the sale was official, Short and his investors came up with another $50,000 for operating expenses.

That money was gone in two weeks.

Short was a sharp entrepreneur who understood supply and demand in the business world. But sports were a different universe —especially pro basketball as a lower-tier sport in its early years.

Economics seemed to determine most Lakers moves. If a player was sold to another team, it was often because the club could no longer afford him or because it simply needed money.

"Hey, guys," Short once told his players in a locker room talk, "I like basketball as much as the next guy, but not when it's going to cost me $50,000 a week."

Short bemoaned the fact he had not sold future Hall of Famers George Mikan and Jim Pollard at the end of their careers. Instead they retired without the club getting anything for them.

"I will never again let a player retire from my roster," Short said. "The Lakers can't afford that kind of luxury.

"Other teams better fixed financially can get by with letting their veterans retire. The Minneapolis club followed the same policy and look at the fix we're in today.

"In this business, when you want to stay ahead of the sheriff, you keep moving."

At one point, the Lakers were again at the edge of financial disaster. If they didn't get $14,000 immediately, they might not survive.

Short wrote them a personal check.

What could the other investors do to repay him? They certainly weren't going to put more of their own money into such a shaky operation. So instead they awarded Short enough stock, at five cents a share, to give him a one-third interest in the team.

Of course, one third of nothing is still nothing.

When Short finally announced he was pulling the plug after the conclusion of the 1959–60 season and heading west, he didn't get much sympathy from the Minnesota faithful by pleading poverty.

"The downfall of the Lakers," wrote Charlie Johnson in the *Minneapolis Tribune*, "can be summarized as follows: lack of professional leadership and management; mistakes in draft choices, trades, player deals, selection of coaches; and unwise expenditures; too much switching of games; and far too much talk of moving."

In other words: goodbye and good riddance.

39 Baylor Beats the Bigots

During the 1958–59 season, the Minneapolis Lakers played the Cincinnati Royals in Charleston, West Virginia.

Despite the fact the civil rights movement was gaining momentum in America, prejudice was still virulent in some parts of the country. Even an African American as famous and respected on the basketball court as Elgin Baylor found he wasn't famous or respected enough for the bigots.

On the day of the game, Baylor and two African American teammates—Boo Ellis and Ed Fleming—were refused service at a Charleston hotel while the White players were invited in. The

Elgin Baylor makes a beautiful, over-the-shoulder pass against the Knicks in Madison Square Garden in 1962. (Getty Images)

Black players were told that they could go to a hotel that accepted African Americans.

That wasn't acceptable to Lakers coach John Kundla who took his entire team, Black and White, to the other hotel, but Baylor felt a bigger statement had to be made. So he refused to play in the game that night, knowing how much his absence would hurt the attendance.

For towns like Charleston that invested money and resources for the right to serve as neutral sites for NBA games, lack of support in the form of empty seats could be devastating.

Lakers owner Bob Short backed Baylor.

"That shows there's a guy who believes in principle," Short said. "I don't argue with principle."

The Charlestown American Business Club, the promoters of the game, appealed to NBA president Maurice Podoloff to intercede.

Podoloff refused.

The Lakers lost 95–91, but Baylor won his point. Cities that discriminated against him or other African American players would pay a price. For the Charleston American Business Club, the loss was $800 to $1,000 after only 2,356 paying customers showed up at the Civic Center.

"They teach us about democracy in school," said a 13-year-old who called the *Charleston Gazette-Mail* after hearing about the treatment of Baylor and his teammates, "but they don't practice it very much around here. It just burns me up."

40 Lakers vs. the Harlem Globetrotters

In the eyes of many, a game between the Lakers and the Harlem Globetrotters, scheduled for February 19, 1948, was going to be a mismatch.

The Globetrotters were regarded by many as clowns, basketball players who were better suited for entertainment than serious competition.

The Lakers, on the other hand, in their first year in Minneapolis, were labeled by their supporters as the best basketball team in the world. They had George Mikan, the most dominant player in the game at any level, and Jim Pollard, who was nicknamed the Kangaroo Kid because of his leaping ability.

But there was much more to this game than just basketball. The Lakers were all White, the Globetrotters all Black.

It was less than a year since Jackie Robinson had broken baseball's color barrier by playing for the Brooklyn Dodgers. President Harry Truman was pushing hard for civil rights in the country. A young preacher named Martin Luther King Jr. was just finding his voice.

And those whose bigotry inflamed their passions yelled just as loud on the other side.

Chicago Stadium would offer a new venue to play this drama out.

Eager to watch it, a crowd of 17,823 packed the arena.

There was heated debate about how good the Globetrotters really were. *Esquire* called them the "world's greatest basketball outfit...not just a passing phenomenon like Philippine yo-yo spinners."

But in the opinion of a Chicago paper, Globetrotters star Reece "Goose" Tatum was nothing more than a "Negro pivot clown."

There was also a dispute over the Globetrotters' winning streak. Team owner Abe Saperstein put it at 101 straight games. Others had it in the 90s. Whatever the number, detractors were quick to point out that the Globetrotters had racked it up against largely inferior talent—teams brought in just to provide bodies for the Globetrotters to dribble over, around, and through as they cavorted in their hilarious shtick.

From the opening tip-off against the Lakers, however, everybody in the arena knew this was going to be more than just an exhibition game played for laughs.

A New Day

The Globetrotters' dramatic victory over the Lakers in their first meeting invigorated a long-standing debate that ultimately brought equality and justice to the court while also elevating both the game and the sport to new heights.

The issue was race. The old taboos were falling in sports. The basketball owners looked at Jackie Robinson and knew that their own unacceptable barriers were about to crumble as well.

When the Globetrotters beat the Lakers a second time in a row, the voices of protest grew louder.

"Baseball proved there is plenty of gold across the color line," wrote the *Chicago Defender*.

Six months after the Globetrotters defeated the Lakers in their first meeting, the Chicago Stags of the Basketball Association of America, the forerunner of the NBA, signed six Black players.

Finally, in 1950, prior to the NBA's second season of existence, Celtics owner Walter Brown announced at the league draft, "Boston takes Charles Cooper of Duquesne."

"Walter," another owner said, "don't you know he's a colored boy?"

"I don't give a damn if he's striped, plaid, or polka dot," Brown said. "Boston takes Charles Cooper of Duquesne."

When Mikan went up for the ball, he found himself with company in the air up there. Tatum also soared. Though six inches shorter, Tatum beat the Laker center to the ball, tapping it to a fellow Globetrotter.

Game on.

"It was electric, as charged an atmosphere as I've ever been in," Mikan said.

The Globetrotters knew their chance for victory hinged on stopping Mikan. They tried everything from body-pounding fouls to knocking his glasses off.

Not a lot of laughs for the 6'10" center. Mikan was so upset that the normally accurate free-throw shooter connected on only 4–11 from the line. However, he still managed to score 24 points, a humongous total in an era before the invention of the shot clock.

But the Globetrotters got their points as well and, after trailing 32–23 at the half, they were even with the Lakers at 59 all with 10 seconds to play.

The ball was in the hands of the Globetrotters Marques Haynes, who would later learn he was playing with a fractured vertebra suffered while crashing to the floor in a battle for the ball with Mikan earlier in the game.

Haynes passed to teammate Ermer Robinson, who hit a one-handed set shot at the final gun to give the Globetrotters a 61–59 victory.

Mikan later said he was "ashamed" of his performance. "I tried to beat the Globetrotters all by myself," he said.

A year later, the two teams met again in Chicago Stadium and exceeded the initial meeting in attendance with 20,046 filling the arena. The results didn't change. The Globetrotters won again.

But the Lakers got a rematch that season and finally won. They then reeled off six straight victories against the Globetrotters, causing Saperstein to end the rivalry in 1958.

No more Lakers. No more bitterly contested games. Leave that to the NBA, Saperstein figured.

Instead he decided that if he went back to the laughs, and the fun, and the rows of giggling kids in packed arenas, he couldn't lose.

Not as long as the Washington Generals were around.

41 Chick to the Rescue

Although his team was struggling to attract fans during the team's first regular season in Los Angeles, Bob Short hoped that would change in the postseason. Surely the excitement of the playoffs would capture the attention of the fans even in a city like L.A., blessed with a myriad of entertainment options.

That hope, however, soon faded.

Despite finishing with a 36–43 record, the Lakers not only made it into the postseason, but also beat the Detroit Pistons in the Western Division semifinals in five games to make it into the second round.

Cheers from the fans? It was more like yawns. Game 1 at the Sports Arena drew 3,549 fans. The Lakers won, but the attendance only increased to 4,253 for Game 2.

There was one more game in Los Angeles, the fifth and deciding game, but that couldn't be used as a barometer of fan interest. With the Sports Arena already booked, the Lakers were forced to play at the Shrine Auditorium, which held only 3,705 for basketball.

Next up for the Lakers was the division finals against the St. Louis Hawks, who had reached the NBA Finals the season before where they had lost to the Celtics.

The operators of the Sports Arena had not been willing to gamble that the Lakers would be in the postseason, because if they failed to qualify, those would be nights of lost revenue.

Besides, why take the risk with a client who was only bringing in around 5,000 customers per event?

So Sports Arena officials booked events without considering NBA playoff dates and the Lakers had to settle for the leftovers. There were none for the first two home games of the second round. That forced them to play the Hawks at the California State, Los Angeles gym where the capacity was only 5,200.

Short was dying financially by the time the teams headed back to St. Louis for Game 5.

What could he do?

He needed publicity.

He needed to broadcast the games on radio, something he had yet to do in L.A., because—amazingly enough—he didn't want to spend the money to secure a station.

What Short really needed and got was the voice of Chick Hearn.

Peoria to L.A.

In Peoria, Hearn broadcast not only Bradley basketball, but high school games as well.

"It was an incredible thrill for me," said one former high-school player from that era, "because I had heard him broadcasting all those Bradley games. The Bradley players were huge heroes to me, and I had heard him calling their names over the years. And here he was, calling my name. I just thought it was the coolest thing I had ever heard."

Talk about cool. That player was Ralph Lawler, and, years later, he would also take his place behind a microphone in Los Angeles— sometimes side by side with Hearn—broadcasting the games of the other team in town, the Clippers.

Hearn grew up as a farm boy in Buda, Illinois, 133 miles southwest of Chicago.

A star basketball player in high school, he continued to play the game at the AAU level upon graduation while working for Austin Western, a manufacturer of farm machinery.

Hearn had dreams of continuing his basketball career at the collegiate level, but when his father, Frank, was seriously injured as a result of his laundry truck skidding off an icy road, Hearn had to keep working to help support his family.

He went to Chicago and took a job with Dun and Bradstreet, a supplier of business information. Still in search of a rewarding profession, he next became a salesman for a pharmaceutical company.

Whatever he did, Hearn needed to make enough money to also support his own growing family. He had married his high-school sweetheart, Marge, and in 1942 they had a son, Gary.

Basketball seemed further and further away.

To satisfy his unquenchable thirst for the game, Hearn settled for doing some refereeing.

Then, his life changed, as did those of so many Americans who went off to serve their country in World War II.

Shipped to the South Pacific, Hearn was put in charge of special services.

In that capacity, he organized a military baseball team, a club good enough to go 82–0.

There was enough interest in the team to broadcast its games on Armed Forces Radio.

To do so, of course, they needed a broadcaster. Nobody connected with the team had any play-by-play experience. Since Hearn was running the show, he was drafted to sit behind the mic, even though he had never done so before.

He wasn't bad. As a matter of fact, he became so good at it and liked it so much that, when he got out of the service, he told Marge, "I think I'm going to try to get into the business."

Hearn pounded on doors in Chicago, but got the same answer time after time: No college degree, no job.

Finally, a little station in Aurora, Illinois, WMRO, offered him employment. They didn't exactly bet the bank on the novice announcer. He would be paid $25 a week to broadcast everything from news to religion, with some sports thrown in as well.

Marge was on board, but Hearn's father wasn't convinced.

"Do you really think radio is here to stay?" Frank Hearn asked.

There wasn't a doubt in Chick's mind. And even if there had been, he was going to be an announcer as long as they would have him, especially since the job included doing the play-by-play for the Aurora Clippers semipro football team.

From there, Hearn moved to another Aurora station where he also hosted a game show, *The Sky's the Limit*, from the top of a hotel.

That station, WBNU-FM, carried a basketball tournament known as the Sweet Sixteen. When an Aurora team qualified for the event and the station's regular play-by-play man became ill, Hearn was again drafted.

He proved to be so good that Bradley University in Peoria offered him its play-by-play basketball job.

No more searching for work satisfaction. Chick Hearn had found his niche.

In 1956, he came to Los Angeles to do USC football and basketball. He soon added a nightly sportscast on radio and became the sportscaster on the Channel 4 news.

Hearn's voice seemed to be everywhere in L.A., even in the ear of Bob Short.

At 2:00 AM on a March night in 1961, the phone rang in the Hearn home. It was Short. He had struck a deal with the CBS radio affiliate in L.A. to broadcast the remaining games of the Western Division finals between his Lakers and the Hawks. Game 5 would be in St. Louis. Would Hearn agree to be there?

Still groggy, Hearn said yes, taking the assignment that would define his career and his life. With one day's notice, he had become the Lakers' announcer.

L.A. won that fifth game 121–112.

When the Lakers and Hawks returned to the Sports Arena for Game 6, they'd be excused for thinking the tickets were being given away. The crowd was 14,844, nearly triple their season average and nearly double the total for their first two playoff games at the Sports Arena.

All because of Hearn? He *was* the only difference from their previous home games.

The Lakers wound up losing the series in seven games. But they gained something even more valuable: a voice that would reverberate for them for decades to come.

42 Sports Arena: JFK, MLK, UCLA, and NBA

By 1999, nearing the end of its third decade of existence and with the gleaming new Staples Center being erected across town, the glow of the Sports Arena had long since faded.

And nobody expressed that opinion better than Charles Barkley. Then a member of the Houston Rockets, Barkley, there to face the Clippers, was asked about the Sports Arena.

"This place?" he said. "Nothing positive. Okay, I want to say something positive. It's positively a dump."

But there were scintillating memories floating around those ancient walls, the mists of time having obscured but not erased unforgettable moments that the Sports Arena's legacy could match against any rival arena.

Those moments include:

- JFK's presidential nomination. With young Ted Kennedy standing on the Sports Arena floor in the midst of the Wyoming delegation, that state announced it was casting the votes to put Ted's older brother over the top.
- A Dr. Martin Luther King Jr. speech there in 1961.
- A victory by Muhammad Ali, then still Cassius Clay, over an aging but still valiant Archie Moore. Those were the days when Clay, campaigning for a title shot, used to predict the outcome of his fights. "They all shall fall in the round I call," he would say. The 20-year-old Clay predicted the 49-year-old Moore would be stopped in the fourth round, and he was.
- UCLA's victory against North Carolina in the championship game of the 1968 NCAA Tournament. After beating the University of Houston 101–69 on the Sports Arena court in the semifinals to avenge a regular-season loss to the Cougars, the Bruins defeated North Carolina 78–55 to win their second straight NCAA title in a streak that would stretch to an incredible seven in a row under coach John Wooden. The Bruins also played the majority of their games there in the 2011–12 season while their home court, Pauley Pavilion, was being refurbished.

Fans arriving for a Lakers game at the Sports Arena in the 1960s were treated to a feature unique to that building.

The turnstiles were wired to the scoreboard so that every time they turned to admit a paying customer, the number of people in the arena shown on the overhead screen was increased by one. The attendance figure was a work in progress.

Those already in their seats could watch the crowd grow from say 100 to 200 to 2,000 to—on good nights—10,000.

It was cheap entertainment for fans before everything from dancers and shooting contests to music and highlight videos became commonplace pregame features.

While the fans may have been amused, and perhaps even placed a bet or two on how high the attendance would ultimately grow, it was not such a pleasant experience for Short—and later Cooke—when that turnstile count on the scoreboard ended up embarrassingly low

The Lakers would leave the Sports Arena after seven seasons but not because the building was decaying or insufficient for their needs.

No, the team departed because of attitude.

The attitudes of the Coliseum Commission and Lakers owner Jack Kent Cooke.

At first, the issue wasn't even the Lakers. It was hockey.

Cooke, a native of Canada, was trying to land an NHL expansion team for Los Angeles. Naturally, he figured the team would play in the same arena that his Lakers called home.

The problem was that the Los Angeles Blades, a minor league club, were trying to move up and become the NHL's L.A. team. And in pursuit of that goal, the Blades had obtained the exclusive rights to the Sports Arena from the Coliseum Commission, overseers of the building.

So Cooke was already in an antagonistic frame of mind—his usual frame of mind, according to many who negotiated with him—when he attempted to secure a new Sports Arena contract for his Lakers.

He was told that the deal, signed by previous owner Bob Short, still had two years to go. When that contract was over, he could negotiate a new deal.

"He's got to fish or cut bait," said L.A. County Supervisor Ernest Debs, chairman of the Coliseum Commission's finance committee.

"I figured I was being euchred out of the entire setup," Cooke said. "They were treating me contemptuously. It was just awful.... I'd only been [in L.A.] three or four years and I didn't know about the machinations of these guys, Machiavellian kind of birds.

"So I said, 'You know, you are making this whole thing so difficult, I'm liable to build my own arena.' And this fellow looked at me and said, 'Ha, ha, ha.'

"Now if he had only laughed, I would have laughed with him, you see? But he actually said, 'Ha, ha, ha.' So I said, 'In that case, I *am* going to build my own arena.'

"I turned to [my lawyer] Clyde Tritt and said, 'Close your briefcase. I've had enough of this balderdash.' And away we went."

All the way to Inglewood. Cooke was the object of more laughs when it was learned that he planned to build his arena way beyond L.A.'s city limits on a plot of land next to Hollywood Park racetrack. It was thought fans wouldn't drive that far on a regular basis to support a basketball team that had yet to capture the hearts of the general public.

Cooke had the last laugh when the Forum was built and became the home of not only the Lakers, but also Cooke's hockey team, the Kings, as well as a destination for many of the world's top musical groups over the next three decades.

It would take 18 years for the Sports Arena to finally get another team, when the Clippers moved there from San Diego. But in the meantime, while the Forum packed them in, the Sports Arena sat dark on many a night.

43 The Clown Prince

If Jerry West was Mr. Clutch, his West Virginia running mate, Hot Rod Hundley, was Mr. Clown.

It's not that Hundley didn't have talent. Entering the NBA as the top pick in the draft, he was a master ballhandler who was comfortable either trying to emulate the moves of Pete Maravich or the schtick of the Harlem Globetrotters.

Thus the name Hot Rod.

It was the Rochester Royals, about to move to Cincinnati, who regarded the three-time All-American at West Virginia so highly that they took him with the first pick in 1957. But before Hundley even dribbled a ball for them, he was part of a seven-player trade with the Minneapolis Lakers. The two key figures changing uniforms were Hundley and the Lakers' Clyde Lovellette.

Hundley spent six seasons in the NBA, all with Lakers—three in Minneapolis and three in L.A.

He dazzled the crowds in those early days in Los Angeles despite the fact he had to share the spotlight with Elgin Baylor and Jerry West.

When the Lakers played in L.A. for the first time in February 1960 to test the market, the game story in the *Los Angeles Times* noted that "the audience cheered the Lakers' Hot Rod Hundley when he pulled his behind-the-back dribbling routine."

Hundley's best seasons were his last one in Minneapolis (12.8 points and 4.6 assists) and his first in L.A. (11.0, 4.4). He was an All-Star in both of those seasons.

But Hundley's ability to entertain, his charm, his wit, and his legendary love of the nightlife were ever-present during his short playing career.

Lakers owner Bob Short tried to settle Hundley down one night when he found him standing in front of the team hotel in St. Louis waiting for a cab to hit the town even though there was a game the following day.

"Listen, Hot Rod," Short said, "you need your rest. I don't want you to wear yourself out chasing all over town. If you'll

Vegas

When the Lakers moved to L.A., Hot Rod Hundley and teammate Rudy LaRusso, a 6-7, 220-pound power forward who averaged 15.6 points and 9.4 rebounds, decided they would be the first two players in town.

So they jumped in their cars—LaRusso in his Oldsmobile and Hundley in his Pontiac Bonneville—and off they went from Minnesota with whatever they could shove into their trunks.

They raced through Salt Lake City and then roared into Las Vegas.

Hundley had never been to Vegas. He stared at the neon jungle, listened to the sound of coins belching out of slot machines and watched the showgirls strutting around.

So this was what heaven looked like.

"We were like guys let out of jail," Hundley said.

He and LaRusso wandered into the Stardust Resort and Casino and over to the blackjack table.

Hundley hit his first hand. Blackjack.

Twenty-four hours later, he and LaRusso were still sitting there.

As they emerged into the clean desert air, they were greeted by the rising sun.

LaRusso, feeling the sweat and booze and cigarettes on his clothes, said he wished he could take a bath.

Hundley grinned and nodded toward the immense pool in front of them.

So in they went with a leap and a splash, dousing their clothes in the cool waters.

They weren't reckless, Hundley insisted. They did stop to take their shoes off.

And then they were back in their cars, the sun behind them as they headed into a bright new day.

go back to your room, I'll send up a beautiful girl. I'll pay for everything."

"Bob, you know I don't work that way," said Hundley, his trademark grin on his face. "The thrill is in the chase, baby."

On second thought, maybe Hundley should have taken Short's money. Rejected, the Lakers owner decided to handle Hundley's problem by taking some of his money.

When Hundley and teammate Bob "Slick" Leonard broke curfew one time too many, Short fined them $1,000 each.

Not a big deal?

In those days, Hundley was making $10,000, Leonard $9,000.

In 1960, Elgin Baylor set the then-NBA record for most points in a game with 71 against the New York Knicks at Madison Square Garden.

Hundley scored seven that night.

Afterward, the two jumped into a cab to check out the bright lights of Broadway.

When the driver began barreling down the canyons of Manhattan as only a New York taxi driver can, Hundley wisecracked, "Be careful, you've got 78 points in this cab."

When his playing days were over, Hundley was away from the game for four years except for his role as a spokesman for a shoe company. He then returned to the Lakers as Chick Hearn's analyst.

It was a chance for Hundley to demonstrate his sharp wit to a much bigger audience.

And get a bigger paycheck from his former employer. Despite being a two-time All-Star, Hundley had never made more than $11,500 as a player. To be Hearn's sidekick, he was paid $15,000.

Hundley left the Lakers after two seasons and spent five years behind the mic for the Phoenix Suns before becoming the play-by-play man of an expansion team, the New Orleans Jazz, in 1974.

Hundley stayed with the club when it moved to Salt Lake City five years later, finally retiring in 2009 after 35 years with the Jazz.

As player and broadcaster, he was in the NBA for more than half a century.

Not bad for a clown.

44 Nice Shot, Baby

It was just a 15-foot jumper.

A wide-open 15-foot jumper.

That's all that stood between the Lakers and an NBA title at the expense of the Boston Celtics.

Back in 1962.

This was before the long and agonizing string of L.A. losses to Boston in the NBA Finals.

The Lakers had lost once to the Celtics in the Finals while they were in Minneapolis, getting swept in 1959.

Then, in their second season in L.A., they were again matched against the Celtics in the Finals, and this time, things were going a lot better. The two teams fought to a seventh game held at the Boston Garden.

They were still even with only three seconds to play.

And the ball was in the Lakers' hands.

Specifically, it was in the hands of swingman Frank Selvy, a man who once scored 100 points while playing for Furman University.

Two would be quite enough here.

The ball had been in Hot Rod Hundley's hands seconds earlier.

"I turned to face the basket," Hundley said. "K.C. [Jones] got through [Rudy] LaRusso's screen to [Jerry] West, so West wasn't open. [Bob] Cousy was on Selvy. Cousy was a terrible defensive player. We used to fight over who would be guarded by him. He would steal the ball a lot because he ran around, but he never guarded his man."

Selvy was standing on the baseline. Hundley whipped him the ball.

"Hot Rod had told me he had had a dream that he made the winning shot," his coach, Fred Schaus, later said. "Damn, he should have taken it."

Cousy had to fight through a screen to get to Selvy.

"The screen delayed him just a second," Selvy said. "I had to get it off fast. I sort of hurried…but I thought it was going in."

So did Boston coach Red Auerbach, who figured his chances of lighting up a victory cigar were about to be extinguished.

"I thought it was all over," said Auerbach.

So did Celtic forward Tom "Satch" Sanders.

"There was very little breathing room in the Garden when the ball went to Selvy," Sanders said. "I thought, *Anybody but him.*"

Selvy's shot clanged off the rim, went up in the air, and came down in the vise-like hands of one of the game's greatest rebounders, Bill Russell.

It seemed, said K.C. Jones, that Russell went "about 12,000 feet above the rim" to secure the ball.

"I'm sure poor Frank still wakes up in the middle of the night and sees the ball hit the rim and go up," Cousy said. "I was so relieved. I don't think Frank had missed that shot since 1928."

As time expired, Elgin Baylor looked for a whistle because he thought Cousy had fouled Selvy.

Or a whistle because he thought he had been fouled.

"Then I was in good position to get the rebound," Baylor said, "and Sam Jones just shoved me out of bounds. He didn't get called for it."

Jones did indeed foul Baylor, as he admitted to him in a conversation 16 years later. But Jones wasn't going to get a whistle blown in his direction. Not in that situation. Not today and not back then.

No referee wants to decide the NBA championship. A player would have to get an opponent in a headlock in order to get a whistle under those circumstances.

Ultimately, it was Boston who decided the outcome, beating the Lakers 110–107 in overtime. It was the Celtics' fourth straight NBA title halfway through a record streak that would stretch to eight in a row.

"I get the blame for missing that shot," Selvy said, "but I don't think that was the ballgame. We could have done better in overtime. I think a lot of people don't realize that I made the last two baskets to tie the game up."

Hundley, however, wasn't about to let Selvy get away unscathed. In the funereal atmosphere of the locker room afterward, Hundley came up to Selvy.

To ease the guilt?

Not a chance.

"It could happen to anybody," Hundley said. "Don't worry, baby. You only cost us about $30,000."

Hundley wasn't finished.

For years afterward, long after both players had retired, Hundley would call Selvy's house when he knew his former teammate wasn't home. When the answering machine came on, Hundley always left the same three-word message: "Nice shot, baby."

Some feel that, had Selvy's shot found the net, all of Lakers history might have been different. The team would go on to lose six more times to the Celtics before finally breaking the streak in 1985, almost a quarter century later.

Even Auerbach, who never liked to fess up to any cracks in his organization's green armor, conceded a different outcome might have rippled through the ensuing seasons.

"We were an aging club," he said, "and if we hadn't won that one, it would have made it rougher psychologically for the guys in the future."

Laker Tommy Hawkins agreed.

"Especially in Boston, they developed that invincible aura," he said. "Teams going in were psyched totally. It was nervous time. It wasn't, 'I hope we can win.' It was, 'I hope we can get out alive without getting embarrassed.' Even athletes have fear when they enter competition. They are in awe of certain things, and Boston had developed that in other teams. If we had won that one game, it might have changed that aura significantly."

45 Lakers-Celtics: Game 8?

The Lakers' collective spirit was broken by the Game 7 overtime loss to the Celtics in the 1962 Finals.

All except for one player, one voice of hope in the shattered locker room.

"Don't worry," center Ray Felix said, "we'll get 'em tomorrow."

The Lakers were in no mood to explain to Felix there was no Game 8.

It wasn't the first or the last time the 6'11" center said something that left teammates shaking their heads.

Despite being an inch taller than Boston's Bill Russell, Felix, like every other center in the league, struggled against the Celtics Hall of Famer, considered by some the greatest player in league history.

In one Lakers-Celtics game, Felix put up a shot only to have it blocked by Russell.

Another shot, another block.

After four shot attempts and four Russell blocks, Felix was desperate. Facing the long-armed, sure-fingertipped, high-jumping Russell once again, Felix overcompensated by throwing up a high-arcing shot that flew over Russell's long reach, so far over that it cleared the backboard and landed in the crowd beyond.

Felix looked Russell in the eye, broke into a big grin and said, "You didn't get that one, baby."

A sportswriter once referred to Felix as "gangling."

Angry, Felix confronted the sportswriter the next time he saw him and told him he wasn't welcome in the locker room.

Felix then turned to a teammate and asked, "What does gangling mean?"

"We'd play high-low [poker], where you have to declare high or low by showing one finger or two," teammate Tommy Hawkins said. "Ray would get confused. He'd have a lock on low and he'd display the high sign and lose the pot. Invariably, he'd forget to bring an overcoat to New York. And he wasn't a guy who remembered every offensive play the Lakers had. He had the ability to forget.

"He'd make the all-eccentric, all-absent-minded team."

Whatever his mental gaffes, Felix displayed enough physically to last 11 seasons in the NBA—the last three with the Lakers. Rookie of the Year with the Baltimore Bullets in 1953–54, Felix's numbers with the Lakers (6.4 points, 6.7 rebounds), while not spectacular, were respectable.

He could play the game as long as no one asked him which game it was.

46 Tight-Fisted Lou Mohs

If Lou Mohs, the Lakers general manager for the team's first seven seasons in L.A., was around today, he'd have trouble holding his temper.

Not to mention his job.

Mohs was old school, from an era where a player in search of a raise came in to see the GM, made his case, and then had to live with what he got.

That sum was usually what the player would have gotten had he not spoken up at all.

On one occasion a player came into Mohs' office accompanied by his agent.

Mohs took one look at the pair, got up, and left the room, returning shortly with the Lakers' attorney.

"You two talk together," Mohs told the agent and the attorney, "and when you're done, let me know, and I'll get this finished because neither one of you knows a thing about basketball."

The same could be said of Mohs.

Oh, he knew about playing sports. At the University of Minnesota, he was on the football team with Bronko Nagurski and earned seven letters in all in seven different sports.

But he had never worked in sports. He had been a circulation manager for the Hearst newspaper chain, living in St. Louis.

Lakers owner Bob Short hired Mohs because of two traits.

One was a great work ethic. Mohs bragged that, while employed to pound away on a rock quarry, "I did so much work they got rid of two of their mules."

The other quality Short liked was Mohs' tendency toward thrift, bordering on outright stinginess.

Mohs bragged about that as well.

After he had taken the Lakers job, Mohs once said, "Ask anybody around here. They'll tell you how tight I am."

That was fine with Short, who was never sure whether his team was going to stay afloat or sink in a wave of red ink.

When he sent Mohs out to L.A. prior to the team's move from Minneapolis, Short told his general manager, "Call me for anything, but don't call me for money."

How could he afford the team's two superstars, Jerry West and Elgin Baylor?

No problem for Mohs. He just wouldn't pay much to the rest of the roster.

Short Money

While Short is also commonly depicted as being tight with money, it was out of necessity. Even after the move to L.A., there was never any certainty the Lakers could survive financially.

But away from public scrutiny, Short often opened his heart and his wallet for his players.

"One year, we got beat in the seventh game in the Finals at Boston," Hot Rod Hundley said. "The [Celtics'] pay for winning was $2,000. Ours for finishing second was $1,000, which was a lot for us back then.

"Short came into [the locker room] and said, 'Here's an extra thousand for each of you.'"

He had decided that his players, who had stayed even with the Celtics until the end, deserved the same money their archrivals had received.

"Short did something," Hundley said, "that was like, in a way, not legal."

But much appreciated.

"We'd be down 20 at the half," Hundley said. "He'd come into the locker room and say, `Here's $200' or 'Here's $300 if you win this game, or if you just play a good game.'

"Once, I left my billfold back in the hotel room. He just gave me a hundred and asked if that would be enough to get by."

"The salaries you pay the Jerry Wests and the Elgin Baylors don't hurt at all," Mohs said. "If it's your last breath, you can pay for a good doctor."

Mohs was very successful at breathing life into L.A.'s first pro basketball franchise.

He drafted players such as West (1960), Leroy Ellis (1962), Walt Hazzard (1964), and Gail Goodrich (1965).

He hired Fred Schaus as the first L.A. Lakers coach, and Schaus led the team to the NBA Finals four times in Mohs' seven seasons.

GM experience? Highly overrated.

47 The Hawk: Lakers and All That Jazz

Tommy Hawkins was part of the Los Angeles baseball and media scene for so long, today's fans could be excused for not knowing he played for the Lakers.

Hawkins, who died In 2017, was a sportscaster on both radio and television in the L.A. market and a front-office executive for the Dodgers in charge of media relations for nearly two decades.

But before all that, the 6'5", 210-pound Hawkins was a two-time All-American at Notre Dame and an NBA forward for a decade, including two tours of duty with the Lakers. He was with them in their last season in Minneapolis and the first two years in L.A. Then, after playing for the Cincinnati Royals, Hawkins returned to the Lakers for the final three years of his career, retiring after the 1968–69 season.

Being a member of L.A.'s first Lakers squad turned out to be great training for Hawkins' subsequent career behind the mic.

The team was so lightly regarded when it first arrived that players were asked to get into vehicles equipped with loudspeakers and drive up and down the streets of the city, announcing their presence.

"Tommy Hawkins here," he would say. "Come see me and the rest of the Los Angeles Lakers on Sunday night at the Sports Arena against the Boston Celtics."

Hawkins was a modest scorer, averaging nine points. He also pulled down 5.7 rebounds per game and was a strong defensive player.

Hawkins' other love was jazz. He hosted a jazz radio show and had a collection of approximately 11,000 jazz records and CDs. Hawkins told the *Los Angeles Times* that if he hadn't grown tall, "I'd probably be wailing on a trumpet right now."

48 Fred Schaus and That Damn Cigar

In 1959, coach Fred Schaus led the University of West Virginia to the championship game of the NCAA Tournament where the Mountaineers lost by only a point, 71–70, to Cal.

Schaus was not only successful, but also comfortable at West Virginia, his alma mater. In each of his six seasons there, the Mountaineers basketball team won the Southern Conference championship, compiling an overall record of 146–37.

Then a year after West Virginia's near-miss against Cal, Lakers owner Bob Short came knocking at Schaus' door. Short was loaded with enticements to sell the Mountaineer coach on coming west to become the first coach of the L.A. Lakers.

For one thing, they had drafted Jerry West, Schaus' star at West Virginia. They also had Hot Rod Hundley, whom Schaus had coached in college.

Plus, Schaus was hardly a stranger to pro basketball. He played four seasons for the Fort Wayne Pistons and one for the New York Knicks. In 1950–51, before the invention of the 24-second clock, Schaus scored 1,028 points, the first player to reach four figures in that department in a single season for the Pistons.

All that was nice, but then Short added the coup de grace. Never known for spending a buck on his Lakers when 50 cents would do the job, Short nevertheless offered Schaus a two-year deal at $18,500 per season. That represented a $3,500 annual increase over his West Virginia salary.

So Schaus took the job, but some wondered how his no-nonsense approach would mesh with the sometimes freewheeling NBA where the strict discipline of the college game was often lacking.

But Schaus was prepared. After all, in college, he had coached Hundley, who could be about as freewheeling as they came.

"He always told me, 'I [don't] care if you drop-kick the ball out of the building, but we'd better be up by 20 when you do,'" Hundley said. "Fred taught me that the game was the most important thing. He never did anything to jeopardize the game."

As a result he was very successful in his seven seasons at the helm. Schaus' Lakers were 315–245, and reached the NBA Finals four times in his seven seasons.

And lost them all to the hated Boston Celtics.

That was a constant source of stomach-grinding frustration for Schaus even though he knew that he would always be at a disadvantage without a center to match up with Boston's incomparable Bill Russell.

"If Russell had been on the Lakers, we'd have won all six," said announcer Chick Hearn, referring to the six championship-round meetings between the two teams in the '60s.

What really made Schaus see red—or rather green—was the sight of Celtics coach Red Auerbach celebrating each title with that trademark victory cigar clenched between his grinning lips.

"They were continually building a better team. We didn't have any money, any draft choices," Auerbach said, "and we still beat them.

"[It] was more satisfying because of the Hollywood syndrome. Every year, the writers out there raved [about] how tremendous the Lakers were. We whipped them with [Wilt] Chamberlain, without Chamberlain, with Baylor, with West.

Coach Fred Schaus (second from left) stands with (from left) Rudy LaRusso, Dick Barnett, and Jerry West after the Lakers defeated the Baltimore Bullets to win the Western Division and advance to the NBA Finals.

"We out-psyched them many times. One time [1966], they came into Boston for the first game and whipped us. That was the day I released the news that I was making Russell coach for the next season. That killed them. They had beat the hell out of us and everybody was writing about Russell being the next coach. They hardly even mentioned the game.

"We used to psyche Schaus pretty good. He became a little confused. It got to the point that he started Baylor in the backcourt."

Auerbach's remarks, made to the *Los Angeles Times,* further infuriated Schaus.

"He always had a gimmick all right. It was called Bill Russell," Schaus said. "It was amazing how great a coach he became after he got Bill Russell. Russell made a hell of a coach out of him. Before that, with Cousy and [Bill] Sharman, he couldn't even win his division."

In the 1966 NBA Finals between the Lakers and Celtics, Boston hung on for a two-point win, 95–93, in Game 7 after leading by 10 with 40 seconds to play.

"I would have loved to have stuffed that damn cigar down his throat," Schaus said. "We came awfully close to putting that damn thing out."

Schaus had been so convinced his Lakers would win the series that he bought a case of champagne for the anticipated victory celebration.

"We carried that champagne from coast to coast," Baylor said. "By the time we lost, the labels had come off the bottles. Schaus wanted to know if we could get our money back. I think we wound up selling the champagne to the Celtics."

Schaus finally got his chance to raise the NBA championship trophy, but alas, it wasn't at the expense of his old nemesis.

After the 1966–67 season, Schaus had replaced Lou Mohs as general manager. And in 1972, with Schaus still the general manager and Bill Sharman as coach, the Lakers won the NBA

The Auerbach Statue

Here's something for the not-to-do list for Laker fans, except for those who are masochistic.

In Boston, don't wander around Faneuil Hall because you are sure to come face to face with the Auerbach statue.

He is depicted sitting on a bench, exuding confidence bordering on arrogance, a rolled-up program in one hand, and the obligatory cigar in the other.

It would be about as enjoyable an experience as it would be for Celtics fans to wander around the front of Staples Center seeing the statues of various Laker superstars.

title—their first in Los Angeles—by beating the New York Knicks in the Finals in five games.

Not only had Schaus put together a championship club, but also one that compiled a then-record 69–13 regular-season mark and a 33-game winning streak that remains untouched to this day.

His mission finally complete, Schaus went back to his first love, college basketball. He coached Purdue and eventually made it all the way back to West Virginia as the school's athletic director.

But he could never quite get the bitter taste of those defeats by the Celtics out of his mouth.

It didn't help that Auerbach remained as derisive as ever even decades later.

In the 1980s, Boston players from the '60s were asked about the old rivalry and, to a man, they expressed sympathy for the losing Lakers.

"I've always felt a little fortunate," Cousy said. "Jerry and Elgin should have had a championship ring long before they got one… Active players are notoriously selfish. It's only when you get into middle age that you develop the quiet compassion."

Not Auerbach.

"Why would I feel sorry for them?" he said in 1984. "They were the enemy."

Schaus was finally able to put the ghosts of the triumphant Celtics away in 1985 when the Lakers beat Boston for the championship.

As the title-clinching Game 6 wound down to its glorious conclusion, Schaus, back home in West Virginia, was too nervous to even watch.

When the Lakers won, Schaus, in the midst of euphoria, was asked if the law of averages had finally favored his old team.

"I never believed in the law of averages in athletics," he said. "That is hogwash. If you execute, you get it done."

49 A Laker Corpse?

On a 1960s road trip, a member of the Lakers' traveling party had too much to drink. So much, that he passed out in his hotel room.

When he was first discovered by a hotel employee, it was thought the man was dead.

Before the drunken guest was identified and revived, coach Fred Schaus was informed that a corpse had been discovered in one of the Lakers' rooms.

"Yeah," replied Schaus without hesitation, "well, I sure as hell hope it isn't Baylor or West."

50 A Clock in His Head

Chick Hearn used that term in reference to Jerry West, saying that the Hall of Famer didn't need to look at the scoreboard to know how much time was remaining.

The idea that there was a clock ticking in West's head was formed on an unforgettable spring night at the Sports Arena in 1962.

It was the NBA Finals, Lakers and Celtics, of course. With the series tied at one, a then-record Sports Arena crowd of 15,180 was on hand for Game 3.

They got their money's worth, with the outcome in doubt as the final seconds ticked away.

The Lakers had been down by four, but West tied the game by hitting a jump shot and then making two free throws.

Four seconds left.

Boston's Sam Jones tried to in-bound the ball, but there was West again, intercepting the pass.

He was 35 feet from the basket, and a second had already expired.

"We were all yelling for him to shoot it at the free-throw line," teammate Frank Selvy said.

No way.

West drove in and laid the ball smoothly into the hoop as time ran out, giving the Lakers a 117–115 victory.

"He knew exactly how much time was left," Selvy said. "You wouldn't find anyone that smart now. They would all pull up and shoot."

"[Red] Auerbach said it was impossible to dribble nearly half the court and make the basket in three seconds," Hearn said. "So

The Logo: Jerry West goes up for another masterful shot. (Getty Images)

he got the film of the game, ran that play a thousand times and it always came out the same: 2.9 seconds."

51 Jim Krebs: His Luck Ran Out

He escaped death in a harrowing situation with potential disaster looming ahead only to die in a situation seemingly free of the slightest hint of peril.

The Minneapolis Lakers selected the 6'8", 230-pounder from Southern Methodist University with the third pick overall in the 1957 NBA Draft.

No surprise there. An All-American at SMU, Krebs had led the Mustangs to three straight Southwest Conference championships and a slot in the 1956 Final Four.

A February 1957, *Sports Illustrated* cover showed Krebs with the headline "Best in the Southwest."

Becoming the best in the NBA would prove much more difficult. Krebs was not only taking a huge step up to the pro level, but also trying to step into the shoes of a legend, striving to fill the hole left by the retirement of Hall of Famer George Mikan a year earlier.

It never quite worked out. Over seven seasons with the Lakers—the last three in Minneapolis and the first four in Los Angeles—Krebs, nicknamed "Boomer," didn't exactly live up to that title, averaging just eight points and 6.2 rebounds.

He retired at 28 after averaging just 14.3 minutes during the 1963–64 season.

"I guess you could say I was a little bitter about that," he remarked of his premature exit from the game.

At least he got out alive.

Krebs was on board the Lakers' DC-3 that landed in an Iowa cornfield in 1960 with, amazingly enough, no injuries.

Not that Krebs hadn't tried to warn his teammates. A month earlier he had received a Ouija board—a game with a pointer to link to a spiritual world, from where, it was claimed, questions could be answered and the future predicted—as a holiday gift.

A week prior to the Lakers' frightening flight, Krebs insisted his Ouija board had informed him of an impending plane crash.

As the club took off from St. Louis in the midst of a snowstorm, teammate Hot Rod Hundley had even said to Krebs, "Hey Boomer, better check your Ouija board."

Minutes later, when a generator blew out and the players found themselves in a life-and-death situation, nobody was making fun of Krebs or his Ouija board.

A year after his retirement, he had no reason to check a Ouija board before going out to help a neighbor cut down a tree near his Woodland Hills home.

Horribly, the tree came crashing down in an unexpected direction, and Krebs was killed. He was 29.

52 Lakers-Celtics: Forgetting Those Unforgettable Moments

In Game 5 of the 1962 NBA Finals, Elgin Baylor accomplished something that has never been equaled in league history.

He scored 61 points.

And if that wasn't enough, Baylor also pulled down 22 rebounds in that game against the Celtics in Boston Garden.

An unforgettable night?

Not for Baylor.

"I don't remember whether we won or lost," he said when asked about it two decades later.

His team won that game 126–121 to take a 3–2 series lead, but it's understandable why Baylor learned to block out final scores. The Lakers went on to lose that series in seven games. It was another painful memory from the '60s, a decade in which they played Boston six times in the Finals and lost all six.

Jerry West had his own monumental achievements against the Celtics negated by the sting of defeat in those years.

In 1965, with Baylor forced to exit with a knee injury five minutes into the first playoff game, West went on to average 40.6 points for the Lakers' 11 postseason games.

Against the Celtics in the Finals, West scored 45 points in Game 2 and came back with 43 in Game 3.

Ultimately, though, the results were the same—Boston winning the NBA title, this time in five games. With Baylor, the Lakers' leading rebounder, missing from the frontcourt, the Celtics' Bill Russell pulled down 30 rebounds in the clinching game.

In the 1963 Finals between the Lakers and Celtics, the Lakers—down 3–1—won Game 5 in Boston by a score of 126–119 to extend the series.

Back at the Forum, the Lakers—down by 14 at halftime of Game 6—cut the lead to one with five minutes to play.

But Boston hung on, with Bob Cousy dribbling away from defenders as time expired. Then the Celtics guard, who was retiring after 13 seasons, hurled the ball into the Sports Arena rafters as his teammates poured onto the court.

"Please tell some of these stories," said Boston coach Red Auerbach sarcastically, his victory cigar framed by a wide smile, "about Los Angeles being the basketball capital of the world."

Instead, it was home to yet another forgettable moment.

53 Dodgers/Lakers: It Almost Happened

He went from door to door to team to team, from selling books to selling out arenas and stadiums.

Jack Kent Cooke, once the owner of the Lakers, the NHL's Kings, the Washington Redskins, and the Forum, entered the business world at the bottom, selling encyclopedias in his native Canada.

Born in Hamilton, Ontario, Cooke played hockey and football in high school and the saxophone in the school band.

He had dreams of becoming a professional hockey player, but that idea came crashing down when the Great Depression caused his father, Ralph, to lose his picture-framing business.

When Cooke, at the age of 21, married his high-school sweetheart, Barbara Jean Carnegie, the two of them took off on a honeymoon through Western Canada, encyclopedias in hand. Whenever they ran short of money, Cooke started banging on doors.

Next he tried selling soap, then landed a job managing an Ontario radio station for a man named Roy Thomson. Cooke was paid $23.85 a week.

That amount, however, soon soared beyond even the dreams of the ambitious Cooke as he and Thomson became partners in a media empire, buying everything from radio stations and newspapers to an ad agency.

By the age of 31, Cooke had his first million.

In the 1960s, having moved to Beverly Hills, Cooke, financially secure for life, poured his competitive energy into everything from racing yachts to playing bridge.

But, as was his nature, he wanted more. He already owned a quarter interest in the Redskins and a minor league baseball team in Toronto.

But, as usual, Cooke was thinking bigger. He thought about acquiring the Los Angeles Angels, an American League expansion team scheduled to begin play in 1961, but that franchise went to singing cowboy/businessman Gene Autry.

A lawyer Cooke met suggested going after the Lakers.

The Lakers? Cooke had never even seen a pro basketball game either in person or on television, but the idea intrigued him.

He approached Lakers owner Bob Short only to learn Short was already negotiating with Dodgers owner Walter O'Malley.

O'Malley envisioned an arena for the team in Chavez Ravine.

Had that deal been consummated, how different the L.A. sports landscape would have been.

Under the terms of the proposal, Short and his Lakers partner, Frank Ryan, would have owned 20 percent of the Lakers, Dodgers, the new arena, and Dodger Stadium, according to Ryan.

"I didn't want to sell," said Short in the book, *Winnin' Times.* "We were talking about a merger."

But the process bogged down when O'Malley became enmeshed in a television deal.

Enter Cooke.

Short resisted him at first, never an easy thing to do with Cooke.

"But my banker told me, 'Everything is for sale.'" Short said.

What were the Lakers worth?

The Boston Celtics had recently sold for $3 million, so Short decided to shoot for the stars and ask for $5 million.

Remember, this was a time when the NBA was still a minor league compared to the NFL and MLB.

Cooke, however, accepted the offer.

"I called my banker back," Short said, "and told him he was right after Cooke took me into the stratosphere."

O'Malley agreed.

"Hell, you gotta sell," the Dodgers owner told Short. "That's a tremendous amount of money for 10 pairs of tennis shoes, as long as you get it in cash."

Short, however, figured he could squeeze out a little more. After all, he had already sold $350,000 worth of season tickets for the upcoming season. He wanted at least half that total back.

So he told Cooke, $5,175,000 would seal the deal.

Cooke didn't blink.

"I wanted the team so damn badly," he said, "had he asked for $575,000 extra, I would have paid him."

As per O'Malley's advice, Short asked for the full amount in cash, and it was handed over to his people in a New York bank vault.

Never again would money be an issue for the Lakers.

54 The Wrath of Cooke

Superstar or secretary, everybody who worked for Jack Kent Cooke felt his wrath sooner or later.

He was a perfectionist who expected the same effort from everybody else that he expended himself.

After he built the Forum, Cooke would call the arena periodically from wherever he was. If the phone rang more than three times, the switchboard operator would be out of a job.

"He is one of the most forceful people I have ever known," said Lord Beaverbrook, a British press agent, in *Winnin' Times*. "He is quick, pungent, full of ideas.

"He has qualities that sometimes provoke dislike: invincible confidence in himself, and a fluent, rushing anxiety to tell you about his work and his projects. Yet Cooke is likable."

"Was I tough to work for?" Cooke asked. "I think not in this respect: No one ever had any misunderstanding about what I wanted done. I was easy to work for. The toughest guy in the world to work for is the fella who waffles, who vacillates. You never know quite what he wants done. Then he raises hell because you failed to do what he failed to communicate to you. There was never any question about my ability to communicate with people."

Cooke had one employee, however, who questioned him: Chick Hearn.

The owner called Hearn into his office the morning after a game against the Philadelphia 76ers. Hearn had no choice but to go, even though the team was leaving on a road trip in a few hours.

Cooke proceeded to turn on a tape recorder, and Hearn found himself listening to his own broadcast from the night before.

As Hearn's crisp play-by-play reverberated through the office, Cooke took notes on a yellow pad.

Finally, he shut off the machine and, obviously annoyed, told Hearn, "You have said nice things about Detroit 15 times. You said something decent about the Lakers three times. I've got to put people in those seats.

"Wait a minute, Mr. Cooke," Hearn said. "What was the score?"

"I don't know," replied Cooke.

"The score was 127–107," Hearn said. "How the hell am I going to say something good about a team getting beat 127–107?"

Cooke backed down, but added, "You will give our team due credit, won't you?"

"I won't be a cheerleader," Hearn said.

"All right," Cooke replied, "be on your way."

On another occasion, Cooke and one of his superstars, Jerry West, had become embroiled in a dispute over West's contract.

West was so furious that he refused to meet with Cooke, choosing instead to go play golf.

Cooke called Hearn from the Forum and bellowed, "You go over to the golf course, you get him by the arm, you put him in the car, and you bring him here."

"I don't have to take this," Hearn responded. "I quit."

And with that, he hung up.

Cooke immediately called back.

"You can't quit," he told Hearn.

"No, I can't," said Hearn, "and I can't bring Jerry West over there, either."

Perhaps Cooke admired people who dared get in his face, because he eventually made Hearn assistant general manager.

Appointing him, however, was one thing. Listening to him was quite another.

In 1975, with Wilt Chamberlain retired, the Lakers, in search of their next great big man, were trying to decide whether to pursue Kareem Abdul-Jabbar or Bill Walton.

Called into a team meeting, Hearn was asked his opinion.

Figuring that Abdul-Jabbar was older than Walton by five and a half years, Hearn said, "I vote to go after Walton."

"What do you mean you vote for Walton?" Cooke said. "The rest of us have agreed on Kareem."

"Then why did you ask me?" said Hearn.

"Because," said Cooke, "you have the right to vote."

Just, apparently, not the right to disagree.

* * *

In his first season with the Lakers in 1966–67, guard Archie Clark averaged 10.5 points in 76 games and shot 45.2 percent from the floor.

Good but not great.

Cooke decided he, not the coach, could make Clark better.

How?

The way you'd make a kid better. Cooke presented Clark with a basket and said, "I want you to hang that up over your garage, my boy, and practice shooting."

No telling how many people in the locker room turned their heads at that moment to stifle a grin as they saw their owner present a hoop to one of their teammates.

The next time Cooke saw Clark, he asked "Well, my boy, are you using my basket a lot?"

"No, I'm not, Mr. Cooke," said Clark, averting the bombastic owner's gaze.

"Why not?" demanded Cooke.

"Because my landlord wouldn't let me put it up, Mr. Cooke," Clark replied.

"Your landlord? Why not?" asked Cooke.

"Because he thought it would ruin the garage, Mr. Cooke," said Clark.

"Well," said Cooke, fuming, "I'll just buy that building from him. What is your landlord's name?"

At that moment, the landlord, also known as All-Star guard Walt Hazzard, emerged from the shower at the end of the locker room.

He had heard enough to know it would be prudent to turn around and head back into that shower.

A year later, both players were gone.

Cooke found out Hazzard was the landlord, and, shortly thereafter, the Lakers failed to protect him in an expansion draft, and he wound up going to the Seattle SuperSonics.

Clark could at least take comfort in the fact he was traded for one of the game's all-time greats. At the end of Clark's second season with the Lakers, he, along with Darrall Imhoff and Jerry Chambers, were sent to the Philadelphia 76ers for Wilt Chamberlain.

Clark wound up playing in the league for a decade. Imagine how long he would have lasted if he could have practiced on Cooke's hoop.

55 The Balloon Game

There are many ways to describe Game 7 of the 1969 NBA Finals between the Lakers and Celtics.

It was the game in which Wilt Chamberlain took himself out with the season on the line.

It was the last game played by Boston's Bill Russell.

It was the last Lakers game coached by Bill van Breda Kolff.

It was one of the most crushing defeats in Lakers history.

But for some, it will ultimately be remembered as The Balloon Game.

The 1969 Finals was supposed to be the series in which the Lakers finally got revenge for those six previous championship-round defeats at the hands of the Celtics. Russell was 35, and his legendary leaping ability and defensive skills were perhaps waning.

And in the 7'1" Chamberlain, the Lakers finally had a giant of their own to match Russell.

With home-court advantage, L.A. won the first two games of the best-of-seven series and was up 3–2 heading back to Boston for Game 6.

The Celtics extended the series by pulling out that game with a 99–90 victory, leaving the championship trophy still unclaimed and both teams headed back to the Forum for the final outcome.

Owner Jack Kent Cooke, who never lacked for confidence, came up with a special touch for the victory celebration he was already playing out in his head. To counter Red Auerbach's trademark victory cigar, Cooke decided on balloons.

"I remember the phone was ringing off the hook on the day of that game," said Lakers public relations man Jim Brochu, "but all the secretaries were in the press lounge blowing up balloons."

Cooke had them stuffed into the rafters of the Forum where they were clearly visible, softly bobbing against a safety net.

When Auerbach entered the arena and spotted the balloons, he said, "Those things are going to stay up there a hell of a long time."

Auerbach's words seemed to ring true early in the fourth quarter, with Boston leading by 17 and less than 10 minutes to play.

The Lakers made a run, cutting the lead to seven with under six minutes remaining.

It was then that Chamberlain injured his right knee going for a rebound and limped off the court.

Should he have stayed in?

He certainly looked less courageous than Jerry West, who had remained on the court and kept his team in the game despite a badly pulled hamstring. West would grind out a triple double, finishing with 42 points, 13 rebounds, and 12 assists.

The fact that West could perform so superbly despite suffering from an injury that would leave most players able to do little more than limp made Chamberlain's decision all the more infuriating.

Mel Counts, a journeyman, took his place and then hit a 10-foot jumper to pull the Lakers within one with less than two minutes left.

It was then that Chamberlain decided he was suddenly well enough to play.

Van Breda Kolff, whose relationship with Chamberlain had long been rocky, told him to remain right where he had placed himself: the bench.

"We're doing well enough without you," van Breda Kolff said.

The Celtics clung to a 103–102 lead as the clock dipped under the 90-second mark.

From the free-throw line, Boston's Don Nelson then launched a shot that appeared long.

It was, hitting the back of the rim.

The ball bounced high in the air above the backboard and came down right through the hoop.

"It was lucky," Nelson said. "Sometimes luck does play a part. There had been nothing we'd been able to do to stop them…. But that one shot brought them back to reality."

Boston hung on to once again beat the Lakers, this time 108–106.

As the Celtics joyously celebrated and the Lakers forlornly headed to the locker room, those balloons, still in the rafters, served as mute evidence of the Lakers' frustration.

"I'll never forget it," West said. "It was the most embarrassing thing I'd ever seen. All it did was hurt us."

Eventually, of course, the balloons came down.

"I sent them all to a children's hospital," Cooke said, "where the kids had a great time with them. Certainly a better time than I did."

56 Wilt vs. Butch: No Contest

Bill van Breda Kolff was "Butch" to his friends and "Coach" to anybody who ever played for him.

Except perhaps for Wilt Chamberlain, who probably had other names for him, unprintable names.

Van Breda Kolff loved to coach regardless of the level of competition or the skill level of his players.

And he proved it by coaching at every level from high school to college to the pros, both men and women. In all, he had 13 head coaching jobs, putting him on the sidelines for approximately 1,300 games.

Van Breda Kolff took the high school job at the age of 61.

"Coaching is coaching," he once said. "Give me 10 players who want to work and learn the game and I'm happy. I don't count the house."

He did, however, work for Jack Kent Cooke, a man who did count the house, seat by seat.

So when van Breda Kolff found himself in an untenable situation with Chamberlain, his superstar center on the Lakers, van Breda Kolff knew that he would be the one to go. No one was going to pay to see him.

Van Breda Kolff was already a big name within the coaching ranks when he came to the Lakers, having taken Princeton to the Final Four two years earlier.

He took the Lakers to the NBA Finals in both his seasons as their head coach, losing both times to the Boston Celtics.

Van Breda Kolff would later go on to coach Detroit, Phoenix, and New Orleans in the NBA as well as the Memphis Tams of the

The incomparable Wilt the Stilt goes up to drop two more points on the Knicks.
(Getty Images)

American Basketball Association and the New Orleans Pride of the Women's Professional Basketball League.

He never mellowed. Describing his style of coaching at Hofstra University at the age of 71, *The New York Times* said van Breda Kolff was the "animated, nonstop-gesticulating, chair-kicking, sideline-pacing, expletive-spewing Butch of days gone by."

But he would be best remembered for his showdown with Chamberlain on the Forum sidelines in the closing minutes of Game 7 of the 1969 Finals against the Celtics.

When Chamberlain volunteered to come back in after taking himself out because of a knee injury, van Breda Kolff uttered the six words that would end his brief time with the Lakers: "We're doing well enough without you."

Who wouldn't want Wilt Chamberlain on the court with the season on the line?

Who would blow a chance to beat the Celtics of Russell and Auerbach?

Who would get in the face of both Chamberlain and Cooke?

Only van Breda Kolff, who would always choose his own principles over all other considerations, no matter the consequences.

The consequences were rough this time.

When the Lakers lost, van Breda Kolff didn't give Cooke the satisfaction of swinging his ax. Van Breda Kolff resigned.

"We played better when he was out," van Breda Kolff later said of Chamberlain. "I have no regrets because, in my mind at the time, I thought it was the right thing to do."

Later looking back on that moment and his career, van Breda Kolff stood his ground, telling *The New York Times*, "I've had some good jobs that I've left, or they fired me. At the time, I thought it was the right thing for me to do. Whether it turned out right later, who cares?"

Another Streak— 3,338 Straight

This one stretched over 36 years and parts of five decades.

It didn't require memorable wins, unbelievable plays, or gravity-defying acrobatics, though all those elements were a part of it.

But it did require great skill, unflinching determination, and the ability to fight through injuries that would have stopped lesser men.

It was the broadcasting streak of Chick Hearn who was behind the Lakers microphone for every game from November 21, 1965, to December 16, 2001.

Nothing separated Hearn from his loyal audience, not prostate cancer, heart problems, a knee injury, nor a damaged cornea, along with the usual assortment of colds, flu, and laryngitis, the most frightening ailment for an announcer.

"To do it in that sport," said fellow announcer Ross Porter, who shared a broadcast booth with Hearn for UNLV basketball, "where you're constantly jumping on airplanes, doing three games in a row in three different cities [was amazing]. You've got weather problems because the basketball season goes through winter. You've always got the threat of laryngitis.

"And I never saw Chick worn out. He always kept his exuberance, his excitement."

It wasn't always easy. Sometimes, it was downright unbelievable.

Like the time in Houston during the 2000–01 season when Hearn became ill prior to a game and reluctantly agreed to go to a nearby hospital.

Doctors told him the problem was his heart and ordered a blood transfusion.

As he laid there, the IV needle stuck in his arm, the blood flowing into his body, Hearn kept his eye on a clock on the wall, silently calculating the absolute latest he could leave for the arena if he still wanted to broadcast the game.

Yes, he still planned on being there, heart problem or no heart problem.

When the time for departure arrived, Hearn informed the doctors he was done.

Whatever blood they had given him, he said, would have to do. He was leaving even if he had to pull the IV out by himself.

With no choice other than to physically subdue Hearn, the doctors followed his orders against their better judgment and watched him walk out of the hospital, slowly but resolutely.

Hearn was *84 years old* at the time.

When the ball was tipped off, there was Hearn describing it for the fans back home, he and his streak both still alive.

"When he made up his mind to do something," said Susan Stratton, his longtime producer, "he was very bullheaded about it. But leave a hospital while having a transfusion? Who would do that?"

Chick Hearn—more than once.

His wife, Marge, remembered another occasion, this one in L.A., when he needed a transfusion on a game day.

With game time approaching and Marge in the room, doctors had given Hearn half of what they felt he needed.

"There's no time for a second one," he told Marge. "Let's get out of here."

And again, leaving his IV bag dangling, Hearn took off.

Before a game in San Antonio, Stratton, working in the production truck, received word that Hearn needed to see her outside the arena.

She found him sitting in a cab in great pain. Trying to remove a contact lens, he had scratched the cornea of his left eye.

Stratton made a call to the Spurs' medical staff, and their eye doctor was contacted. Hearn was driven by a Spurs employee to the doctor's office, and, by 6:30, an hour before game time, Hearn was at his usual broadcast perch ready to go to work.

"I don't know how he did that," Stratton said.

He did it in secret as always, never wishing to let his audience know he was ill or in any way unable to perform his duties at his normal high level.

For example, although Hearn suffered from a knee problem for years, few knew it.

On one trip, he was badly hobbled by fluid in the knee. A doctor came to his hotel room, drained the liquid, gave him a cortisone shot, and Hearn didn't miss a moment of action.

The show must go on, and it always did.

"It never dawned on Fran to count the games," said Marge, referring to her husband by his given name, Francis. "He didn't even know how many in a row he had until they told him it was a thousand.

"And he didn't get serious about the streak until it reached 2,500. After that he really wanted to keep it going, but he didn't brag about it. He was not one to do that."

"There were a number of times during my 15 years with the team," said analyst Stu Lantz, a former player himself, "that he shouldn't have been at work.

"Two times, they took Chick off the air at halftime because he had laryngitis so bad, no one could understand a word he was saying.

"There were other times when…he felt terrible. Truly felt terrible. But, when the light went on and the game was about to start, he went to work."

"I don't know how you can compare his streak to others," said Lakers forward Rick Fox. "Cal Ripken's streak maybe. But Cal just had to show up. I'm sure he didn't play every one of those 2,632 straight games as well as Chick announced every game."

The streak would not have happened if owner Jack Kent Cooke had not expressed his unhappiness with his superstar announcer's outside work. Though Cooke appreciated that Hearn was much in demand because of his versatility, he felt that being the Lakers announcer should be good enough for any broadcaster.

In 1965, several years after taking the Lakers job, Hearn missed a game to do a golf tournament.

It was the only time he was ever absent from a Lakers game by choice.

Later that year, Hearn was in Fayetteville, Arkansas, to broadcast a football game between Arkansas and Texas Tech. It was late autumn—November 20—and the weather was brutal.

The Lakers were scheduled to play the San Francisco Warriors in Las Vegas that night. Cooke had chartered a private jet to get Hearn there in time.

"What do you think?" Hearn asked the pilot.

"I don't like the way the sky looks," the pilot said.

"Whatever you don't like, I don't like," Hearn said.

So Hearn spent the night in his Fayetteville hotel room while the Lakers raced up and down a court over a thousand miles away.

Cooke fumed, and Hearn was chagrined. Never again would he risk missing a Laker game.

The next night, the Lakers played the Philadelphia 76ers in the L.A. Sports Arena. Hearn was back in his familiar spot behind the microphone and there he stayed in good times and bad past the turn of the century.

In December 2001, an examination revealed that Hearn had suffered a slight heart attack and also had a blocked aortic valve.

He was told he needed surgery that couldn't wait until the end of the season.

The streak or his life?

Hearn didn't hesitate.

"Let's do it," he told the doctor.

And thus the streak ended. But before the season ended, Hearn was back on the job at age 85, describing his team's run to its third straight championship.

58 Pulling a Willis Reed

It has become a sports cliché. Every time an athlete suffers an injury of any type and there is uncertainty about that athlete's participation in an upcoming game, inevitably, someone will wonder, "Is he (or she) going to pull a Willis Reed?"

On May 8, 1970, the question being asked from Brooklyn to the Bronx was, "Will Willis Reed play?"

That evening at Madison Square Garden, the New York Knicks were facing the Lakers in Game 7 of the NBA Finals.

The Knicks desperately needed Reed, their 6'9", 235-pound center, to take his place in the middle as a counterbalance to L.A.'s Wilt Chamberlain. The Lakers center had missed nearly all of the regular season because of a knee injury, but had recovered sufficiently by the postseason to average 22.1 points and 22.2 rebounds.

But if Reed was to play, it would have to be largely on one leg. His right leg was seriously hobbled by a torn muscle that stretched from thigh to hip.

The injury had occurred in the first quarter of Game 5 at the Garden when Reed fell as he tried to get around Chamberlain on a drive to the basket.

As he looked at Reed, lying on the court with pain shooting through his body, teammate Walt Frazier said to himself, "There goes the championship."

It had been an up-and-down Finals with neither team able to win two in a row.

Although they trailed by 10 points when Reed went down, the Knicks rallied to win Game 5. Back in L.A., with Reed out, Chamberlain scored 45 points and pulled down 27 rebounds, and the Lakers took Game 6 to force the showdown finale.

Reed had been a powerful force in the first four games of the series, averaging 31.8 points and 15 rebounds.

As the time approached for Game 7, the question remained: Would Reed play? Even his teammates didn't have the answer.

"We left the locker room for the warmups," Bill Bradley told *The New York Times*, "not knowing if Willis was going to come out or not."

Back in the locker room, Reed was being given a cortisone shot.

"It was a big needle," Reed told AOL News years later. "I think I suffered more from the needle than the injury. I still had some pain afterward, but I could restrict some of my movement if I dragged the leg."

There was no doubt, however, what he was going to do.

"I wanted to play," he said. "That was the championship, the one great moment we had all played for…I didn't want to have to look at myself in the mirror 20 years later and say that I wished I had tried to play."

When Reed came limping out of the locker room and the crowd spotted him, a roar went up and bounced off the walls of the Garden and down the canyons of Manhattan.

A sense of completeness enveloped his teammates.

"It was like getting your left arm sewed back on," teammate Cazzie Russell said.

"We were flabbergasted just like everybody else when he came out," Frazier said. "The noise got louder and louder, and it reached a crescendo.... He wasn't limping. I'm sure he didn't feel it because of the adrenaline rush. It was like he was walking on air."

That's how it appeared, but Reed didn't feel that way.

"It was a tough spot," Reed said. "It was a heck of a predicament to be in. I knew I wasn't 100 percent. The fans were roaring. I was getting a standing ovation. Everybody was yelling, 'The Captain is here.' Everybody was saying that he's walking, but I sure couldn't walk very well. I was in a lot of pain."

"He gave us a tremendous lift just going out there," said Reed's coach, Red Holzman.

The Lakers, who had been warming up, paused to watch Reed tentatively take a few shots.

Knicks forward Dave DeBusschere observed the Lakers looking at Reed and said, "We got them."

"I'll never forget [watching] three of the greatest players that ever played [West, Baylor, and Chamberlain] just standing mesmerized, staring at Willis," Frazier said. "That gave me so much confidence."

That confidence level and the cheers of the crowd soared even higher after Reed, who failed to even leave the floor on the opening tip-off against Chamberlain, hit his first two shots in the game.

He didn't hit another, finishing 2–5 from the field with three rebounds and four fouls in 27 minutes.

But it didn't matter. Reed's mere presence on the court had provided the emotional wave that the Knicks—further powered by Frazier's 36 points, 19 assists, and five steals—rode to a 113–99 victory and the NBA title.

"Maybe if I'd missed those first two shots, it would have been different," said Reed. "But after that, the crowd was so into it, and Walt was just fantastic."

"It was Willis, and the courage that he showed," Frazier said. "It was so inspirational that once we saw him on the court, it really galvanized our team.... It was like a Hollywood ending."

59 Nice Guy Finishes First

Baseball's Leo Durocher used to say, "Nice guys finish last."

Durocher obviously didn't know Bill Sharman.

It would be hard, if not impossible, to find anybody who didn't consider Sharman one of the nicest people they ever ran across in the NBA.

Off the court.

On the court, his nice-guy demeanor was noticeably absent. It was consumed by a competitive streak that burned inside him and drove him to never settle for anything less than first.

And he was incredibly successful in pursuing that goal.

Sharman played for the Boston Celtics for a decade, beginning in 1951, and was a member of their first four championship teams.

He was a superlative shooter, especially at the free-throw line where he shot better than 90 percent in three different seasons and led the league in that category seven times. Sharman once made 55 free throws in a row, then a league record.

But, it was on defense that his competitiveness was the most glaring.

In his book, *Heinsohn, Don't You Ever Smile?*, former Boston teammate Tommy Heinsohn wrote, "Sharman was like a treacherous bulldog that would suddenly bite and refuse to let go.... Bill didn't have the quickness, but he intimidated his man. He played him in his socks. He picked him up and stayed with him all the way to his girlfriend's apartment."

Jerry West once hit seven jumpers with Sharman on him. Sharman became so incensed that he threw a punch at West after the seventh shot. Fortunately it was one of the few times Sharman missed his target.

"Bill was tough," West told the *Los Angeles Times*. "I'll tell you this, you did not drive by him. He got into more fights than Mike Tyson."

Maybe Durocher was right after all.

The Bo Jackson of his era, Sharman was such a good athlete that he was also able to play professional baseball during the first half of his NBA career.

He spent five years in the minors and was briefly called up by the Brooklyn Dodgers in 1951 but never got into a game.

When he turned to coaching, Sharman was just as successful.

Sharman's Competitiveness

Long after he was done playing and coaching, the competitiveness was still ingrained in Sharman.

It came out one night in the 1980 playoffs. A group of team personnel and writers went to dinner in Phoenix during the Lakers-Suns series.

As the meal was being concluded and the check paid, Sharman and the team's head physician, Dr. Robert Kerlan, were discussing the best way to get back to the team hotel. Sharman favored one route, Kerlan another.

"See you back there," said Sharman, the old glare in his eye.

He loaded his group into his rental car. Kerlan did the same with his group, and the two roared out of the parking lot.

Sharman raced down the desert streets, cutting corners when permissible, determined to beat Kerlan back to the hotel.

Sharman may have been 53 years old, with more than enough victories in his life to mellow him, but he still wasn't about to lose, even far from a basketball court, and go quietly into the night.

He coached the Cleveland Pipers of the American Basketball League to a title.

He coached the Utah Stars of the American Basketball Association to a title.

In the 1971–72 season, he joined the Lakers—a club that despite a dream team roster with Jerry West, Elgin Baylor, and Wilt Chamberlain—was still looking for its first championship in Los Angeles.

Sharman delivered again and did so in grand style. His team won a record 33 straight games, a then-record 69 regular season games, and the NBA title by beating the Knicks in five games.

Sharman thus became the only man ever to win professional basketball championships in three leagues.

He wasn't finished bringing glory to the Lakers. In 1976, Sharman became the team's general manager and helped usher in the Showtime era under new owner Jerry Buss.

Sharman's competitiveness, however, had a downside. Coaching instead of playing meant he could no longer express his unflinching desire for victory in a physical manner.

Only vocally.

For Sharman, that meant yelling, screaming, protesting, cajoling, and imploring.

He got hoarse, very hoarse. No big deal.

In Sharman's case, though, it turned out to be a very big deal. He permanently damaged his vocal cords, which eventually forced him off the sideline and into the front office.

But Sharman stayed with the Lakers, going from general manager to team president to special consultant, a title he held until his death in 2013.

He was voted into the basketball Hall of Fame twice as a player and a coach. Only two others—John Wooden and Lenny Wilkens—have been so honored.

Wooden wrote a letter of recommendation for Sharman's selection the second time, saying, "If Bill Sharman isn't in the Hall of Fame as a coach, no one should be."

There could be no higher praise.

Stumpy

The nickname is perfectly understandable.

In the land of giants known as the NBA, Gail Goodrich stood just 6'1" and weighed 170 pounds.

Too short?

He'd been hearing that since he tried to make his Poly High team in the San Fernando Valley, though he was only 5'2" and all of 99 pounds at the time.

Goodrich eventually turned the chuckles to cheers by leading his high school team to the city championship and being named player of the year.

Same deal in college. Never thinking small, he decided to go to UCLA and arrived just in time to help John Wooden start his legendary dynasty, playing on the Bruins' first two championship teams.

Goodrich scored 27 points against Duke in the 1964 NCAA title game, and 42 against Michigan in the 1965 final.

A sharpshooter with long arms, big hands, and impressive court awareness, Goodrich was able to compensate for his lack of height by mastering the skills necessary to excel in the backcourt.

Pro ball? Why not? He felt confident he could exceed expectations at yet another level.

This was one stump, he vowed, that nobody was going to step on.

Playing for 14 seasons, Goodrich not only succeeded in the NBA, but also stretched his comparatively short frame all the

Coin Flip

Unhappy with his Lakers contract, Goodrich wanted out of Purple and Gold after the 1975–76 season.

He signed with the Jazz, but, in those days, it wasn't as simple as that. The team losing a free agent was entitled to compensation in the form of players, draft picks, or cash.

If no agreement was reached, the commissioner, then Larry O'Brien, would step in and dictate the terms.

Lakers owner Jack Kent Cooke wanted three draft picks for Goodrich, even though he was 33 and past his prime. He requested the Jazz's first-round selections in 1977 and '79 and a second-rounder in 1980.

Though not thrilled with the price, New Orleans general manager Barry Mendelson finally agreed. Anything was better than putting the matter in O'Brien's hands and winding up with perhaps an even bigger cost.

Cooke, however, then offered an alternative. The Jazz had made a conditional deal for forward Sidney Wicks, who, like Goodrich, was a former Bruin. Cooke asked for Wicks.

No thanks, said Mendelson, we'll stick with the first offer.

Back then the No. 1 overall pick was determined by a coin flip between the two teams that finished last in their respective conferences. For the 1979 Draft, it came down to New Orleans (26–56) and Chicago (31–51).

On a conference call, O'Brien flipped the coin.

Bulls general manager Rod Thorn, who had gathered a crowd for the occasion, called heads.

It was tails.

So, after all he had done while playing for the Lakers, it turned out Goodrich made one last contribution in departing for three draft picks.

Less than three years later, just like magic, that '79 pick—by virtue of the coin flip—turned into Earvin Johnson.

way up to an elite peak reached by only the true superstars, the Naismith Memorial Basketball Hall of Fame.

A Laker for three seasons, Goodrich spent two with the Phoenix Suns, came back for six more with the Lakers, and then finished his career with the New Orleans Jazz.

Goodrich led the Lakers in scoring four times. A five-time All-Star, his career scoring average was 18.6.

He played with towering superstars, but his speed enabled him to often compensate for his relatively short stature.

"When you come down on the break," one of Goodrich's Lakers coaches, Bill Sharman, told him, "if you have an open shot, take it. If the other guys complain, we'll just tell them to get down faster."

As far as L.A. is concerned, Goodrich was the ultimate champion, winning high school, NCAA, and NBA titles there.

Redemption at Last

In movie terms it was *Groundhog Day* meets *A Nightmare on Elm Street* except the nightmare was on Prairie Avenue in Inglewood, and instead of Bill Murray, it was Bill Sharman.

It was the spring of 1972 and in the minds of basketball observers, certainly those gathered in the Forum, it was time. Finally.

After seven frustrating trips to the NBA Finals and a dozen years trying to emulate the success of their Midwest forebears, the Los Angeles Lakers seemed poised to win their first title.

That would still leave them four behind the Minneapolis Lakers, but at least they could feel they had done their part to carry on the tradition. At least they would have a banner of their own.

Backups

Even a team of superstars needed competent reserves who could fill any gaps left by the inevitable bouts of pain and exhaustion experienced by starters like West, Chamberlain, and Gail Goodrich.

And the bench definitely aided the Lakers' march to the championship.

Guard Flynn Robinson was known as "Instant Offense." While averaging only 9.9 points, he made the most of his 15.7 minutes of playing time by shooting 49 percent from the floor.

But Robinson's most indelible legacy is the source of laughter he once supplied for the entire team.

Not everyone knew Robinson wore a hairpiece, but no one could forget after he was exposed while driving down the floor one night.

With the spotlight on him, it was the worst possible time for the wig to come loose, but that's what happened.

The front of the toupee popped up while the back end stayed attached.

"It looked like the bill of a cap," announcer Chick Hearn said.

To his credit, Robinson maintained his focus, launched a shot and scored despite the peals of laughter from the crowd.

Then, there was Keith Erickson. There were bigger stars on the team, but no greater athlete. It wasn't just that Erickson played on both Lakers and UCLA championship basketball teams. His athletic talent went far beyond hoops. He played volleyball well enough to make the 1964 U.S. Olympic team. Put a bat in his hand and watch him excel in baseball. Put a racquet in his hand and watch him do the same in tennis.

How good was he? Coach John Wooden said Erickson was the finest athlete he ever coached.

Enough said.

The only time Erickson sometimes struggled to make his presence felt was when he was behind the microphone as Chick Hearn's analyst.

Hearn was the consummate broadcaster, able to handle every aspect of the job. That made it difficult—sometimes impossible—for his broadcast partners to get airtime.

But Erickson could laugh about it.

On an off night in Indianapolis one season, members of the Lakers traveling party, including Hearn and Erickson, went out to dinner.

After the meal and a few drinks, Hearn was nudged into giving an after-dinner speech. He went on and on, covering a wide range of unrelated subjects.

Finally exhausted, he plopped back down in his seat.

"Your turn, Keith," someone said.

Erickson stood up, and with a big smile, said, "I agree with everything you said, Chick."

Guard Jim Cleamons was a seldom-used reserve on the team, averaging only 5.3 minutes. But he had a unique distinction that may never be equaled. Cleamons was later an assistant coach on the 1995–96 Chicago Bulls, the team that broke the Lakers' record won-lost mark of 69–13 by going 72–10. That got him into the team photo of the two greatest squads in NBA history.

It seemed inevitable that the Lakers would win. No team had ever entered the Finals with better credentials. They had amassed the best regular-season record to that point in NBA history at 69–13, and that included a record 33-game winning streak.

They had gone 8–2 in the first two rounds of the playoffs, sweeping the Bulls and beating Kareem Abdul-Jabbar and his Bucks in six games.

Only the Knicks lay ahead and they were not the Knicks who had beaten the Lakers in the Finals two years earlier. Willis Reed, who had supplied crucial inspiration by limping into Game 7 in 1970, was limping again, hampered by a knee injury. But this time he wouldn't make it to the court. Dick Barnett was severely limited by an injury, and Cazzie Russell had been traded.

What could possibly stop the Lakers now?

Only a devastating injury to a superstar. They had been there before and, for one horrifying moment, thought they were reliving a bad memory a la *Groundhog Day*.

There was no panic after New York won Game 1 at the Forum, 114–92, thanks largely to a 53 percent shooting night.

The Lakers were confident the Knicks couldn't maintain that pace, and, indeed, they didn't. With New York forward Dave DeBusschere injured in Game 2 and the Lakers back to form, L.A. won that game at the Forum and Game 3 in New York's Madison Square Garden.

It was in the first quarter of Game 4 that the nightmare surfaced. Wilt Chamberlain fell on the hardwood at the Garden and injured a wrist. As he stood there, clutching it in pain, the Lakers saw 1969 all over again. In the Finals that year, Chamberlain left Game 7 against the Celtics with just over five minutes to play, and the Lakers wound up losing by two.

Chamberlain had taken himself out of that seventh game, but this time he refused to leave.

It was a decision that may well have been the series' deciding factor. With their big man remaining in the middle, the Lakers pulled out Game 4 in overtime, 116–111. Chamberlain played ferociously in the extra period even though he had five fouls.

As Game 5 loomed, it was decision time for Chamberlain once again. At first, he said he wouldn't be able to play. But then he received a shot to lessen the inflammation in his wrist and headed out onto the Forum floor.

It wasn't exactly a replay of the Willis Reed moment, but what it may have lacked in terms of comparable inspiration, it more than made up for in substance.

Sore wrist and all, Chamberlain was unstoppable at times, getting 24 points and 29 rebounds to lead the Lakers to a 114–100 victory and their first L.A. championship.

So how did it feel to West to finally hold the championship trophy that had eluded his grasp for so long?

"I played terrible basketball in the Finals," West said, "and we won. And that didn't seem to be justice for me personally because I had contributed so much in other years when we lost. Now, when we won I was just another piece of the machinery."

Most players would consider themselves a vital piece of machinery if they averaged 19.8 points, 8.8 assists, and four rebounds in the NBA Finals as did West. But he was right. By his lofty standards, his numbers—especially a 32.5 field goal percentage—were below par.

"It was particularly frustrating," he said, "because I was playing so poorly that the team had to overcome my performance.

"Maybe that's what a team is all about."

Certainly that team, arguably the best in NBA history.

The Punch

It was the most devastating punch ever thrown in an NBA game, a blow that would even make a Mike Tyson sit up and take notice.

It nearly killed a player, damaged two careers, and sent shock waves through the league.

Thrown by Laker forward Kermit Washington, the punch shattered the face of Houston forward Rudy Tomjanovich.

It would have been tragic and unnecessary even if it had come in the midst of a fight between Washington and Tomjanovich. What made it even worse—if that's possible—was that Tomjanovich was trying, at the time, to serve as peacemaker, not combatant.

The fight in that December 9, 1977, game at the Forum was between Washington and Houston's Kevin Kunnert.

Fellow Laker Kareem Abdul-Jabbar had already pulled Kunnert away when Tomjanovich came rushing up with the intent, he would later say, of breaking up the slugfest.

Washington would later claim what happened next was "an honest mistake," that all he saw was "a blur" rushing at him from behind.

Looking at a film of that devastating moment, however, it is clear the 6'8" Washington had already turned around. He saw Tomjanovich rushing up and planted his feet before burying his right hand in the face of the 6'8" Rocket.

Everything was suddenly blurred for Tomjanovich, who suffered a broken nose, double fracture of the jaw, swelling around the head, a concussion, an eye injury, and facial cuts.

All that from one punch.

"I remember thinking the scoreboard must have fallen on me," Tomjanovich later said.

In his book, *Giant Steps,* Abdul-Jabbar wrote that the sound of Washington's fist hitting Tomjanovich's face "sounded like a watermelon had been dropped onto a concrete floor.... Even as Rudy was going down, there was blood pouring out of his face."

A doctor equated the injuries to those a man might sustain from being thrown through a car windshield at 50 miles an hour.

The fans, who were in an uproar, were suddenly silent. Horror replaced hysteria.

While the fallen Tomjanovich was crushed physically, Washington was crushed emotionally.

Starting there on the court and continuing on in the ensuing days as the hospitalized Tomjanovich underwent three operations, Washington searched within himself for some explanation of how he could have committed such a terrible act.

"My God, I don't want to hurt anyone," Washington later told the *Los Angeles Times.* "I'm just trying to earn a living. Maybe I ought to just be a teacher."

NBA commissioner Larry O'Brien decided this had to be a teachable moment. There had been many ugly incidents on NBA hardwood, but this one went beyond anything seen before. Or, as it turned out, seen since. This was unacceptable.

O'Brien fined Washington $10,000, then a league record, and suspended him for 60 days.

His days as a Laker were numbered. He didn't even finish his suspension in Purple and Gold. Eighteen days after smashing Tomjanovich to the Forum floor, Washington was traded to the Celtics.

He played four more seasons, one with the then–San Diego Clippers and three with the Trail Blazers, before retiring at 30.

Washington, however, couldn't shake the feeling that he had more basketball left in him. Six years later, he tried a comeback, but lasted only six games with the Warriors before quitting for good.

While his uniform changed over the years, his image never did. Some would always perceive him as a loose cannon who could go off at any time.

Tomjanovich spent the rest of the 1977–78 season recuperating but came back to play three more years with the Rockets, later becoming a scout, an assistant coach, and a head coach.

As head coach, he led the Rockets to back-to-back titles in the mid-'90s and, ironically, finished up his coaching career spending half a season leading the Lakers.

Tomjanovich quit 43 games into the 2004–05 season, explaining that he shouldn't have taken the job only a year removed from bladder cancer.

As for the Washington incident, Tomjanovich said it had long since been relegated to his rearview mirror by the time he joined the Lakers.

"Someone once told me," he said in the book, *The Punch*, "that hating Kermit would be like taking poison and hoping someone else died."

63 They Played It for Laughs

There are superstars, there are stars, and then there are characters. Here are a pair of the latter:

Nobody identifies Johnny Neumann with the Lakers. Few if any fans even remember he was on the roster. After all he was on eight teams in seven seasons, beginning with the Memphis Pros of the American Basketball Association.

Neumann played less than one full season with the Lakers, getting into 59 games in 1976–77.

Yet he left a lasting mark with the club for the one game in which he wasn't wearing Purple and Gold.

Sitting in his usual spot on the bench, Neumann was called upon by his coach, Jerry West, to go in.

It's a routine that has been repeated hundreds of thousands of times. The coach points, the player leaps off the bench, pops open the buttons on his warmup outfit, flings it in the direction of a ball boy, and rushes to the scorers' table to check in.

When Neumann went through that routine that night, however, there was one hilarious difference. He had forgotten to put on his basketball shorts and was standing there in his underwear for all to see.

Said announcer Chick Hearn, "He got the biggest ovation of his career."

Billy Thompson spent two seasons with the Lakers in the latter half of the 1980s. He had some talent, but he also had some bad habits that left his coach, Pat Riley, fuming.

For one thing, Thompson was late, habitually, to practices and shootarounds. Despite lectures, fines, and decreased playing time, the man remained seriously in need of a watch.

Riley cracked a smile one day when Thompson showed up on time.

But that smile quickly faded when the Lakers coach saw that Thompson had two left shoes.

Teammates were all smiles one night in Cleveland after Thompson announced he was going to leave a pair of tickets for a fan he had met at the airport.

No problem, Thompson was told. He was given an envelope and asked to write the fan's name on it. The tickets would be placed in the envelope and left at the will call window. When he showed his ID, the fan would get the tickets.

Thompson thought for a moment, then wrote on the envelope: the guy from the airport.

64 Monopoly as the Game of Life

Jerry Buss loved to play Monopoly. Evenings in the family home in Pacific Palisades would often center on marathon sessions of the game involving Buss, his wife, and four kids.

But Buss didn't stop playing when he left the house. He continued to roll the dice in the actual world of real estate. Instead of the fictional Boardwalk and Park Place, he was wheeling and dealing to acquire huge chunks of tangible property throughout the Southwest.

Always in Buss' mind, however, was the idea that the ultimate acquisition would be a sports team, and the bigger the better.

He started relatively small, investing in a new sports concept: (WTT) World Team Tennis.

It was during the tennis boom of the 1970s, when Jimmy Connors and Chris Evert were appealing to a whole new generation, and every hip weekend warrior in search of exercise had a racket in his or her hands.

The idea of the WTT was to take high-profile tennis stars and put them in a team situation, awarding points for singles, doubles, and mixed doubles victories.

The league wanted an L.A. franchise. This was ideal for Buss and his attorney, Jerry Fine, who purchased the rights to a WTT club to be named the Los Angeles Strings, for $50,000, splitting the cost while bringing in limited partners.

The public, however, wasn't sold on the new Los Angeles team. In its first year of operation, the club lost $200,000.

Fine wanted out. That was fine with Buss, who was determined to stick with the venture, establish his credentials as a stable, competent sports owner, and use those credentials to obtain a more conventional team in a more established league such as the NFL or NBA.

"This is going to be my education in sports," he said.

The Strings began at the L.A. Sports Arena, but moved to Jack Kent Cooke's Forum. That allowed Buss to get to know Cooke. And when rumors circulated that Cooke was going to dump his Southern California sports empire because of his impending divorce, Buss saw a possible path to his dream acquisition.

He told Cooke, if the rumors were true, he wanted a shot at the Lakers and Kings. And since real estate was his game, Buss was interested in the Forum as well.

Cooke didn't exactly open the door to negotiations, but he didn't shut it either. He just left the possibility out there, tantalizingly.

When Cooke moved to Las Vegas, Buss stayed in contact with him. Every few weeks, Cooke would call and say, "Why don't you come up and talk to me this afternoon?"

Jerry Buss shows off his Naismith Memorial Basketball Hall of Fame ring.

Buss would be on the next flight out of L.A.

Finally, on a Tuesday in May, 1979, Buss heard the words for which he had longed.

"Are you ready?" said Cooke from Vegas.

Buss was practically in the air while the words were still echoing in his ears.

The trigger point had been the conclusion of divorce proceedings. Cooke would pay out somewhere between $41 million and $49 million, depending on whose numbers are accurate. There is no disputing, though, the divorce's listing in the *Guinness Book of World Records* as the largest ever to that point.

Planning to move to Virginia to be nearer to the Washington Redskins, which he owned, Cooke was ready to divest himself of his California holdings and leave the state behind.

But at what price?

Buss was about to begin the biggest game of Monopoly ever played.

Once a week, Cooke and Buss, each fortified by a small army of lawyers and tax advisers, would meet at the Desert Inn in Las Vegas.

Taxes were the critical issue in the negotiations. With the kind of money these two men were talking about, the government might turn out to be the big winner.

Unless…

Cooke and Buss began to discuss a trade, not of players, but of assets and properties.

Buss had plenty of property, but Cooke coveted New York's Chrysler Building. Who wouldn't?

Buss obtained the lease to the property, but the stakes continued to rise, the lawyers multiplied, and the sessions intensified.

Both Cooke, the former door-to-door encyclopedia salesman, and Buss, the former ditchdigger, loved the action. They had built fortunes from scratch by always staying ahead of the competition, but now, each had met a rival who could match the other move for move. Each was determined to walk away from the table a winner. In the end, both did.

First Night

Buss knew it was a silly thought, but he still entertained it when he first walked into the Forum after purchasing the arena.

Having just spent more than $33 million for this building, shouldn't he at least get a key for it?

Buss had a lot of other thoughts that first night in the Forum, and there was nothing silly about any of them.

After the building had emptied out for the day, he took a folding chair down to the floor, sat at where midcourt would be, and pulled out a cigarette.

The building was quiet and dark except for the hum of a generator and a few scattered lights faintly illuminating Buss.

He thought about the path that had led him to this spot, full of unexpected twists and turns, and the road ahead, surely leading to a bright future.

He looked into the silent darkness and imagined the roar of the crowds, the sight of a sold-out arena, and the glitter and glamour of the celebrity-filled courtside seats.

Buss imagined the Lakers racing up and down the court, fast breaks unfolding, slam dunks exploding, and championship banners unfurling.

He could almost hear the scraping of skates on ice, the slapping of stick on puck, and the banging of bodies into the boards as the Kings battled for the ever-elusive Stanley Cup.

Buss knew there would be other sounds, from the music of the world's top recording artists to the giggles of children watching the Harlem Globetrotters.

There would be so much more as well, from circuses to indoor soccer to roller hockey.

Nights like this, when he would be alone in his new palace, would be rare.

But on that night—the night he planted his flag in the Southern California sports landscape—being a solitary man alone with his thoughts was all he needed.

When the last agreement was signed, the briefcases closed and the handshakes over, the monumental deal broke down as follows:

- Buss got the Lakers, the Kings, the Forum, and Cooke's 13,000-acre Raljon Ranch, nestled near the Sierra Nevada mountains
- Cooke got the Chrysler Building and property in Massachusetts, Maryland, and Virginia.
- The former holders of the Chrysler lease got property owned by Buss.

It wasn't purely a trade. There was money involved, $67.5 million of it. Buss would pay $33.5 million for the Forum, $16 million for the Lakers, $8 million for the Kings, and $10 million for the ranch.

In all, there were nine pieces of property involved, spread over three states with a dozen escrows and a total of over 50 lawyers and accountants.

Somewhere, Bob Short had to be shaking his head.

65 Sand Dabs?

Jack Kent Cooke had no doubt Magic Johnson had the talent to succeed in a spectacular way in the NBA.

But did he have the determination and the confidence?

That question was answered at the Forum, not on the court, but in one of the offices above.

Having made the decision to select Johnson, Cooke decided to negotiate a deal with him before the draft was even held.

The Lakers owner invited the 19-year-old college star; his father, Earvin Sr.; his lawyer, George Andrews; and his adviser, Dr. Charles Tucker, to lunch.

The meal was to be served in the Trophy Room, where the four walls were loaded with tributes to Cooke and his accomplishments.

Most 19-year-olds would be intimidated by the man and the surroundings. But as Cooke was soon to learn, Johnson was not like any other 19-year-old.

When it came time for the meal, Cooke said, "I'll order."

He told his chef to bring sand dabs, a fish found in abundance in the Pacific Ocean. Because there are none in Lake Michigan, Johnson had never heard of sand dabs.

When the food arrived and Johnson had taken a few tentative bites, Cooke said, "Well, Earvin, how do you like your sand dabs?"

"They're all right," said Johnson, not a fan of fish in general.

Suddenly, it got very quiet in the room. Cooke wasn't used to anyone but yes men.

"All right?" he said, his voice rising. "Only all right?"

Not flinching, Johnson said he wanted something else, like a hamburger or pizza.

Despite his initial outburst, Cooke was actually pleased Johnson had disputed the owner's meal choice. That told the Lakers owner he had selected someone who, despite his youth, was not going to be intimidated by any aspect of the huge role he was about to take on.

66 The Dog Days of Jerry West

Once new Lakers owner Jerry Buss had a style of play in mind and a trigger man to perform on the court, he needed someone to run the show from the sideline.

His first choice for head coach was Jerry West, the man who had been there the previous three years.

But West had no intention of sticking around. He had enjoyed some success with a 145–101 regular-season record. But getting West, ever the perfectionist, to truly enjoy any season is nearly impossible.

And certainly not his three seasons as coach, considering none of his teams advanced beyond the second round of the playoffs.

West became so frustrated that, at one point, he referred to his superstar center, Kareem Abdul-Jabbar, as a "dog."

Looking back only after time had healed some of the agony West had felt as a coach, he conceded that the good had probably outweighed the bad.

"We had glaring weaknesses on the team," West said, "and yet, we prospered in the three years. I think we turned the franchise around in my three years, put it on a path where we could continue to win.

"I can say I'm glad I had an opportunity to do what I did, but two of those years were the most miserable years I have ever spent on this earth. No player is as lonely as a coach. You don't know about this until you become a coach. I learned some bitter lessons."

It was obvious Buss was going to have to look elsewhere for a coach to launch the Showtime era.

67 The Architect of Showtime

It was Chick Hearn who first brought up Jack McKinney as a possible Lakers coach.

Jerry Buss was thinking of a more colorful, more charismatic figure like UNLV head coach Jerry Tarkanian.

If Tark didn't have to worry about the recruiting phase of the game, the phase that had landed him in so much trouble throughout his college career and sucked up so much of his energy and focus, imagine how effective he could be, went the argument of those who wanted to see him coach in the pros.

There had been talks between the Lakers and Tarkanian while Jack Kent Cooke was still the owner. In June of 1979, with the ownership of the team having recently changed hands, both Cooke and Buss agreed to meet at a Beverly Hills hotel with Vic Weiss, a friend of Tarkanian who was representing him in negotiations. Weiss was an agent/businessman/boxing manager/high-stakes gambler.

At the meeting, Buss and Cooke presented Weiss with a lucrative financial offer to Tarkanian.

Weiss said he'd get back to them, but never did. He never got back to anyone because he disappeared that night, his body found stuffed into the trunk of his car three days later. He had been killed execution style with two gunshots to the head. The case was never solved, but it was believed by some to be a mob hit.

Tarkanian was stunned by the murder. Was it a bad omen, bad karma?

All he knew for sure was that the Laker job didn't look so attractive anymore, certainly not as attractive as the sweet deal he had at UNLV that included a large salary, the resources to compete for a national title and the opportunity to battle the NCAA over it's policies.

So Tarkanian stayed, making McKinney the Lakers' leading candidate, even though he was once described as "like Jack Ramsay, only without charisma."

That was not a compliment. If serious, studious Ramsay—the Trail Blazers coach was McKinney's mentor—was your standard for charisma, you were dull at best.

But McKinney wasn't being considered for his ability to put fans in the seats, but rather to put victories in the win column.

He had been quite successful at that at both the high school and college level before moving on to the NBA as an assistant coach.

Buss hired McKinney, giving him a one-year contract worth $125,000.

When McKinney said he had hoped for a three-year deal, Buss told him, "I don't know if you're even a good coach."

As it turned out, he was.

At first glance, it appeared to be a job with a high probability of success.

Kareem and Magic on the same team? Just roll the ball out there and let them play.

But as Phil Jackson found when he had Kobe and Shaq on the same team, and as countless other coaches with superstars would also point out, the problem is that there is only one ball for all those big names to share.

In joining the Lakers, Johnson was entering Abdul-Jabbar's turf. The big center was the accepted leader of the team, the captain of the squad. He was a serious, often distant figure, not likely to be amused by the gregarious kid with the infectious grin and the sparkling enthusiasm.

Before even tackling that issue, McKinney designed the fast-breaking, high-octane offense that became the trademark of the Showtime era. It was the offense Buss had envisioned, the offense

Kareem and Magic

Despite McKinney's best efforts to bring Kareem and Magic together, no one could dispute the glaring difference in perspective between the hardened veteran and the effervescent rookie.

That was evident in the first game of their first season together.

It was in San Diego where the Clippers were then located. The game, tied in the final seconds, was won by Abdul-Jabbar on a skyhook as time expired.

Johnson came rushing up to the Lakers center and threw his arms around "Cap," as he called him, as if the team had just won an NBA title.

"Hey," Abdul-Jabbar told him, "we've got 81 more of these."

Unfortunately for McKinney, he had only a fraction of that amount remaining in his brief tenure as Lakers coach.

that outlasted McKinney and his successor, Paul Westhead. Pat Riley, Westhead's successor, adeptly adopted that style—with some adjustments—during his early years as Lakers coach.

After assembling the offense, McKinney sat down with his two superstars individually.

He told Abdul-Jabbar, the man whose trademark skyhook made him an unstoppable offensive force in a half-court offense, that he wanted him to run because the Lakers were about to launch one of the great fast-break offenses of all time.

Abdul-Jabbar said to count him in.

In his book, *Jack McKinney's Tales from the Saint Joseph's Hardwood,* the coach recalled sitting down with Johnson two weeks into training camp.

"I'm disappointed," McKinney said. "When we drafted you, I thought you'd take charge and run the show."

"Coach," Johnson replied, "I couldn't tell Kareem, Jamaal [Wilkes], and Norman [Nixon] what to do. These guys are All-Pros."

McKinney said, "Magic, somebody has to do it. Just yesterday after practice, Kareem said to me, 'Coach, when is that young buck going to take over like you said he would?'"

Johnson was stunned.

"Kareem said that?" he asked.

"Yep, yesterday," McKinney assured him.

"Well, if Kareem said that," Johnson responded, "then I'd better do it."

Years later, McKinney wrote, "The fact that Kareem had never so much as mentioned Magic or Magic's role falls under the category [of] coach's prerogative. I stretched the truth a little, but you can't dispute the results."

68 The Downfall of Jack McKinney

When Jack McKinney was hired to coach the Lakers, the person he wanted by his side was Paul Westhead.

No surprise there. Whenever a basketball opportunity came up, Westhead was always the first one McKinney called.

Their relationship began at St. Joseph's University in Philadelphia when McKinney was an assistant coach and Westhead was a player.

When McKinney moved up to head coach, he made Westhead, a graduate by then, his assistant.

When Westhead coached in Puerto Rico one summer, it was because McKinney had gotten him the job.

When Westhead went to Brazil representing the U.S. State Department, it was because McKinney had recommended him.

When McKinney had to leave a basketball clinic in Italy to interview for the Lakers job, Westhead took his place.

So, of course, once he became head coach, who did McKinney ask the Lakers to hire as his assistant?

Is it really necessary to ask?

Thirteen games into the season, things were going well for McKinney. Although they had just lost to the Golden State Warriors 126–109, the Lakers were still 9–4, Earvin Johnson was beginning to look like Magic, and the offense was starting to kick into the high gear that would characterize it for nearly a decade.

It all seemed to lay ahead for McKinney on the night of November 7, as he and his players flew home following the Warriors game in Oakland. He was the coach of a team on the verge of greatness, the leader of a squad filled with potential and promise.

But all those bright tomorrows could wait. The tomorrow immediately ahead, November 8, was the Lakers' first day off since the start of the preseason, a chance for a welcome, if brief, respite.

McKinney slept in, awakened by a call from Westhead, who asked him to play tennis. Westhead had reserved a court at his Palos Verdes condominium complex.

It sounded like a good idea to McKinney. He jumped in the shower, then threw on some shorts, poured a cup of coffee, picked up his racket, and walked into his garage—but found it empty.

Then it all came flashing back to him. His wife, Claire, had told him she was taking the family car to attend a class she was taking with Cassie Westhead, Paul's wife. She mentioned this earlier while she got dressed in the bedroom and he was drifting in and out of sleep.

McKinney looked at his watch. Westhead had probably left for the courts already.

If there were cell phones in those days, McKinney could have called Westhead to pick him up and thus might have remained coach of the Lakers for a decade or more.

But back then, there was no way to reach him. McKinney could jog the mile and a half to the courts, which would sap much of his energy, or…

His eyes settled on his son John's bicycle in the corner of the garage.

Why not?

McKinney secured his racket on the back, got on, and made his way down the street.

Coming to a steep hill, McKinney started down. An eyewitness said that McKinney was taking the hill cautiously, slowing down even more as the incline increased.

But then, the bike seemed to lock up, coming to a jarring halt. McKinney, however, kept going, and was flung over the handlebars headfirst without a helmet.

Because he had struggled to hang on, there was no time to bring his hands forward to break his fall. Instead, his skull smashed into the asphalt. Even after McKinney lost consciousness, his body kept sliding down the hill another 18 feet.

Finally, it stopped, the only motion being the pool of blood slowly expanding from around his head.

69 The Substitute Teacher

When the paramedics arrived after an onlooker had reported the accident, the man they found in the street was so badly injured that they questioned whether he would survive.

Head coach Jack McKinney had a severe concussion; broken cheekbone and elbow; and cuts and bruises all over his body. He was not conscious.

Hospitalized in intensive care, McKinney faced a long road to recovery.

When he regained consciousness and his wife showed him a newspaper story about the accident, McKinney said, "Is this me they are talking about?"

In the meantime, there was a team to coach. Paul Westhead stepped in for his fallen friend. Having served in the unlikely role of Shakespearean scholar/basketball coach at the college level, Westhead saw a similarity in his new role.

"I'm a substitute teacher," he said. "Once you go into the classroom, you have to teach. Sometimes it's just for a day and sometimes it's for a whole year."

No one except McKinney's doctors felt it would be for a whole year.

As he recuperated, McKinney became impatient. The Lakers were maintaining the momentum he had set in motion, and he wanted to be part of it.

That was fine with Westhead.

"Even if we go [undefeated] the rest of the season," he said, "it's still Jack McKinney's team."

Buss wasn't so sure of that. Not after McKinney came out to a game and walked right by his boss.

"Jack, how are you?" Buss said. "How are you feeling?"

McKinney didn't answer, didn't even acknowledge him. His mind not yet right, he hadn't recognized Jerry Buss.

Deep down, McKinney knew he wasn't ready.

After the Lakers

McKinney was understandably bitter when he was let go.

He imagined his coaching career was over at 44. The chance to lead a team headed for a dynasty was lost in a five-minute bike ride.

"I thought I was fine,' McKinney later said. "I thought Buss was being mean, but he knew what he was doing. I didn't know what I was doing. He was a businessman running a very successful business and he had to make a decision.... It was a good decision, though, at the time I thought it was horrible."

"He was just deeply hurt," Buss said. "He felt, basically, it was his team. What had he done to lose it? I guess the answer is: he had an accident."

McKinney went on to coach the Indiana Pacers, a job Buss got him, though McKinney didn't know it at the time and wouldn't have accepted the position had he known.

He spent four years in Indiana, finishing with a losing record and then coached the Kansas City Kings for their first nine games of the 1984–85 season, quitting after going 1–8.

"I just can't do it anymore," he told his mentor, Jack Ramsay.

"[McKinney] was a great coach," Pat Riley said. "If he hadn't had the accident, he might have won five or six titles for the Lakers in the '80s."

Perhaps the ultimate compliment to McKinney was the answer to a question posed to Kareem Abdul-Jabbar: Who was the greatest coach he ever played for?

"John Wooden and Jack McKinney," said Abdul-Jabbar, including a man who coached him for only 13 games.

"Of course, I have to wonder how long I would have gone on with the Lakers," McKinney once said, "but I've learned to accept it and finally found peace of mind."

He went on to work for a sporting goods company and did some scouting for NBA clubs. McKinney died in 2018 at age 83.

"I couldn't walk straight," he said, "but I wanted to be out there."

The more Buss consulted with doctors, the more he became convinced McKinney wouldn't be sufficiently recovered to return before season's end.

When Westhead led the Lakers into the playoffs and all the way to the NBA Finals against Philadelphia, Buss decided not to bring McKinney back at all. He wanted Westhead to become the permanent coach.

"Maybe McKinney would have won it," said Buss after the Lakers beat the 76ers for the title. "Maybe he wouldn't. This guy won it. I had a sure against a maybe. I'll go with the sure every time."

Westhead, however, insisted he was not so sure about taking his best friend's job.

"Jack will not be the coach of this team," Buss said. "Do you want the job or do we get somebody else?"

Westhead took it.

"Shoot, I'd have taken it, too," said McKinney years later, "but at the time, that hurt."

Not only had McKinney and Westhead been close, but their wives and kids had also bonded.

But that ended when Westhead had accepted the dream job, which turned out to be a nightmare for McKinney.

"They can't share our joys," said Cassie Westhead of the McKinneys, "and we can't share their sorrows."

70 The Curious Case of Spencer Haywood

It was one of the strangest sights ever seen on an NBA court.

And it was on a practice court.

Preparing to face Philadelphia in the 1980 NBA Finals, the Lakers were going through stretching exercises at the start of practice when the coaches realized forward Spencer Haywood, stretched out on the floor seemingly frozen in the position of a hurdler poised to leap, wasn't participating.

On closer inspection, they realized he was sound asleep.

Another bizarre moment in Haywood's bizarre season.

There were others. He also fell asleep in the middle of a team film session, claiming exhaustion.

It had long been known Haywood had an erratic personality. He would shower before games, he said, to remove the pollen from his body.

But teams put up with him because he had talent.

The 6'8", 225-pounder had been an All-American at the University of Detroit, a center on the gold medal–winning 1968 U.S. Olympic men's basketball team, and had spent 10 seasons in the pros by the time he joined the Lakers for the 1979–80 season.

From then on, he engaged in a battle of wills against Paul Westhead, who took over the head coaching position after Jack McKinney's devastating bicycle accident.

Haywood lost his starting job early in the season due to injury. As the season wore on, he became more and more vocal about what he saw as an unfair lack of playing time. His grumbling turned into sulking, and his behavior became a distraction to a team positioned to win a championship.

Pay Cut

When it came time to vote playoff shares after the 1980 postseason, the players gave Haywood only a quarter share, the ultimate insult considering he had been with the team all season.

"It's more than he deserved." said Kareem Abdul-Jabbar.

Disgusted with his role as a bench player, Haywood made a scene in the locker room at halftime of one game, saying, "I don't need this [bleep]. I'm independently wealthy."

Although his teammates weren't sympathetic, he won over the Forum fans, who chanted his name during games.

That prompted *Phoenix Gazette* columnist Joe Gilmartin to write, "The Lakers need two psychiatrists' couches, one for Haywood and one for all the fans."

Haywood survived despite his disruptive behavior and inappropriate naps. But then after Game 2 of the Finals, he got into an argument with teammate Brad Holland over the use of the tape cutters.

Another teammate, Jim Chones, jumped in and pushed Haywood away.

"You crazy, Wood?" Chones said. "Man, you're lettin' us down."

For the final time.

The Lakers hierarchy immediately held an emergency meeting in Jerry Buss' office. They quickly decided that Haywood, who was still in the building, would be suspended from the team, a highly unusual move in the midst of a championship series.

As he headed for his car after hearing the news, Haywood told reporters, "I waited 10 years to play on a championship team, and now [the Lakers] do this to me. You tell me if it's not vicious to do something like that."

Then he got into his car and drove off into Lakers history, a weird footnote to a championship season.

71 Silk

Anyone who ever saw Jamaal Wilkes cock the basketball behind his right ear and smoothly toss up a jump shot would understand why his nickname was "Silk."

He preferred the background to the spotlight, a low-key spot on the highest-profile team of the 1980s.

But opponents weren't fooled. They knew that when the ball got into his hands, Wilkes could make his presence felt in dramatic style. It would take perfect defense or a double team to have a chance against one of the surest shots in the game.

Chick Hearn described Wilkes' jumper as "a 20-foot layup." Coach Paul Westhead said the release from Wilkes' soft hands was like "snow falling off a bamboo leaf."

Born Keith Wilkes, he first excited L.A. basketball fans as a member of the UCLA Bruins (1972–74) where he was a two-time All-American. His teams reached the Final Four all three seasons, winning the championship twice.

Typically, he was overshadowed by Bill Walton at UCLA.

Typically, on arguably his greatest shooting night as a pro—37 points, including 16 in the third quarter of the Lakers' title-clinching game against the 76ers in the 1980 NBA Finals—he was overshadowed by Magic Johnson.

Ever humble, Wilkes never complained about a lack of media attention.

As a matter of fact, the only time he ever complained about the media was when a remark to a *Los Angeles Times* reporter that Wilkes felt was the off the record appeared in print.

The next time he found himself surrounded by the media, including that reporter, Wilkes said, "I can't speak right now. There's a liar among us."

72. Coach Westhead: To Be or Not to Be

It was just a *Sports Illustrated* photo, a way to illustrate the unusual chemistry that had resulted in a winning formula for the Lakers.

The players were seated at student desks with coach Paul Westhead at the front of the classroom, serving as the teacher.

Seemed fair enough.

After all, how many teams are run by a man who not only coached basketball at the college level, but taught Shakespeare and English literature as well?

Westhead even tossed in some lines from the legendary English playwright when addressing his teams, though the message was often lost on them.

But what the *Sports Illustrated* editors did not know was that the message had grown stale.

Westhead was a novelty when he took over the Lakers on an interim basis in 1979 after head coach Jack McKinney suffered a near-fatal bicycle accident.

Though he sometimes spoke to the players in what seemed like a foreign language, they just nodded and went about doing what they did so well.

As long as the Lakers kept winning, the players didn't care what the coach said.

He once quoted from *Macbeth* in the huddle, saying, "If it were done when 'tis done, then 'twere well it were done quickly."

After a collective blank stare from the players, Magic Johnson finally responded, saying, "You want me to get it into the Big Fella?"

But the players were no longer amused when they felt Westhead was adversely affecting the highly successful fast-breaking system installed by McKinney by installing a new offense, a Westhead offense, one that shut down the running game far too often in order to feed Kareem Abdul-Jabbar in the post. And they were no longer supportive after Westhead decided to shake up the starting lineup the season after winning the NBA title by replacing Michael Cooper and Jim Chones with Butch Carter and Jim Brewer.

Westhead further damaged his relationship with the players by failing to inform either Cooper or Chones that they were being benched, waiting instead until the pregame introductions.

When the press asked Westhead about the changes, he explained that it was to create a "balance of energy."

Norm Nixon and Westhead

After Westhead led the team to the NBA championship, Nixon perceived what he considered a lack of respect from his coach during the ensuing summer of 1980.

Nixon had finished the season with a dislocated left finger.

After undergoing surgery and having his cast removed, the Lakers guard bumped into Westhead in the Forum offices.

"I'd like you to come over," the coach told him, "and play with our rookies [in the summer league] to get ready for the season."

Still undergoing physical therapy on the finger and insulted at being asked, as a veteran on a championship team, to play with rookies, Nixon replied, "Sure, have Kareem pick me up on his way out there."

End of conversation.

To the players, that was just another of Westhead's word games.

When the Lakers struggled against Houston in the first round of the 1981 playoffs, guard Norm Nixon was less than inspired by Westhead's approach.

"He told us about a man in a boat," Nixon said, "and how you had to throw the rope out to him and how we all had to pull him in.

"When you're getting ready to play for a championship, you don't want to hear about no man in a boat. You can talk about getting effort out...pulling together. But really and truly...you don't want to hear no [bleep] about holding on to no rope. You want to hear about going out and kicking some ass on the court."

Said another Lakers player, who insisted on anonymity, "If you had [Westhead] give you a talk before the game, when you left the locker room, you didn't want to play."

Even owner Jerry Buss seemed to be questioning Westhead by the time the 1981–82 season started. Westhead had pushed for the Lakers to get free agent Mitch Kupchak.

When the team did so, Buss said, "Is Westhead a real genius? We'll find out. He asked me to get the talent. He wanted it this way. Now we'll find out what he can do."

So by the time that *Sports Illustrated* photo came out, the idea that Westhead was the teacher and the players his fawning pupils infuriated many of the Lakers.

73 No More Magic

For those who traveled with the Lakers, the tension between Paul Westhead and his players at the start of the 1981–82 season was clearly evident on a strip of grass in the midst of the ribbons of asphalt surrounding Houston Intercontinental Airport.

There sat Magic Johnson, looking up at the sunny sky on a November morning, oblivious to the cars whizzing by as he immersed himself in the music coming out of his headphones.

A few lanes over, the team bus sat idling. The rest of the Lakers were waiting for Johnson to get on board so they could get to their hotel and enjoy some rest prior to that night's game against the Rockets.

But Johnson showed no inclination to move, no desire to rejoin his teammates. That grassy island was a perfect metaphor for his state of mind.

The Lakers had just arrived from San Antonio, where the Spurs had blasted them 128–102 the night before.

But it wasn't the loss that had left Johnson so discouraged. It was *how* they lost.

He blamed it on Westhead's new-look, Kareem-centric offense, an offense that robbed the players of the freedom they had enjoyed to react to the opponent's defense quickly and decisively rather than standing around waiting for the coach's system to kick in. "Westhead's new system had a major impact on the team's morale," said Johnson in his book, *My Life.* "Now there were fewer high fives and less camaraderie. Previously, we had been five guys running all over the court. Now we were four guys looking to pass in to one. The ball moved, but the bodies didn't."

Abdul-Jabbar was the beneficiary of the new system, but that didn't mean he shut his eyes to its deficiencies.

"[Westhead] was establishing his thing with the team," Abdul-Jabbar said. "The problem was he left the ways that we were successful, and that made it hard for us to get things done. It was like wearing somebody else's suit. You are not going to look that great."

"I sense he felt he had to prove himself," guard Brad Holland said. "His attitude was, 'I'm going to show everyone we can win my way.'"

Westhead insisted his motivation was based on the need to improve the Lakers' half-court game and his concern about Johnson's ability to get back to full speed following a knee injury the previous season.

The pressure was growing, with nerves tightening on both sides.

Prior to a game against the Indiana Pacers on the night of November 15, owner Jerry Buss, fuming over what he saw as an ill-advised turn away from the Showtime offense that had put fans in the seats and a championship banner on the Forum wall, called general manager Bill Sharman and special consultant Jerry West into his office and told them, "I would like to fire Westhead."

He asked both of them if they had a strong argument for keeping Westhead, and neither did.

Sharman did, however, appeal for a little time—a week—to see who might be out there to replace Westhead, while also giving him time to change his approach.

Down on the floor, the Lakers beat the Pacers 124–123 in double overtime for their fourth win in a row.

The losing coach was Jack McKinney, the man who had designed the system Buss had embraced and Westhead had turned his back on.

Although he didn't dream his job was on the line, Westhead was feeling the vibes of discontent spreading through the organization. On a flight to Salt Lake City for a game against the Jazz two days later, he snapped at trainer Jack Curran over the size of the snack on the plane. It was decidedly out of character for the usually easygoing Westhead, especially since Curran's only involvement in airplane food was eating it.

Finally the issue burst into the public eye on an ugly night in Salt Lake City.

Following the Lakers' 113–110 victory over the Jazz, their fifth straight victory, reporters came into the locker room for what they anticipated would be a routine postgame session.

It was anything but.

When they approached Johnson, he was waiting with a shocking announcement.

With a calm, but resolute voice, he said, "I want to be traded."

* * *

In Johnson's mind, the beginning of the end of his Laker career, once thought to be decades away, came in a team huddle during a timeout in that November 18, 1981game against the Jazz.

When Johnson asked a ball boy for water, Westhead yelled at his superstar.

"Earvin, shut up," the coach said. "Get your ass in this huddle and pay attention."

"I am paying attention," Johnson insisted.

"You should be looking at me," Westhead said.

The heated discussion continued in an equipment room after the game.

"I'm tired of your horseshit attitude," Westhead said, "and I'm not going to put up with it anymore. Either you start listening to me or you don't have to play."

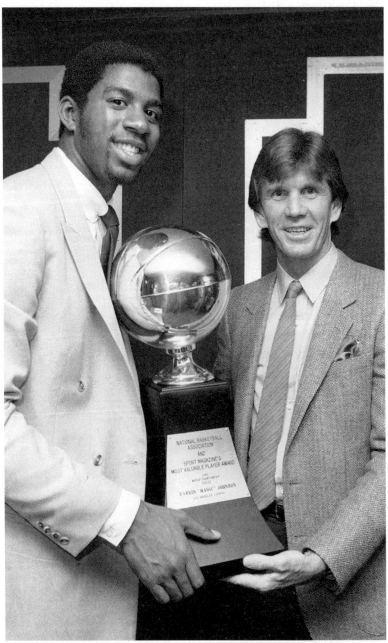

Magic and Paul Westhead pose together as Johnson is awarded the 1980 NBA Finals MVP trophy.

"I'm tired of it, too," Johnson said. "So maybe you shouldn't play me at all.... Why don't you send me somewhere else?"

By the time he reached the locker room, Johnson had decided to take control of the situation.

"I want to leave," he told reporters. "I'm not happy now.... I can't deal with it no more."

Up and down the row of locker stalls, the other Lakers, getting dressed and listening to their music, were suddenly stretching their long bodies to hear the stunning words of their celebrated teammate.

But when Johnson was done and reporters began looking around for others to comment, all the players turned back into their stalls simultaneously as if somebody had drawn up the move for them on a clipboard.

Most, if not all, felt the same as Johnson, but none were willing to publicly support him.

"They were scared to come forward," Johnson later said. "They wanted [the unhappiness revealed], but they didn't say nothing. They were happy as long as they didn't have to say anything."

"I can't say nothing," Norm Nixon told a reporter privately, "because if I say something, they would probably think I was behind the whole thing, that I made Magic say those things.... If

The Boarding Pass

At the Salt Lake City airport the next morning when the Lakers arrived for their flight home, rumors were flying that Westhead was about to be fired.

Mitch Chortkoff, beat writer for the *Santa Monica Evening Outlook*, came up to his fellow reporters and, with mock seriousness. said, "The airline just made a horrible mistake."

"How?" he was asked.

"They just gave Westhead a boarding pass," Chortkoff replied, "that said, 'Coach.'"

anybody else in the NBA had done what Magic did, they'd have run him out of the league."

Years later, Westhead finally spoke out. "My opinion at that moment," he said, "was that Magic Johnson was wrong in what happened in the game. He obviously responded emotionally to what he thought was the embarrassment of being told off."

Prior to Johnson's dramatic words, Westhead had been asked in his postgame press conference about the criticism of his offense.

"The almond tree," he said, "bears its fruit in silence."

74 Tragic Johnson

Jerry Buss was seated above the ice at the Forum, halfway up the arena, watching his Kings play, when he saw a pack of reporters heading in his direction.

He didn't know what they wanted, but he figured it couldn't be good. Hockey writers don't normally turn their backs on the ice in the middle of a game to seek out the team owner.

In the age before the internet, this was how Buss learned Magic Johnson had demanded to be traded.

"I think everybody is very frustrated," Buss told the hockey writers who had swarmed down on him. "The main thing you learn the longer you're in sports is, don't overreact. Don't panic. Sit back and talk to everybody, then make the moves that are necessary based on what you've discovered."

It sounded good, but deep down, Buss knew he had sat back too long. Angry with himself, he felt a sharp sting of regret for not following through on his gut feeling to fire Westhead after meeting with Jerry West and Bill Sharman a few days earlier.

Buss knew his favorite player, Magic Johnson, would pay the price for that indecision.

Still, Buss had no choice at that point. His hand had been forced by his impetuous young star and Buss knew that, if he didn't act then, his players' discontent would only deepen, imperiling the season.

At that point, it was more than salvageable. The Lakers were 7–4 and, after stumbling badly at the starting block, had won five in a row.

What he needed, Buss figured, was to keep Magic in a Lakers uniform, put the ball back in his talented hands, find someone to reignite the Showtime offense, and then get out of the way.

It may be hard to believe, but Westhead claimed he was totally oblivious to the ax that was about to come crashing down on his head.

When he returned to L.A. the morning after Johnson's media meltdown, Westhead went out to lunch with his wife, Cassie, and daughter, Monica.

He explained to them how he was going to tell Buss that Johnson needed to be brought under control.

Realizing he was clueless, Monica blurted out, "Dad, you're going to get fired."

When Westhead was indeed terminated a few hours later, the national media and fans across the country blamed Johnson, labeling him "Tragic Johnson" and calling him a crybaby.

A cartoon in San Antonio on the next Lakers visit there depicted Johnson in diapers.

Even Jim Murray, the Pulitzer Prize–winning columnist of the *Los Angeles Times,* weighed in with criticism, labeling Jerry Buss an "unfit owner."

Murray later admitted he had misjudged the situation.

"Like everybody," he said, "I was outraged that a basketball player got the coach fired. It looked like a clear-cut case at the time.

Later on, it came to light that he was not the only one. The whole team was mutinous…. I was wrong, but I had a lot of company."

"I was disgusted," said Johnson of the overall media reaction. "I couldn't even listen to the radio no more. Nothin. I dealt with it, but it was tough. But even tougher than all that was the booing of the fans."

While Buss may have had regrets about enabling the controversy to grow, Westhead had none about starting it.

"I did the absolute right thing," he said in retrospect. "I would not have changed anything. If I had been losing and then got fired, I'd say, 'Maybe I ought to rethink this and get this pattern reshuffled because it didn't work.' But it worked."

Not for him.

75 Who Is the Coach?

It took only a few seconds for Jerry West to walk from his seat in the Forum press lounge to the microphone during a news conference held a few hours after the firing of coach Paul Westhead.

But in those few seconds, West, who always seemed to make the right decision on the court in the crucial seconds of clutch time, made one of the most far-reaching decisions in Lakers history.

Owner Jerry Buss had just announced that Westhead was gone, West was being named "offensive coach," and assistant Pat Riley would "stay as coach."

West had already tried coaching the Lakers, enduring three gut-wrenching seasons on the sideline. There was no way he was going back to that.

Buss had left him an opening with his confusing statement, and West grabbed it like a loose ball.

"I'm going to be working for and with Pat Riley," said West when he took center stage. "I feel in my heart he is the head coach."

That left everybody in the media scratching their collective heads.

Reporters turned back to Buss and asked, who is the *head* coach? Who is going to pick the starters?

"Well," said Buss, his definitive statement uttered just a moment earlier now muddled in uncertainty, "obviously that's the job of the coach. I'm sure they should be able to get together and decide that sort of thing."

One of those in attendance that day was *Los Angeles Times* sports editor Bill Dwyre. When Dwyre got back to his office, he phoned Lakers PR director Bob Steiner and asked, "What in the world are you guys doing?"

"Bill, we proved one thing," replied Steiner, "that we don't know how to run a press conference."

76 Riles' Roots

Anybody who didn't think Pat Riley was coaching material, who looked at the long hair and the stylish clothes and figured he belonged in a courtside seat rather than the coach's hot seat, should have paid less attention to his jeans and more to his genes.

Riley's father, Lee, had been a minor league outfielder, who played briefly in the majors and then became a minor league manager.

Although he didn't realize it at the time, watching his father run a team inspired Pat to seek a similar role after his body no longer allowed him to compete as an athlete.

Lee used to order his older sons to take young Pat down to a rough neighborhood in their hometown of Schenectady, New York, to play basketball in order to toughen the kid up.

"I'm going to teach you to never be afraid," Lee told his son.

Pat needed to be tough to play for legendary coach Adolph Rupp at the University of Kentucky and to carve out a nine-year career in the NBA without the natural talent of some of his teammates.

He applied what he had learned from both his father and Rupp when he became a coach.

But not at first.

When the Lakers went into their first slump under Riley, owner Jerry Buss had a talk with him, unknowingly uttering words similar to what Pat had heard from his own father years earlier.

"Don't be afraid to coach," Buss said. "Make a statement. This is your team."

Perhaps it was the echo of his father's voice or the realization of his potential, but whatever the cause, Riley responded, grabbing the reins of the Showtime team and driving it to four titles and six trips to the NBA Finals in seven seasons.

"I had been giving the players too much responsibility," he said. "The players have a responsibility to play, but I have a responsibility to coach."

True, Riley would not have had such success without the vast array of talent at his disposal. Those under his command included Magic Johnson, one of the greatest point guards in NBA history; Kareem Abdul-Jabbar, one of the greatest centers; a Hall of Fame forward in James Worthy; and a complementary cast of stars that included Michael Cooper, Jamaal Wilkes, Kurt Rambis, Norm Nixon, Byron Scott, Bob McAdoo, and many others over the years.

But determined to prove he was more than just a pretty face in a sweet spot required only to roll the ball onto the court, Riley worked his stars as if they were a bunch of journeymen.

His practices could be brutal, his film sessions seemingly without end, his locker room theatrics over the top, his paranoia about the media—whom he referred to as "peripheral opponents" or "buzzards"—startling.

He once closed a practice to reporters after claiming a writer, whom he refused to name, had revealed a play he had designed to another team.

Responded one writer to Riley: "We wouldn't know a play if we saw one."

He once yelled at a writer for playing tennis with Bob McAdoo on the road, blaming the writer for McAdoo's decision to pick up a racket.

During a Lakers practice, Riley once ordered a cleaning crew working in the Boston Garden to get out of the arena, claiming they might have recording devices in their brooms.

Riley's methods can sometimes backfire, as was the case in 1989.

The team soared into the playoffs that year, winning 11 games to sweep the first three rounds.

Finishing so quickly meant the Lakers had to wait for an Eastern Conference opponent to be crowned. Determined to maintain the players' rhythm and fend off rust, Riley took the club up the coast to Santa Barbara for a vigorous workout that mirrored a preseason training camp/boot camp.

But this was not the preseason. It was the end of a long, exhausting year when bodies were worn down, making them far more susceptible to injury than rust. So it was no coincidence, in the minds of some in the Lakers organization, that both Magic Johnson and Byron Scott blew out hamstrings after those marathon

Santa Barbara sessions: Scott before the NBA Finals began and Johnson in Game 2.

Without two key members of their squad, the Lakers were unable to deal with the Detroit Pistons, losing in an embarrassing sweep.

In the playoffs, Riley's team had gone from 11–0 to 0–4.

But for him, the good times far outweighed the bad. In the defining moment of his coaching career, Riley, ever in search of motivation, turned back to his roots, to his father.

The year was 1985. The Lakers, facing the Celtics in the Finals, were trying to avoid losing to their archrivals for the second season in a row and the ninth time overall.

But one game into the series, the Lakers were already looking over the abyss after getting trounced 148–114 in a game that came to be known as the Memorial Day Massacre.

That's when Pat Riley reached back to Lee.

As he was departing Pat's wedding in 1970, Lee had told his son, "Just remember what I always taught you. Somewhere, someplace, sometime, you are going to have to plant your feet, make a stand, and kick some ass. And when that time comes, you do it."

Lee's words became especially memorable to Pat because it was the last time he ever saw his father. Lee died shortly afterward of a heart attack.

But his words lived on. Riley used them in the locker room prior to Game 2.

The Lakers won that game and went on to win the series in six games.

Somewhere, Lee Riley was smiling.

77 Destiny's Child

It should come as no surprise that Luke Walton became the head coach of the most glamorous and one of the two most successful franchises in NBA history

Basketball greatness is in his DNA, on his driver's license, and in his résumé.

The first name on his license comes from Maurice Lucas, a tough, multitalented competitor who was not only an effective shooter and rebounder, but could also fill the role of enforcer on the court when necessary. Lucas played in both the American Basketball Association and the NBA, and was the leading scorer on the Portland Trail Blazers team that Bill Walton led to the 1977 NBA championship.

Luke's last name, of course, comes from his father, Bill, who also led the UCLA Bruins to two NCAA championships and might have been one of the NBA's all-time greats had his career not been severely limited by foot and leg injuries.

Luke was the Forrest Gump of basketball. Wherever there were historic figures and historic moments, there was Luke.

Not only was he exposed to the skills and methods of his father and Lucas, but he was on teams run by some of the most successful coaches to ever walk a sideline.

In college, Luke played at Arizona for Lute Olson, a Hall of Fame coach.

In the pros, he played for the Lakers under Phil Jackson, winner of a record 11 NBA championships.

And when he turned to coaching, Luke became an assistant under Steve Kerr, leader of the Warriors dynasty.

Luke has taken advantage of his proximity to all these hoop geniuses, absorbing their knowledge like a sponge.

He laughs now about how far he has come from his cocky days playing for University of San Diego High School. Back then, he scored 35 points one night in a game attended by his father.

When Luke got home, he found Bill waiting for him, anxious to go over what he had observed from his seat.

Lonzo Ball listens as head coach Luke Walton gives instruction during the second half of a January 2018 game against the Atlanta Hawks at Staples Center.
(Jayne Kamin-Oncea/USA TODAY Sports)

Luke wasn't about to openly question his famous father, but he thought to himself, "I just scored 35 points. What can *he* tell me?"

Drafted by the Lakers in 2003 with the third pick in the second round, 32nd overall, Luke, a power forward, was never a dominating player, averaging only 4.9 points, 2.9 rebounds, and 2.3 assists over nine seasons with the Lakers.

But to make up for what he lacked athletically, he tried to compensate mentally, determined to learn as much as he could about every aspect of the game.

Impressed, Jackson supported Luke and rewarded him with playing time, feeling that this enthusiastic young player gave him an additional coach when he was on the floor.

When the Lakers were temporarily shut down by an NBA lockout, Luke used the time to advance his worth as a coach by taking a position as an assistant with the University of Memphis team.

After retiring as a player, he became the player development coach for the D-Fenders, the Lakers' entry in the D-League, before joining the Warriors for the 2014–15 season. He became a trusted member of the staff as Golden State went on to win the NBA title.

So trusted that, when Kerr was forced to temporarily give up the reins of his club before the start of the following season due to a slow recovery from offseason back surgery, he chose Luke to run the team despite the fact that he had only been an NBA assistant for one year.

Kerr would still be back in the locker room for home games or on the phone for consultation when the team was on the road, but in the heat of the game, Luke was on his own in terms of setting the tone, communicating with the players, and making the minute-by-minute substitutions and adjustments.

Was he ready?

Was he ever. The Warriors broke from the starting gate with a surge unlike anything ever seen in NBA history. Under Luke, the team won its first 24 games, shattering the old mark of 15–0 to start a season, established by the Washington Capitols in 1948 and equaled by the Houston Rockets in 1993.

By the time Kerr returned to the sideline, the Warriors were 39–4, a sizzling pace that led to a regular-season record of 73–9, beating the record 72 regular-season wins by the Michael Jordan–led 1995–96 Bulls.

As far as the NBA record book is concerned, however, Luke's win total for the Warriors that season was a big, fat zero. Because Kerr was officially the team's head coach from the first day of training camp, he got credit for all 73 wins.

Even though he didn't feel he deserved the first 39.

"I think it's ridiculous," Kerr told ESPN 19 games into the season. "I'm sitting in the locker room and watching the game on TV and I'm not even traveling to most of the road games. Luke's doing all the work with the rest of the staff. Luke is 19–0 right now. I'm not."

The NBA could take Luke out of the record book, but not the spotlight. People were watching, especially the Lakers, who would soon be seeking a new coach of their own.

They hadn't been satisfied with the men in that position since Jackson left.

Mike Brown lasted one full season, but was then fired five games into the following season when the team started 1–4.

Next came Mike D'Antoni, he of the seven-seconds-or-less offensive philosophy. But, with twin towers Dwight Howard and Pau Gasol, the Lakers didn't have the personnel for the run-and-gun-and-gun-and-gun attack D'Antoni had implemented in Phoenix. He had come to L.A. with a reputation for being a poor defensive coach and did nothing with the Lakers to alter that perception. In the two years before he arrived, the Lakers were fourth and then sixth in the league defensively, according to NBA Advanced Stats. In his two seasons at the helm, they dropped to 11th and then 25th defensively. In that second year, the Lakers finished 27–55, the team's worst season since it came to L.A. After those two years, D'Antoni resigned when the Laker hierarchy declined to pick up the option year on his contract.

Next, the team decided to go old school, signing Byron Scott, a veteran coach and a former member of the Lakers' celebrated Showtime squads. His mission was to bring experience, stability, and patience to a young roster that lacked all of that. He, too, lasted two seasons.

What now? The Lakers decided they would be better served with a young coach to match their young roster. And they knew the ideal candidate to fill that role, a familiar face with a familiar last name.

When the Lakers offered the job to Luke, he didn't have to ask Bill for advice. His father had already been very public about his feelings. "Head-coaching jobs are open for a reason," Bill told Phoenix TV station KTVK. "What he has right now, it doesn't get any better than that."

Indeed, there was an argument to be made for turning down the opportunity. Why leave the best team in basketball with the potential to maintain a dynasty for years to come, to join a bad team with turmoil in the front office and unrealistic expectations from a fan base spoiled by decades of excellence?

Luke wouldn't be dissuaded. This was a head-coaching job with his former team, and a chance, unrealistic though it might have seemed at the time, to resurrect the glory of earlier eras.

The odds of that happening seemed pretty unlikely at first. Luke took over a team that had won 27, 21, and 17 games in its previous three seasons.

No new coach had ever been handed a weaker Laker team. The 17–65 mark in 2015–16 was the worst in team history, including the Lakers' years in Minneapolis.

Slowly the rebuilding began. The team won 26 games in Luke's first season and 35 in his second year.

And then, at the dawn of free agency in 2018, the Lakers suddenly became relevant overnight when LeBron James agreed to swap his Cavaliers uniform for the Purple and Gold.

Would Luke be intimidated by the idea of coaching the best player on the planet and maybe the best of all time?

Not a chance. After all, superstars have been a part of his life since the day he was born.

78 Beat L.A.!

It is a chant heard all over the country, not only against the Lakers, but also the Dodgers and every other team that has the letters "L" and "A" on its uniform.

But strangely enough, that chant didn't begin at a game involving a Los Angeles team.

It started at Boston Garden in the seventh game of the 1982 Eastern Conference Finals between the Celtics and the 76ers.

The Lakers may be No. 1 on Celtics fans' enemies list, but the 76ers are a solid No. 2.

Yet as bitter as it was for the Celtics faithful to watch their team not only lose on their green parquet home court, but also to get shellacked 120–106, their hatred of the Lakers was still the overriding emotion.

So with the 76ers on their way to the Finals against the Lakers, Celtics fans swallowed their pride and began chanting, "Beat L.A.! Beat L.A.!" in the closing seconds of the game.

Think the Yankees would ever hear Boston fans chanting for them in Fenway Park?

Okay, so that's even less likely, but this was still pretty hard to believe.

Like so many before him, a fan in 2010 implores his team to "Beat L.A."

Hit the Road

Another item for the to-do list: Lakers fans can never truly understand the hatred other cities have for the Purple and Gold until they have sat in the middle of a crowd chanting, "Beat L.A.!"

It's an experience guaranteed to get the adrenaline flowing and the pride showing, especially if the Lakers are winning.

Where can fans find such chanting? Pretty much any NBA city, other than L.A., of course, will do.

Not that it mattered. With the Lakers fast break back in high gear after Pat Riley replaced Paul Westhead as head coach, there was no chance that mere chants could impede their run to the 1982 NBA title. They won it in six games.

79 Out Like Magic

As Magic Johnson groped his way through the smoke, searching for fresh air and safety, he realized he had company on a frightening night in Philadelphia.

Other guests from all walks of life were following him down a hallway in the Lakers' hotel after a fire had broken out.

Minutes before, the crisis on the minds of the players was the fact they had fallen behind the Philadelphia 76ers 2–0 in the best-of-seven 1983 NBA Finals.

But after fire alarms went off in the 19-story, 79-year-old Bellevue Stratford Hotel, that was the least of their worries.

As it turned out, the blaze had been limited to a stairwell between the third and fourth floors where the drapes had caught fire.

But until that became evident, all the Lakers and the other hotel guests knew was that they were caught in a potentially suffocating cloud of smoke. A burning smell filled their nostrils.

"We went down a couple of flights on the stairs," Johnson said, "but the smoke became too strong.

"I was scared. One lady came up to me and nearly fainted. I told her to calm down. Inside, I was trying to calm *myself* down."

Johnson and his group, who had started on the eighth floor, made it down as far as the third before the smoke turned them back.

Searching around, Johnson spotted a fire-escape ladder. As he surveyed the device, designed to slowly drop to the ground when someone stepped on it, a voice behind him said, "Go ahead, you can do it."

Turning around, he saw it was the voice of Kareem Abdul-Jabbar.

Johnson stepped onto the first rung as if he were entering a tub of hot water, but soon relaxed as the brief ride ended with a soft landing on the ground. Behind him came all the other guests.

Johnson later marveled at the fact that all these guests, some of them middle-aged, would follow a 23-year-old kid in a potentially life-threatening situation simply because he was Magic Johnson. Did they think he really possessed some sort of magic to make an exit suddenly appear?

Teammates Michael Cooper and Kurt Rambis also served as rescuers that night. Cooper went door to door to alert other guests while Rambis helped team physician Robert Kerlan, who was disabled, get out.

When the fire department arrived, there were priorities. They paused to get a few Lakers autographs before proceeding to handle the blaze that was out in 15 minutes.

Shaking his head at the Lakers' latest misfortune, Jamaal Wilkes said, "The only thing left to happen now would be for the plane not to make it home safely."

That was not a problem, but back on the ground in L.A., the Lakers' troubles continued. With James Worthy having missed the entire postseason because of a fractured leg and the playing time of both Norm Nixon and Bob McAdoo cut down drastically because of injuries, the Lakers were swept by the 76ers.

80 West's Spies

Kids on the block in his Baldwin Hills neighborhood first alerted Norm Nixon that there were suspicious figures prowling around.

It was 1983, at the end of a long and frustrating postseason for the Lakers point guard. Hampered by shoulder and knee injuries, he had struggled through the first three games of the NBA Finals against the Philadelphia 76ers, then sat out Game 4.

Nixon wouldn't get a chance to return. With James Worthy having missed the entire postseason because of a fractured leg and Bob McAdoo joining Nixon on the list of walking wounded, the Lakers were swept.

Now what?

"Hey Norm, somebody is going to get robbed," one of the kids told him.

"What do you mean?" Nixon asked.

"There's been cars parked at both ends of our street with telescopes, guys looking into houses," another youngster said. "People are setting somebody up."

Starting to pay attention, Nixon indeed began to notice furtive figures parked nearby. He first thought it was a drug dealer.

The situation concerned drugs all right, but not in the way Nixon imagined.

The truth came out several days later when he arrived home at around 2:30 AM. As he walked up to his door, a figure emerged from the shadows.

"Hey, man," the person said, "I have to talk to you."

"Whoa, what the hell is going on?" Nixon demanded to know.

The man said he'd be right back. Thinking he might need help, Nixon went into his house and awakened his brother, Ron, who was staying with him.

Soon came a knock on the door. Nixon tentatively opened it. It was the man he had encountered a moment earlier.

"Norm," the man said, "I just want to tell you that we've been following you for the last two weeks. We were hired by...Jerry West."

Nixon couldn't believe it. Yes, he and West had had their differences when West was coach and Nixon was a rookie. Nixon felt West picked on him because he was an easy target, easier than going after the veterans. West said he was just trying to prod Nixon into reaching his potential.

Nixon claims West once screamed at him for taking a shot at the end of a quarter with too much time left on the clock.

Standing on the sidelines, West had an obstructed view of the play. According to Nixon, when Kareem Abdul-Jabbar said he took the shot, West yelled at Nixon for passing the big center the ball too early.

Nixon took his jabs at West. In a crowd of national media, Nixon was once asked if he ever saw West play.

"No," Nixon replied, "and I never saw him coach either."

But despite all that, it was hard for Nixon to accept the fact West was having him tailed like a criminal.

When Nixon challenged the veracity of the claim by the late-night visitor, the man responded by enumerating everywhere he and his cohorts had followed Nixon during the previous few weeks.

"I've got a job to do," the man said, "but I like you and I felt an obligation to tell you. Now I've got to go back to work."

Sure enough, when Nixon pulled out of his driveway the next day and looked in his rearview mirror, he saw a car following him.

Burning with indignation, he finally stormed out onto his street a few days later and confronted two men sitting in one of the stakeout cars.

They claimed they had been hired to watch another home on Nixon's block by the owners who had been having problems with burglars.

He didn't buy that, but the car took off before he could pursue the matter further. So Nixon decided to pursue it at the source. He went to see West, who was then the Lakers' general manager.

According to Nixon, West admitted he had hired people to follow the point guard because he believed Nixon not only had a drug problem, but was also involved with drug dealers.

Nixon vehemently denied both charges at the time and to this day. He correctly pointed out that West's surveillance didn't turn up a shred of evidence, that Nixon never missed a game or a practice or any other team function for any reason other than injury, that he was always there on time, and never had any radical swings in his performance on the court. He hardly displayed the behavior of a druggie.

A quick guard with an accurate jumper, smooth passing ability, and excellent court vision, Nixon's stats were remarkably consistent. Starting with his second season in the league, 1978–79, Nixon, over a seven-year period, averaged between 17 and 17.6 points with the exception of one season when he slipped a bit to 15.1. His assist average over those seasons ranged from 7.2 to 11.1, his field-goal percentage from 46.2 to 54.2.

And he did all that despite sharing a backcourt for several seasons with assist wizard Magic Johnson.

When Nixon's claim about being followed at West's directive was first revealed in the book *Winnin' Times,* West initially denied it forcefully and then conceded it was true.

After that, the cars disappeared from Nixon's street, but Nixon himself soon disappeared from the Lakers roster. Several months after being confronted by Nixon, West traded him along with Eddie Jordan and two future draft picks to the then–San Diego Clippers for Byron Scott and Swen Nater.

Several years after the deal, West insisted there was nothing personal about his decision to trade Nixon.

"There were times I know he wasn't enamored with me," West said, "and he probably isn't enamored with me today, which is fine. But my feeling about him is, I liked him a lot. I still like him a lot. He was a tremendous player for us."

81 They Played It for Laughs, Part II

Two of the more colorful characters on the Showtime Lakers were forward Mark Landsberger and guard Mike McGee.

Sent on one occasion to a Lakers autograph session, Landsberger was asked by one fan, after receiving his signature, if he could write his number underneath.

Presumably, one would think, his jersey number.

Not Landsberger. He put down his phone number.

When the Lakers would come out for the start of the second half, Landsberger would always wander over to the press table on the sidelines and stretch his neck, trying to see the halftime stat sheet and check out his numbers for the first 24 minutes.

On one particular occasion, Landsberger strained as always to see what he had done in the first half.

The problem: he hadn't played in the first half.

On the road the day before a game, Landsberger, leaving a practice, asked two reporters if he could tag along with them for lunch.

When they welcomed him, he left the court still wearing his Lakers uniform.

"Mark," warned trainer Jack Curran, "that's the only uniform I brought along for you. Why don't you take it off before you go?"

Lansberger assured Curran he'd be fine.

He wasn't. When he spilled a chocolate shake at the restaurant, the brown foam ran down Landsberger's side.

The next day, he played in a nationally televised game with a long, brown streak mixed into the Purple and Gold.

McGee, a first-round pick by the Lakers in 1981, struggled to learn the offense for several seasons.

After watching him look completely lost in yet another practice, coach Pat Riley threw up his hands in disgust as McGee walked off the court and said, "I keep calling Mike McGee, Mike McGee, but there's never anybody home."

McGee looked at him in all seriousness and said, "I was home all day, Coach. What time did you call?"

82 25 Years, $25 Million

With the average NBA salary today at $7.4 million, signing a player to a $1 million deal isn't going to make headlines.

How about a million a year for *25 years*?

Now imagine that deal being signed nearly 40 years ago, when only two NBA players, Kareem Abdul-Jabbar and Moses Malone, were even making a million a year.

When Lakers owner Jerry Buss gave Magic Johnson the 25-year, $25-million contract in 1981, the longest and richest in sports history at the time, it not only generated blaring headlines, but also shook up the league, all of professional sports, and especially Abdul-Jabbar. He was so upset that Johnson was getting such a contract after only two seasons in the league that he labeled his teammate the "favorite child" and asked to be traded.

After all, Abdul-Jabbar was a 12-year veteran at the time and the best center in the game.

Abdul-Jabbar was riled that Johnson was guaranteed a seven-figure salary for the next quarter century regardless of his performance or his health.

Actually, Johnson's deal extended even further since the new contract wouldn't kick in until the one he was operating under at the time expired in 1984. That meant Johnson would be getting his million a year until 2009–10, when he would be 50 years old and long retired.

As Buss explained, however, it was a relatively economical deal for him. He was taking $5 million and putting it into a first trust deed with an annual interest rate of 20 percent or $1 million. That is the money he would give Johnson.

But Buss saw the value of the contract in more than just monetary terms.

"I always felt other sports sometimes got a lot of press," he said, "because their players were paid so much money. Anybody who makes an outlandish salary obviously attracts attention. That was what was behind my contract with Magic. I think it created a lot of attention for the Lakers."

Ultimately, Abdul-Jabbar was placated with a little sweeter deal of his own.

"You guys will come back in a few years and admit that I got a bargain," Buss told the media after Johnson's deal was signed.

It didn't take that long.

83 Coop

In the flashy era of the 1980s, on flashy teams like those of the Showtime Lakers, how could a defensive specialist stand out?

By playing with the flair of a Michael Cooper.

He was quick and tough, possessing leaping ability dramatically demonstrated by the Coop-A-Loop, a play in which he would soar above the rim in order to slam dunk a perfectly-timed pass from Norm Nixon or Magic Johnson. Cooper's ability to get into opponent's heads through trash-talking matched the best that Larry Bird could utter. Cooper's defensive skills electrified crowds and provided the trigger for the game-changing fast breaks that became the trademark of the Showtime teams.

Even on the star-studded Lakers, Cooper stood out with his over-the-calf socks, the strings dangling on the front of his shorts, and his finger-pointing salute to his wife, Wanda, in the Forum seats as he ran back down the court after scoring.

But his status as an elite defender was even more amazing considering he overcame a potentially crippling injury as a toddler.

After slashing a knee on a coffee can at the age of two, he required 100 stitches on the wound and needed to wear a brace until he was nearly 10.

Once the brace came off, however, Cooper soared like a bird, excelling on the court at Pasadena High School, Pasadena City College, and the University of New Mexico.

But then disaster struck again, causing him to tumble back to earth as a result of a torn knee ligament suffered in a summer league game.

It was the summer before his rookie season and there had been no guarantee, even before the injury, that the 60th-overall pick would even make the Lakers roster.

Cooper wound up playing only seven minutes that season. As a result, he found himself perched precariously on the bubble as either the 12th or 13th man on a 12-man roster at the start of the next season, 1979–80. With one spot left to fill, it was down to either him or Ron Carter, a one-year veteran who had actually played the season before. Assistant coach Paul Westhead opted for Carter. Head coach Jack McKinney decided on Cooper.

That shaky start stayed with Cooper for a long time. Despite becoming at times the best sixth man in the league and one of the few opponents Bird didn't like seeing on the court, Cooper remained insecure.

Although he was primarily a reserve, Cooper's minutes per game still averaged in the high 20s for most of his 12-year career. But if someone else was inserted into the game in Cooper's regular spot in the rotation, he would begin to sulk, putting a towel over his head.

"I had to get him in fast," said coach Pat Riley of the instances where the towel came out, "or I would lose him."

On one road trip, Riley told Cooper, who was injured, that he would not play until the Lakers got home in order to keep the healing process on track.

In his mind, Cooper believed Riley was just looking for an excuse to get rid of him. Cooper vowed passionately to a reporter that he would come back in another uniform and make the Lakers pay for their decision to cut him.

After Cooper had calmed down, the reporter asked him if he really meant what he had said.

Looking at trainer Jack Curran, Cooper said, "No, I'm...I'm... Jack, what's that word?"

"Paranoid," Curran said.

"Yeah, I'm paranoid," Cooper said. "I figure, if you leave, you may not come back. They don't have time to wait on stragglers."

It took awhile, but he finally felt secure in Purple and Gold.

"He cleaned out the skeletons from his closet," Riley said, "and he found some self-esteem."

It was the esteem that his teammates and opponents had felt for him from the beginning.

84 The Aging Hippie

Nobody knew quite what to make of Kurt Rambis when he arrived.

With goofy, horn-rimmed glasses, straggly hair, and a wardrobe that Magic Johnson described by saying he "came to practice looking like he'd just crawled out of bed," Rambis certainly didn't look like he belonged on the Showtime Lakers. Johnson said he looked like "an aging hippie."

On a team of Clydesdales, Rambis was the plow horse. Alongside teammates who could play above the rim, Rambis was better suited for sliding across the floor.

On a club of superstars, he was Clark Kent—thick black specs and all.

Yet in his unique way, Rambis was a big part of the Lakers' championship runs of the '80s.

He was successful because he knew his place. And that place was under backboards, collecting rebounds in the face of opponents, collecting bumps and bruises and getting floor burns on the hardwood.

After selecting Rambis in the third round of the 1980 Draft out of Santa Clara University, the New York Knicks cut him in the preseason. They later signed him to a 10-day contract but never put him in a game.

Refusing to give up, Rambis went to Greece where he found a style of basketball that suited him.

"The Greeks let the Americans get beat up over there," he said. "It's a rough game. I like a good, rough game."

After signing with the Lakers as a free agent in September 1981, Rambis made his first impression with his new team on a freezing January night in Indianapolis, pulling down 14 rebounds in 25 minutes and playing crushing defense.

Then against Detroit, Rambis snared 16 rebounds in 35 minutes.

When coach Pat Riley was asked if, considering those stats, he had decided to make Rambis the starting power forward, Riley replied, "I think that Kurt has made that decision for himself."

After seven seasons that included four world championships, Rambis went on to play for Charlotte (Hornets), Phoenix, and Sacramento.

Rambis Youth

They wore the same horn-rimmed glasses complete with the strap in the back, had the same unkempt hair, and looked as if they were wearing hand-me-downs like their hero.

The Kurt Rambis fan club sat together at the Forum, calling themselves Rambis Youth.

Said Rambis, "It sounds like a political group ready to take over something, but I don't know what."

But ultimately his blood flowed Purple and Gold. Of course, that could be at least partially explained by the fact he wound up marrying Linda Zafrani, a longtime Lakers front-office employee and close friend of Jeanie Buss.

Rambis came back to the Lakers, bouncing on and off the roster for two seasons. He then had several stints as a Lakers assistant, including his role as defensive guru under Phil Jackson. Rambis was also the Lakers head coach for most of the strike-shortened 1999 season and went on to become head coach of the Minnesota Timberwolves for two seasons.

By then, the hair was much shorter and actually combed, the glasses were long gone, and the clothes were stylish, but the competitive edge remained as sharp as ever. It's no surprise Minnesota forward Kevin Love became the league's leading rebounder in 2010–11 under Rambis.

When Phil Jackson was hired by the Knicks in 2014 to be team president, he brought Rambis on board as associate head coach, a position he held for four seasons except for the 28 games in 2015–16 in which he served as interim head coach. In 2018, Rambis returned to the Lakers in an advisory capacity.

85 From Cold Shoulder to Hot Touch

Byron Scott was living his dream.

As a kid growing up in Inglewood, he was a huge Lakers fan. At nearby Morningside High School, he had worked hour after hour to perfect his game in order to make that dream come true. He continued that routine at Arizona State.

Someday, he told himself, he would put on a Lakers uniform and high-five his teammates.

Scott did indeed put on Purple and Gold after the then-San Diego Clippers traded him to the Lakers prior to the 1983–84 season.

The high-fiving part, however, was going to take a little longer. In the beginning, the Lakers didn't even want to shake Scott's hand.

It's not that they had anything against him for joining the team. The problem was how he joined it. He had been traded as part of a four-player deal that included Norm Nixon.

Nixon was popular with his Lakers teammates, especially Magic Johnson and Michael Cooper. The three of them became an inseparable trio off the court, known as "The Three Amigos."

When one of those Amigos was shipped south by general manager Jerry West, there was a suspicion that it had as much to do with West's personal feelings about Nixon as it had to do with basketball considerations.

So when Scott arrived, several players shunned him. When he drove down the lane in practice, they shut him down as aggressively as if he was wearing Celtic green.

What could Scott do? Just keep his mouth shut and hope he could win over his new teammates.

"It didn't help that Byron played poorly during his first few weeks," said Magic Johnson, referring to the fact that Scott shot only 36.4 percent from the floor in his first 16 games with the team. "It was never easy for a rookie to fit in with the Lakers, but Byron took it well and kept his chin up.

Terminology

It was a term that popped into Scott's head when he was discussing the Lakers' chances of winning a third straight NBA title after beating the Celtics in the 1987 Finals and the Pistons in 1988.

Scott talked about a Lakers "three-peat."

It was such a colorful and unique word that the media and fans quickly picked up on it and have used it to this day not only in basketball, but also for any sports team that has a chance to win three straight championships.

Scott's coach, Pat Riley, thought so much of the term that he copyrighted it.

But that should not obscure the fact that Scott was the man who coined it.

Thanks to his accomplishments on the court, however, Scott will be remembered in Lakers lore even without being credited for the term "three-peat."

Such is not the case with Bruce Jolesch.

Ever heard of him?

Probably not unless you were a die-hard Lakers fan in the early 1980s when Jolesch was briefly the Lakers' public relations director. He was also a stats freak.

Walking by press row after a game, he once casually mentioned that Magic Johnson had gotten a triple double.

Jolesch's comment drew a bunch of blank stares since nobody knew what he was talking about. That's because he had just invented the term.

"It means," he said, "that Magic had double figures in points, rebounds, and assists."

Jolesch soon left to pursue other career opportunities, but he left behind a term that is used on all levels of basketball to this day.

"As time went on, Coop [Michael Cooper] and I started hanging out with him. Before long, the three of us were a tight group."

As the pressure from his teammates and the pressure from being in his hometown subsided, Scott began to relax and put the pressure on opponents.

He finished that first season shooting 48.4 percent from the floor, and, in 11 seasons with the Lakers, wound up with a 49 percent accuracy rate.

Scott not only made his way into the good graces of his teammates, but, by the time he retired after the 1996–97 season, he had also made his way into the Lakers' top 10 in many career statistical categories. Scott is ninth in total points (12,780), fourth in three-pointers made (595), fourth in steals (1,038), and tied for eighth in games played (846).

Those numbers don't even count the three seasons Scott spent away from the Lakers, two with Indiana and one with the Vancouver Grizzlies.

Before he was done, Scott had more high fives than he could have dreamed of.

86 The Guarantee

For Pat Riley, always in search of motivation for his players, even the parade that follows every Lakers championship wasn't off limits.

Normally, it is a time to revel in the glory of the moment. But when Riley stepped up to address the crowd after the team had beaten the Celtics in the 1987 Finals, he guaranteed the Lakers would repeat. At the time, no NBA team had won back-to-back

Riley watching the Lakers from the sideline. (Getty Images)

titles in 19 seasons, the Celtics being the last to do so in 1968 and 1969.

"Riley's guarantee put the goal right in front of us," Magic Johnson said.

And it put enormous pressure on Johnson and his teammates, who already went into most seasons in the '80s as the oddsmakers' favorite.

Even Riley couldn't have imagined just how difficult it would be to live up to his prediction in the 1989 playoffs. . After sweeping the Spurs in the three-game, first-round series, the Lakers were forced to go seven games in each of the three ensuing rounds, against the Jazz, Mavericks, and Pistons.

In the Finals against Detroit, the Lakers faced a team dubbed the "Bad Boys" for a reason.

Against the Lakers in that series, the Pistons went from "bad" to "vicious," according to Magic Johnson.

Perhaps forgetting Kevin McHale's clothesline tackle of Kurt Rambis and various other Celtics-Lakers confrontations in previous NBA Finals, Johnson said the Pistons played the Lakers "a lot nastier than the Celtics ever did. They'd foul you and they'd hit you one more time after that. They'd even stand over you to make sure you knew who had done it. Like a boxer whose opponent was already on his knees, they liked to give you one more elbow to your head."

Add to that the fact Detroit won Game 1 at the Forum 105–93, with former Lakers guard-forward Adrian Dantley hitting 14–16 from the floor for a game-high 34 points, and the task of repeating seemed even more daunting.

L.A., however, won the next two games to gain the edge in the series.

Then, in Game 4, came the seemingly inevitable clash: Magic and Isiah Thomas—the best of friends who kissed each other's cheeks before the opening tip-off of every game—temporarily kissed off their friendship in the heat of battle.

When Johnson, who had been getting battered by the Bad Boys, saw Thomas driving to the basket, he responded with an elbow to Thomas' rib cage.

Tumbling to the floor, Thomas got up, shoved the ball at Johnson, and then pushed him.

Game on.

Detroit won that game and the next to take a 3–2 lead.

In Game 6, Thomas scored 43 points, including an astounding 25 in the third quarter, but late in that period, he severely sprained an ankle. Although he returned to the game, Thomas was no longer able to maintain his torrid pace, and the Lakers were able to avoid elimination and keep Riley's guarantee alive by pulling out a one-point win.

Thomas threw away his crutches for Game 7 and played a painful 28 minutes. He hit only 4–12 from the floor, but managed to hand out seven assists, make four steals, and serve as a symbol of inspiration for his teammates.

As a result, the Pistons, down by 15 in the fourth quarter, made a furious run, but the Lakers ultimately fought them off for a three-point victory, 108–105, making good on Riley's guarantee.

When Brent Musburger, interviewing Riley in the postgame celebration, asked if he wanted to guarantee a three-peat, Kareem Abdul-Jabbar shoved a towel in Riley's mouth.

The only guarantee this time was that the Lakers were tired of the burden of great expectations.

87 Numbers Game

There have been 50 different jersey numbers used by the Los Angeles Lakers. Below is a list of the most memorable player to wear each number:

00—Benoit Benjamin

0—Kyle Kuzma (over Nick Young and Orlando Woolridge)

1—Anthony Peeler (over Caron Butler, Kentavious Caldwell-Pope, D'Angelo Russell, Jordan Farmar, and Smush Parker)

2—Derek Fisher (over Lonzo Ball)

3—Anthony Davis

4—Byron Scott

5—Robert Horry (over Jim McMillian and Dick Barnett)

6—Eddie Jones

7—Lamar Odom

8—Kobe Bryant

9—Jim Chones (over Nick Van Exel)

10—Norm Nixon

11—Bob McAdoo (over Frank Selvy)

12—Vlade Divac (over Pat Riley)

13—Wilt Chamberlain

14—Darrall Imhoff (over Sam Perkins)

15—Jim Price

16—Pau Gasol

17—Rick Fox (over Andrew Bynum)

18—Kurt Rambis

19—Tony Campbell

20—Tommy Hawkins

21—Michael Cooper
22—Elgin Baylor
23—LeBron James (over Cedric Ceballos)
24—Kobe Bryant (over Keith Erickson)
25—Gail Goodrich (over Eddie Jones)
26—Dan Schayes
27—Jordan Hill
28—Tarik Black
30—Julius Randle
31—Kurt Rambis (over Mel Counts)
32—Magic Johnson (over Bill Bridges)
33—Kareem Abdul-Jabbar (over Hot Rod Hundley)
34—Shaquille O'Neal
35—Rudy LaRusso
37—Ron Artest/Metta World Peace
40—Mike McGee
41—Elden Campbell (over Glen Rice)
42—James Worthy (over Walt Hazzard)
43—Mychal Thompson
44—Jerry West
45—A.C. Green
49—Mel McCants
50—Steve Mix
52—Jamaal Wilkes (over Happy Hairston)
53—James Edwards
54—Mark Landsberger (over Horace Grant)
55—Billy Thompson
66—Andrew Bogut
70—Frank Selvy
73—Dennis Rodman
88—Christian Eyenga

Among the Minneapolis Lakers, the Hall of Famers were:
17—Jim Pollard
19—Vern Mikkelsen
22—Slater Martin (later used by Baylor)
34—Clyde Lovellette
99—George Mikan

 **0.4**

He may have worn No. 2 on his Lakers jersey, but for fans, he will always be 0.4.

Derek Fisher made a career out of hitting big shots in crucial situations, but nothing he ever did could match the shot he made in San Antonio in Game 5 of the 2004 Western Conference semifinals.

With the series tied at two games apiece, Tim Duncan scored with four-tenths of a second remaining to give the Spurs a 73–72 lead.

With both Kobe Bryant and Shaquille O'Neal covered, the inbounds pass went to Fisher

Can a man catch a ball, turn, and shoot in less than half a second?

Fisher swung to the left of the key and received the pass. His hands in the air, San Antonio's Manu Ginobili was eyeball to eyeball with Fisher as the Lakers guard fired a desperation shot. When it left Fisher's fingertips, the clock showed one-tenth of a second.

As the 0.0 flashed on the scoreboard, the ball went through the hoop.

The Lakers dashed off the court, not even daring to look at the replay.

They could have stuck around. The tape clearly showed the shot was legal.

"It went up," said teammate Karl Malone, "and I'm thinking, *Oh, it's got a chance.* Then, I'm thinking, *Oh, it's got a good chance.* Then, I'm like, *Dang, we won.*"

Fisher's play for the ages gave the Lakers a 74–73 victory. They would go on to win Game 6 and advance to the next round, ultimately losing in five games to the Pistons in the NBA Finals.

Fisher's résumé includes other big moments. Against the Magic in Game 4 of the 2009 NBA Finals, he hit the game-tying three-pointer with 4.6 seconds remaining in regulation and another three-pointer with 31.3 seconds left in overtime of a 99–91 Lakers victory. Those clutch shots gave them a 3–1 chokehold on a series they would win in five games.

And there was his unforgettable night for the Utah Jazz in a 2007 playoff game against the Warriors. Fisher and his wife, Candace, had been in New York that day for surgery on his infant daughter, Tatum, who was suffering from cancer of the eye.

Assured the surgery was successful, Fisher flew back to Utah with his family that night, had a police escort to EnergySolutions Arena, made it onto the court late in the third quarter, and hit the three-point shot in overtime that put the game in the refrigerator, as Chick would say.

"To wake up this morning and take my daughter to the hospital, not knowing if I was going to see her again...to [see] her coming out of it and being well, and then flying back home and helping the team win a game...had I thought about it, I wouldn't have been able to do it," Fisher told the *Pittsburgh Post-Gazette.* "I was on autopilot and it just happened."

Fisher may have been in the spotlight on nights like that, but he didn't get much attention when he first joined the Lakers in 1996, and it wasn't because he stood just 6'1".

He was the 24th pick in the draft, and that summer the eyes of the franchise and the fans focused on two other acquisitions, Kobe Bryant and Shaquille O'Neal.

But through the years, the Lakers would come to appreciate Fisher, not only for his memorable shots, but also for his maturity and stability.

When Shaq and Kobe were feuding, when the Lakers were losing, when the mood turned dark, or when the luck turned bad, through his calm voice and reasoned approach, Fisher, team co-captain, often turned that chaos back into order, anger into resolve.

It was not only the Lakers who depended on his leadership. In the NBA lockout prior to the 2011–12 season, it was Fisher, president of the Players Association, who served as a key negotiator and public spokesman.

"Derek has such an aura of leadership about him," Jeanie Buss said, "that there's no way to predict how far he might go in whatever direction he chooses."

When the Lakers traded him to the Houston Rockets late in the 2011–12 season, Fisher, at 37, could have chosen to finish his career there. Instead, he immediately negotiated a buyout of his contract, signed with the Oklahoma City Thunder, and then, the old veteran on a team of young guns helped his new squad eliminate his old team, as the Thunder knocked the Lakers out of the playoffs in the second round.

No matter where he goes, however, Fisher will never get away from 0.4.

89 Big Shot Rob

Vlade Divac was seething with frustration and mired in denial.

Only seconds separated the Sacramento center from seeing his team take a commanding 3–1 series lead against the Lakers in the 2002 Western Conference finals.

With the Kings ahead 99–97, Divac had watched Kobe Bryant drive to the basket only to see his shot bounce off the rim. Shaquille O'Neal's follow-up shot had also come up short.

But the ball was still loose and still in the vicinity of the basket with less than three seconds to play. Divac's only thought was to get it out of there

So he batted it away, past the free-throw line and past the top of the key.

But the ball ended up in the last place he wanted to send it: the hands of Robert Horry.

The man they called "Big Shot Rob" lived up to his nickname once again. Calmly, he watched the ball bounce once before it reached his hands. He launched it with half a second remaining. By the time the buzzer sounded, the ball was sailing through the hoop to give the Lakers a 100–99 victory and even a series L.A. would go on to win in seven games.

"A lot of us on the bench were trying to figure out if the ball had really gone in," Laker Mark Madsen said, "if the clock had expired, if his foot was on the line, but it was another classic Robert Horry finish."

Not in Divac's mind.

"It was just a lucky shot," he said in the postgame press conference. "You don't need to have skill to do that. You just throw it up and if it goes in, it goes in."

Perhaps Divac was bitter because he had failed to win a championship in seven seasons with the Lakers or because his departure, not his arrival, helped launch another Lakers dynasty. He was traded for Bryant in 1996.

Whatever the reason, Horry fumed at Divac's remark.

"It wasn't no luck shot," Horry said. "I've been doing that for all my career. He should know. He better read a paper or something."

Indeed, any check of sports sections over the years Horry played—or simply Googling his name—will show his amazing number of big shots such as:

- 1995 NBA Finals, Game 3: Playing for the Houston Rockets against the Orlando Magic, Horry scored 11 of his 20 points in the fourth quarter and hit a three-pointer with 14.1 seconds remaining to turn a one-point lead into a four-point advantage. Houston went on to a 106–103 victory and a sweep of the series.
- 2001 NBA Finals, Game 3: Playing for the Lakers against the 76ers, Horry scored 12 of his 15 points in the fourth quarter and made his third three-pointer of the game with 47.1 seconds left to expand a one-point advantage into a four-point lead. The Lakers went on to win 96–91.
- 2002, First Round, Game 3: Playing for the Lakers against the Trail Blazers, Horry made the game-winning, series-clinching three-pointer from the corner, a 22-footer with 2.1 seconds remaining.
- 2005 NBA Finals, Game 5: Playing for the Spurs against the Pistons, Horry hit a three-pointer with 5.9 seconds left in overtime to give his team a 96–95 victory.

See a pattern here? There's another pattern as well. Horry played for three teams in 16 seasons—the Rockets, Lakers, and Spurs— and all of them won championships with him on their roster.

He has seven rings in all. He was never the biggest star on any team or the one with the most impressive stats or awards. But when it was time for a big shot, all the other big shots looked to Rob.

90 Panic in the Bathroom

When he was the Lakers' general manager, Mitch Kupchak was known for his cool, calm presence in the front office despite being the man on the hot seat.

That wasn't always the case. When first told he was about to become general manager, his initial reaction was panic.

That's understandable. Kupchak had been in the front office about 10 days at the time, and the mere notion of a then-unimaginable promotion was delivered to him while he was standing over a urinal.

It came from then–general manager Jerry West who was known to be excitable, to put it mildly.

"About the second week I was there, I'm standing in the bathroom at the Forum," Kupchak said, "when the door flies open and Jerry walks in, face red, smoke shooting out of his ears, every other word a four-letter word. He's ranting and raving, talking to me, but not really talking to me, even though there's nobody else in there. I'm petrified."

"You know, I've had enough," West said. "I'm telling Dr. [Jerry] Buss I'm quitting and I'm recommending you for the job."

And with that, West stormed out, leaving Kupchak staring at a bathroom wall, thinking, *I don't know if I'm ready for this job.*

That was 1986. As Kupchak soon learned, West was tempted to quit every other week when his anxiety over the fortunes of the team, real or imagined, got the best of him. But ultimately, reason would overtake rage, and West would calm down and come back to a job he never really left.

West was right in one regard. Kupchak was going to inherit his position.

Fourteen years later.

That Kupchak would even be in line for such a job would have been incomprehensible to him when he first joined the Lakers organization.

He was a 6'9", 230-pound power forward in those days, a former North Carolina Tar Heel who had played for the then-Washington Bullets for five seasons.

In 1981, Kupchak joined the Lakers, signing a contract worth nearly $8 million to play for four years and spend an additional seven in the front office.

Just 26 games into his first season with the team, those front-office days suddenly seemed a lot closer when he suffered a devastating fracture of his left leg, damaging cartilage and ligaments. The injury was so severe that a team physician equated it with what might happen to the victim of a major car crash.

Strangely enough, Kupchak's leg had buckled as he ran down the court untouched.

It was a long time before he ran down a court again, and he never did so as effectively as he had before the injury.

Kupchak missed all of that season and the next. He then struggled through the following three years, playing a total of 147 regular-season games over that span. He averaged just 5.1 points and 3.1 rebounds during those three seasons, hardly resembling the player he had been before.

Kupchak then slid over to become West's apprentice. When West finally left in 2000, doubters wondered whether Kupchak was qualified to replace the man who had done so much of the heavy lifting in building two Lakers dynasties.

Kupchak's Knee

After 25 games as a Laker, Kupchak felt he had turned a corner when he awoke on the morning of December 19, 1981.

"I slept well last night for the first time in weeks," he said over breakfast. "I'm really relaxed with things now."

The Lakers played the then–San Diego Clippers at the San Diego Sports Arena that night. Kupchak, having taken a pass from Magic Johnson, was coming downcourt when he saw a Clipper in his path.

Swerving awkwardly to avoid the defender caused Kupchak's knee to explode like a blown tire.

The player he was trying to avoid?

Joe "Jellybean" Bryant.

Kobe's father.

Until West got back into the NBA two years later—agreeing to run the Memphis Grizzlies operation—there were whispers that he was pulling the strings behind Kupchak and that Kupchak might as well have been sitting on his lap.

"I saw all the criticism of Mitch and I knew he didn't deserve it," Jerry Buss said. "People would ask me, 'What are you going to do about Mitch Kupchak?' And I would reply, 'Support him 100 percent, just like I always have.'"

Kupchak, never one to pat himself on the back, chose to let his accomplishments speak for him.

There have been questions about some of his moves.

He traded Shaquille O'Neal to Miami for Lamar Odom, Brian Grant, and Caron Butler. Kupchak's critics said he should have at least acquired Miami's best player, Dwyane Wade, in exchange for O'Neal.

But since everybody knew Kupchak was under orders from Buss to dump O'Neal, Kupchak was forced to deal with a buyer's market.

He took a chance by using a 2005 first-round draft choice on a 17-year-old high school player named Andrew Bynum. While

Kupchak's opinion of Bynum's talent was vindicated, he was a bad choice because he turned out to be a liability in terms of maturity and durability.

Kupchak made the most of a bad situation when negotiations with Trevor Ariza broke down after the 2008–09 season, moving quickly to sign Ron Artest.

No one, of course, can argue with Kupchak's most celebrated move, trading Kwame Brown, Javaris Crittenton, Aaron McKie, the draft rights to Marc Gasol, and two future draft picks to the Grizzlies for Marc's brother, Pau, and a draft choice.

In the decade after West finally left and Kupchak took over, the Lakers won four titles and went to the Finals six times. Not bad for a guy who once stood in a bathroom, thinking he was watching his career go down the drain.

Kupchak may have thrived in his position, but ultimately he couldn't survive when his immediate supervisor, Jim Buss, was relieved of his duties as head of basketball operations by his sister, Jeanie, in 2017. She also fired Kupchak before replacing her brother with Magic Johnson.

Kupchak is now general manager of the Charlotte Hornets.

91 The Great Voice Is Stilled

It would have been tough enough for Lakers play-by-play announcer Chick Hearn, at age 85, to get through the 2001–02 season, which included exhibition games, 82 regular-season games, and 19 post-season games.

Add his open-heart surgery and a hip replacement, and it is hard to believe he was still behind the mic when the Lakers completed a three-peat by sweeping the New Jersey Nets in the Finals.

The medical problems began in December 2001, when Hearn had the heart surgery, ending his streak of consecutive Lakers broadcasts at 3,338 games.

But despite his advanced age and his condition, his heart beat as furiously as ever for his life's work.

While still lying in intensive care several days after the surgery, Hearn pulled agent Lon Rosen close to him and said, "Lonnie, you make sure until I'm better, they don't take away my job."

There was more chance Jerry Buss would sell the Lakers than take away Hearn's job.

His recovery from heart surgery had gone well, and Hearn was zeroing in on a return to the team in March. But while putting gas in his car in mid-February, he heard his wife, Marge, yell from the front seat that the vehicle was rolling.

Hearn tried to get back in and stop it, but the car door hit him, knocking him to the pavement.

The car rolled harmlessly to a stop in some shrubbery. Hearn wasn't so fortunate. He had broken his hip.

As he was being wheeled in for surgery, Hearn was asked by a doctor, "Chick, at your age why are you still pumping your own gas?"

Sharp as ever, he replied, "So I can afford to pay you."

Despite this latest setback, Hearn wouldn't concede that the season was lost for him. Two months after the hip surgery, he delicately sat down before a microphone and broadcast a game.

"How could you not be amazed at him?" said team trainer Gary Vitti.

Hearn not only did the home games, but traveled as well.

At season's end, Hearn told Marge, "I think maybe I'd like to spend more time at home with you."

"Good," she said, "then make this season coming up your last."

"I think I will," he said.

In August, he and Marge were sitting by the pool in the backyard of their Encino home that overlooked the San Fernando Valley when Hearn remarked that a large planter needed to be turned because the plant wasn't getting enough sun.

"That's what gardeners are for," Marge said.

But Hearn, still recuperating from hip surgery, tried to do it himself once Marge had gone in to make dinner. He pulled hard, lost his balance, fell backward, and cracked his skull on the cement.

Massive hemorrhaging of the brain ensued, and he died several days later on August 5, 2002.

His funeral was the only one in memory involving any L.A. figure—including politicians, movie stars, and athletes—that was televised live on every local channel, beginning to end. His broadcast perch at Staples Center was opened up to the public, and 18,000 fans filed by. A statue of him was erected outside the arena.

Actress Dyan Cannon said the Lakers without Hearn were "like a car without an engine."

Chick

He was born Francis Dayle Hearn. So how did he become Chick?

After playing basketball for East High in Aurora, Illinois, Hearn joined an AAU team. When it qualified for a national tournament in Denver, a send-off luncheon was held for the club.

Hearn was in desperate need of basketball shoes at the time, the ones he had having worn down nearly to his socks.

So he was delighted when he was presented with a gift-wrapped shoe box.

Opening it in front of the crowd, he reached in and pulled out…a dead, rotted chicken.

The laughs soon subsided, but the prank had a life of its own. Francis Dayle Hearn became known as Chicken Hearn, and eventually, just Chick.

"Nothing ever galvanized Los Angeles like Chick Hearn," said actor Jack Nicholson, "except for an earthquake."

Hearn spanned the decades and spanned the dynasties, from Baylor and West to Magic and Kareem to Kobe and Shaq. His voice, the only one to ever do Lakers play-by-play, was the one constant, a reassuring presence, praising, scolding, teaching, and imploring in a colorful, creative manner like no other.

There would be other voices and other memorable Lakers moments in the years ahead. But as Jeanie Buss put it, "It's never going to be the same."

92 Phil and Jeanie

Nearly until the end of her teens, Jeanie Buss was known to the public only as one of the J kids of Jerry Buss and his wife, JoAnn, along with siblings Johnny, Jimmy, and Janie. Eventually Jesse and Joey would come along from another mother.

Jeanie told her father that she wanted to get involved in the family business, even though she was still a student at USC.

That business had been solely real estate until Jerry bought the Los Angeles Strings of World Team Tennis.

In terms of his own life or that of his kids, he had never been one for wading into the pool. Better to take the plunge and see if you can survive.

So at the age of 19, Jeanie was appointed general manager of the Strings and told she would be conducting the upcoming draft on her own.

That would seem to be a daunting task for any teen, but because her father had shown so much faith in her, Jeanie felt she could handle it.

His confidence was rewarded. The Strings won the WTT championship in their first season with Jeanie in charge.

A career had been launched.

As Jerry's empire grew, so did Jeanie's responsibilities. She created the Forum Tennis Challenge Series and ran a roller hockey team. She brought concerts and various other attractions to the Forum, and was eventually made president of the arena, then vice president of the Lakers in charge of business operations. In addition to handling everything from the team's sponsors and broadcast partners to marketing, Jeanie is the public face of the team. More than anyone else in her family, she interacts with the fans. Jeanie not only hosts team events, but also oversees the delicate task of making sure all the celebrities who flock to games get the seats they want.

The length fans will go for Lakers tickets, especially during the playoffs, can sometimes be comical.

One fan, claiming to be a celebrity, wanted access to the Chairman's Room, where the stars hang out at STAPLES Center.

When his request was denied, the fan sent photos of himself with celebrities.

Close enough? No way.

Jeanie likes to say that, while Magic Johnson and Rob Pelinka make the basketball decisions, she is the one who generates the revenue to fund those decisions.

Looking back on the summer of 1999, Jeanie is glad she doesn't have input in basketball decisions. Because if she had, she would have vetoed the hiring of Phil Jackson.

"We had two of the biggest stars in the league in Shaquille O'Neal and Kobe Bryant," she said, "and the last thing we needed was another big ego to disturb the already delicate balance between those two.

"As far as Phil the person goes, I…knew little. To me, he was a motorcycle-riding, Grateful Dead–loving hippie."

Didn't exactly sound like the start of a great relationship.

But when Jeanie accepted Jackson's dinner invitation, things began to change.

Quickly.

Despite the fact Jackson is older by 16 years, Jeanie felt a strong attraction to him on that first evening, and he was equally intrigued with her.

Before things progressed too far, however, she insisted on telling her father what was going on.

His reaction?

"I'm glad you are dating someone older," Jerry said, "someone who will appreciate you.

Jerry West was not so appreciative. When he learned of the relationship, he asked Jackson why he couldn't have found someone else among all the women in L.A.

West would never concede the connection, but, a year later, he left the organization.

The motorcycle-riding, Grateful Dead–loving hippie and the subject of a *Playboy* layout eventually became engaged and were together overall for more than 15 years.

93 What If...

For decades, he was Public Enemy No. 1 to Laker fans, his mere image eliciting anger and boos.

But on the night of December 8, 2011, longtime Celtics coach/ general manager Red Auerbach dropped down to No. 2 on L.A.'s Least Wanted list, replaced by then-NBA commissioner David Stern, who, until that day, had been almost universally admired and respected for spearheading the creation of the modern NBA and transforming it into a league with blockbuster television ratings, soaring marketing revenue, and huge international appeal.

None of that mattered in Lakerdom 45 minutes after the team appeared to have pulled off a trade that might have revitalized the Lakers, who were coming off a season in which they had been swept out of the playoffs in the second round by the Mavericks, then lost Phil Jackson to retirement.

Instead, Stern quashed the deal.

Laker general manager Mitch Kupchak had reached an agreement on a three-team trade involving the then–New Orleans Hornets and the Rockets that would have put a Purple and Gold uniform on Chris Paul, then considered one of the top two point guards in the league, along with Derrick Rose. The Hornets would have gotten Lamar Odom from the Lakers and Kevin Martin, Goran Dragic, Luis Scola, and a 2012 first-round pick from Houston, while Pau Gasol would have gone to the Rockets.

Had George Shinn still owned the Hornets that night, it would have been a done deal. But with Shinn steeped in ever-mounting debt and stalled in his attempt to sell the team, the NBA had stepped in a year earlier and purchased the club on a temporary basis, thus avoiding the possibility that a desperate Shinn would sell to a buyer who would move the team out of New Orleans.

When the trade was made by Hornets general manager Dell Demps, his boss was Stern.

Hours earlier, the NBA commissioner had signed off on a new collective bargaining agreement with the players' union, ending a bitter five-month lockout.

One of the issues in the negotiations was the frustration of small-market owners over their inability to remain competitive because of the power of the big-market teams to grab star players. And much of that frustration was aimed at the Lakers who, time and again under Jerry Buss, had lured away big names.

And now they were going to do it again by teaming Paul with Kobe Bryant? It wasn't quite as simple as that since they would be losing Odom and Pau, two other key figures on the Laker roster.

Still, Stern found himself inundated with angry reactions from small-market clubs.

Cavaliers owner Dan Gilbert fired off a bitter, blistering letter to the commissioner in which he called the trade "a travesty," and wrote, "I just don't see how we can allow this trade to happen."

Gilbert asked the commissioner to put the deal to a vote of "the 29 owners of the Hornets," referring to the fact that, since the league had bought the team, each owner had a piece of it.

Comparing the big-market and small-market teams to the Globetrotters and the squad of sparring partners who served as their straight men, Gilbert wrote, "When will we just change the name of 25 of the 30 teams to the Washington Generals?"

Some other owners heatedly concurred with Gilbert.

Less than an hour later, with the ink certifying the transaction barely dry, Stern made his shocking announcement: the deal was dead.

A reaction to the outrage? Absolutely no connection, insisted the commissioner's office.

Now it was the media's turn to react with outrage.

"NBA owners revealed themselves to be vindictive, onerous, agenda-driven, and spectacularly petty," wrote ESPN's Michael Wilbon, "when they complained to the point that David Stern, in a completely gutless move by all involved, essentially vetoed a perfectly legitimate trade."

Wrote Ian O'Conner, also for ESPN, "David Stern never looked so small or weak."

Jeanie Buss said that several owners told her that the uproar was ignited by the circumstances. After Stern had implored the owners to ratify the new collective bargaining agreement with assurances it would be a step toward parity, they did so only to be hit with the news that the Lakers had gotten another superstar, this one from a team owned by the league.

"Look at the timing," Jeanie was told. "If you guys would have just waited…"

Stern insisted he had not nullified the trade.

In a statement issued the day after the deal was killed, he said, "Since the NBA purchased the New Orleans Hornets, final responsibility for significant management decisions lies with the commissioner's office in consultation with team chairman Jac Sperling. All decisions are made on the basis of what is in the best interests of the Hornets…. We decided, free from the influence of other NBA owners, that the team was better served with Chris in a Hornets uniform than by the outcome of the terms of that trade."

Yet one week later, Stern allowed the Hornets to trade Paul to Los Angeles after all. The Los Angeles Clippers. He was sent there in exchange for Eric Gordon, Chris Kaman, Al-Farouq Aminu, and a first-round draft choice. As a group, this threesome clearly didn't match up with the foursome—Odom, Dragic, Martin and Scola—that the Hornets would have gotten in the first trade.

So, as it turned out, it was Demps, not Stern, who had made the right move. Paul had already decided that his days in a Hornets uniform were numbered. He had told the team that, rather than sign a contract extension, he wanted to enter the free-agent market. Knowing that, Demps got the most value for his departing point guard.

In 2017, Stern further justified his veto by throwing Kupchak under the bus on the *Nunyo & Company* podcast.

"In the course of [that] weekend," Stern said, "we thought we could redo the deal. We really thought that Houston would be ready to part with [Kyle] Lowry, and we had a trade lined up for Odom that would have gotten us a good first-round draft pick. Not me, but my basketball folks.

"But Mitch Kupchak at the time panicked and moved Odom to Dallas. So the piece wasn't even there for us to play with.... [It was] just about what was good for the then–New Orleans Hornets."

Doing what he felt was good for the Lakers, Kupchak traded Odom and a 2012 second-round pick to the Mavericks three days after the commissioner put his thumb down on the original trade, and received in return an $8.9 million trade exception and a 2012 protected first-round pick.

Others may not agree with Stern's rationale for his unorthodox move, but one thing is certain. The course of basketball history in L.A. and beyond was forever altered on that night in 2011.

What if Paul had been allowed to go to the Lakers?

With a dream backcourt of Kobe and Chris, the Lakers would not have been shackled with Steve Nash, who, because of leg and back injuries, turned out to be damaged goods after he was acquired in a 2012 trade with the Suns. But would Paul and Bryant, minus Pau and Odom, have been enough to make the Lakers serious contenders once again?

Would they have still made their 2012 trade with the Magic to obtain Dwight Howard? Would he have played with a better attitude as a member of a winning team? Or would the Lakers, able to attract superior talent with the Kobe/Chris backcourt, have gone in a different direction?

Would the presence of Paul on the court have taken some of the pressure off Bryant, enabling him to play fewer minutes, thus reducing the wear and tear on his body, possibly preventing the injuries that hobbled him over his final few seasons, extending his career?

Would a better Laker team have saved the jobs of Mike Brown, Jim Buss, and Kupchak, thus keeping Magic Johnson out of the front office?

Might that have caused LeBron James to have second thoughts about signing with the team?

Even as the years go by, the what ifs never stop.

94 Harsh Reality

It's a fall as steep, as stunning, and as strange as any ever seen in the NBA.

Lamar Odom went from a valued member of a two-time defending NBA champion to the league's Sixth Man of the Year Award to oblivion.

In 2010, he helped the Lakers beat the Boston Celtics in a seven-game NBA Finals.

In 2011, his superlative play off the bench earned him recognition that he said was "a long time coming."

Then, prior to the start of the 2011–12 season, Odom was part of a three-team trade that would have brought guard Chris Paul to the Lakers. After NBA commissioner David Stern disallowed the deal, Odom was so hurt by the idea the Lakers had agreed to ship him out of town without warning that *he* pushed for a trade.

He was sent to the Dallas Mavericks, but was never able to get out of his funk. After 50 games and career-low averages of 6.6 points and 4.2 rebounds, Odom was deactivated for the rest of the season.

Some blamed it on the distraction of his marriage to Khloe Kardashian and their reality TV show. Others pointed to the emotional effect of two tragedies during the summer of 2011, the murder of his 24-year cousin and the death of a pedestrian in an accident involving a car in which Odom was a passenger. Still others felt he never found a comfortable role on the Mavericks, a team coming off an NBA title.

Whatever the reason, he was branded an underachiever, a charge he faced over and over during his 14-year career.

Odom has been the victim of his own potential. People look at his 6'10", 230-pound body, his skill level, and the versatility to play any position, and they feel anything less than superstardom is a disappointment.

He has teased teammates and fans alike with flashes of brilliance. Watching Odom grab a rebound, run coast to coast, gobbling up huge chunks of hardwood with his long legs, befuddle defenders with a dazzling spin to the hoop, and ultimately score on a soft layup, the normal reaction is: why doesn't he do that every time?

"He is the only player to come into this league," Pat Riley said, "who had the ability to play like Earvin Johnson."

Talk about high expectations.

It's not that Odom has been unproductive. Far from it. Prior to his meltdown season with Dallas, he averaged 14.6 points, 8.9 rebounds, 4.0 assists, and shot 46.9 percent from the floor in a career that included five seasons with the Clippers, one with the

Heat, and seven with the Lakers. Over that period, he went to the NBA Finals three times and won two titles.

Through it all, he remained the ultimate team player, never acting selfishly on the court. He accepted a role on the Lakers bench, though he had the talent to start for most teams, and has always deferred to teammates if he thought it was in the best interest of the team. Odom truly left his ego in the locker room.

A good trait, right?

Not to Odom's critics, who said he was too laid back.

Actually, if he lacked a strong will and a competitive spirit, he wouldn't have been able to persevere through a life that was once far removed from the glitzy world of the Kardashians.

Odom grew up in South Jamaica, Queens, where drug dealers brazenly operated outside his front door.

He lost his mother, Cathy Mercer, to colon cancer when he was 12. The job of raising Odom then fell to his grandmother, Mildred.

A first-round draft choice of the Clippers, Odom ran into trouble during his third pro season, receiving two suspensions in 2001 for violating the NBA's drug policy. (He admitted using marijuana.)

In June 2003, finally back at full strength after two injury-plagued seasons, Odom suffered a devastating emotional setback when his grandmother died.

But the most crushing loss of all still lay ahead. In 2006, on the same date Odom's grandmother had passed away three years earlier, his seven-month-old son, Jayden, succumbed to crib death.

"It's so unexpected," Odom said. "I don't think nothing could prepare you. It's just one of those things that's out of your hands. Sometimes, you've just got to accept it as God's work."

95 Metta World Peace, Man of Many Names and Many Faces

How does a player who goes to the effort of legally changing his last name to Peace then commit the most violent foul of the 2011–12 season?

The crushing elbow to the head of the Oklahoma City Thunder's James Harden, a foul that resulted in a seven-game suspension, was just the latest example of the inscrutable nature of Metta World Peace, aka Ron Artest, aka Indiana Ron.

The perfect illustration of both the euphoria and the anguish the man then known as Artest can generate came at the end of Game 5 of the 2010 Western Conference finals between the Lakers and Phoenix Suns.

With the Lakers clinging to a three-point lead, just over a minute to play, and the ball in their hands, specifically in Artest's hands, he took a shot from three-point range. He missed and then, with just two seconds expired on the 24-second clock, took another shot from three-point territory.

And missed again.

That earned him a cold stare from his coach, Phil Jackson.

"If I were Ron, I wouldn't have gone back to the bench to face Phil after that second shot," said Jeanie Buss.

Yet a minute later, Artest was the most popular guy on the team. His teammates hugged him, Jackson was delighted with him, and his transgressions were overlooked.

After Phoenix had tied the game on a three-pointer by Jason Richardson with 3.5 seconds remaining and Kobe Bryant missed a shot on the subsequent Lakers possession, Artest grabbed the loose ball and banked it in as time expired.

The Lakers won 103–101 and went on to win the series in six games.

Ron Artest—sometimes you can't play with him, but sometimes, you just can't play without him.

Jackson knew that when he supported the signing of the 6'7", 260-pound defensive specialist after negotiations with Trevor Ariza collapsed in the summer of 2009.

Jackson was confident he could get Artest to contribute in a meaningful way despite his erratic history. After all, hadn't Jackson gotten significant production out of Dennis Rodman, no easy task, when both were with the Chicago Bulls?

Artest is often compared to Rodman. From the blond dye jobs to their head-scratching behavior, both often seemed in need of a firm hand to keep them under control.

And Jackson, Zen Master though he may have been, could supply a firm hand when necessary.

At least Artest never dressed up in a wedding gown a la Rodman.

But Artest brought his own baggage to the Lakers. His most outrageous behavior occurred during 2004's riotous night in Auburn Hills when he triggered one of the wildest melees ever seen in the NBA by going after a fan in the stands.

It began as an on-court fight between Artest, playing for the Pacers, and the Pistons' Ben Wallace. It was fierce, but nothing that hadn't been seen before. Artest fouled Wallace from behind, and Wallace turned around and pushed Artest in the face. Players from both sides poured onto the floor and punches were thrown.

While that was going on, Artest went over to the scorers' table where he laid down on his back as if he'd had nothing to do with the chaos.

It appeared as if the refs were about to get control of the situation when a beverage came flying out of the stands and splattered Artest.

He snapped, jumping up and leaping into the paying customers, wildly throwing punches. As he was joined by teammate Stephen Jackson, fans began throwing punches of their own at the Pacers pair.

All sorts of objects from the stands came crashing down on the floor.

"It's the ugliest thing I've seen as a coach or player," Detroit coach Larry Brown said.

After he got back on the floor, Artest was approached by a shouting fan in a Pistons jersey. Artest punched him in the face.

Artest was suspended by the league for the rest of the season, a total of 73 games.

There have been other Artest incidents over the years. He was benched for asking for time off to promote a rap album, destroyed TV monitors at New York's Madison Square Garden, and claimed he drank cognac in the locker room during halftime when he was with the Bulls.

He was supposed to be the new, reformed Ron Artest, a model citizen, when he joined the Lakers, but how realistic was that?

He reported overweight and had to play himself into shape. He struggled to learn Jackson's triangle offense and never seemed to master it.

After returning home following a Christmas Day game in 2009, Artest mysteriously fell down a flight of stairs, losing consciousness. He suffered a concussion, required stitches to the back of his head, and injured an elbow.

He said he had slipped while carrying a box down the stairs.

In his second season with the team, Artest clashed with Jackson because he felt the coach was unfairly criticizing him in public.

In his third season, Artest clashed with new Lakers coach Mike Brown, saying derisively, "His background is video coordinator or whatever, so he's all stats."

But there have also been highlights for Artest in Purple and Gold. In Game 7 of the 2010 NBA Finals between the Lakers and Celtics, Artest scored 20 points, second only to Kobe Bryant's 23, played tough defense on Boston's Paul Pierce, had five rebounds, five steals, and hit a crucial three-pointer with a minute to play in his team's 83–79 title-winning victory.

Artest added a big assist the next season, raffling off his championship ring, with the money going to mental-health programs.

At peace with himself or at war, Metta or Ron, there is one thing he will never be called: boring.

96 Kobe's 81

It was January, a time when sports fans are focused on the Super Bowl and debating who deserves to be awarded the college football championship.

Basketball? The attention of the average fan doesn't really kick in until the spring, until the NCAA tournament, until the start of the NBA playoffs.

For the Lakers, January 22, 2006, seemed like a particularly ho-hum night since they were facing the Toronto Raptors, who entered Staples Center with a 14–26 record.

But when Kobe Bryant takes the floor, ho-hum can quickly turn to hoo-hah. And it did that night.

It was a drama that started slowly, but just kept building.

Bryant scored 14 points in the first quarter, hitting 5 of 9 from the floor. He came back with 12 points in the second period, connecting on 5 of 7.

January 22, 2006: Kobe shoots over Morris Peterson in the first quarter. Kobe's final tally of 81 was the second-highest point total in a single game in NBA history.

Then, with his team trailing by 18 in the third quarter, he exploded with 27 in that period (11 of 15) and 28 in the final quarter (7 of 15), accounting for all but three of his team's points in that final 12 minutes.

Bryant's game total: 81 points.

In hitting 28 of 46 from the floor, including 7 of 13 from three-point range, and 18 of 20 from the free-throw line, Bryant had amassed a single-game point total exceeded only by Wilt Chamberlain's monumental 100.

Oh, and by the way, the Lakers won 122–104.

"Not even in my dreams," said Bryant after his amazing performance. "That was something that just happened. It's tough to explain…. I was just locked in…. It turned into something special. To sit here and say I grasp what happened, that would be lying."

Teammate Lamar Odom said the Raptors' big lead was what turned another superior Bryant shooting performance into a history-making event.

"He was ticked off," Odom said.

Apparently so. After his team trailed 71–53 in the third period, Bryant scored 51 of his 81.

"You're sitting and watching, and it's like a miracle unfolding in front of your eyes and you can't accept it," Lakers owner Jerry Buss said. "Somehow, the brain won't work. The easiest way to look at it is, everybody remembers every 50-point game they ever saw. He had 55 in the second half."

When he got hot, Bryant was like a machine running in high gear, and the Raptors were unable to yank the power cord.

"We tried three or four guys on him," said Toronto's Chris Bosh, "but it seemed like nobody guarded him tonight."

Along the way, Bryant obliterated the Lakers' single-game record of 71 points set by Elgin Baylor in 1960, but Bryant, conscious of the criticism that he shoots too much, stressed that his prime focus was not the record book.

"These points tonight mattered," he said. "We needed them. The points I put in the basket were instrumental. It means a lot more.... It's about the W. That's why I turned it on."

Even coach Phil Jackson, not one to heap effusive praise on his players, made an exception that night.

"That was something to behold," he said. "It was another level. I've seen some remarkable games, but I've never seen one like that."

It was not the first or the last time Bryant would leave a crowd with their jaws hanging open and an opposing defender with his head hanging down.

Time and again, he made shots that have left an indelible image in the minds of those who saw them, from his off-balance, 27-foot, buzzer-beating, bank shot in the face of Dwyane Wade's smothering defense to defeat the Heat; to his behind-the-backboard shot that somehow found the net (an attempt more fitting for a game of H-O-R-S-E); to his final minute, double-team beating, reverse-direction, sideline-hugging, high-arcing shot over the straining fingertips of LaMarcus Aldridge in an overtime victory over the Trail Blazers in which Bryant scored 65 points.

This book would have to be expanded to 400 pages to mention all the buzzer beaters, dunks, bank shots, and all the gravity-defying and eye-popping baskets that Bryant made while thrilling teammates and tormenting opponents over his 20-year career.

The kid, who famously air-balled four crucial three-point attempts in a series-eliminating loss to the Jazz in his first post-season, was often criticized for shooting too much and paying too little attention to open teammates. But he has grown into one of the greatest clutch shooters of all time, a worthy replacement for the Lakers' original Mr. Clutch, Jerry West.

Along with his designation as the Closer, Bryant is also known as the Warrior. And not because he ever played for Golden State. It's because he played through injury after injury, gritting his teeth, ignoring the pain, denying he was even hurt.

Best player ever, surpassing Jordan, Kareem Abdul-Jabbar, and Bill Russell?

He's certainly In the conversation.

97 Kobe's Farewell 60

They may just be the two greatest shots Kobe Bryant has ever made. Known for his buzzer beaters, rim rattlers, and gravity defiers, for shots taken from well beyond the arc or with two or three defenders encircling him, Bryant exceeded the degree of difficulty of all of them with two simple shots from 15 feet away, with the clock stopped and not a defender in sight.

It was April 12, 2013. Facing the Warriors at Staples Center in the 80th game of a grueling regular season for the Lakers, Bryant, in the closing minutes, pushed off with his left foot to get around a defender, was fouled, and immediately collapsed on the hardwood after hearing a popping sound. Staying down in a sitting position clutching his left heel, he knew full well what had just happened. He had ruptured his left Achilles tendon.

Nearly every other player, knowing this, would have limped off or been carried off the court. But Bryant was not like any other player. He fought off injuries with the same tenacity that he fought off defenders. He was, said Dr. Steve Lombardo, the Lakers' team physician through Bryant's two decades with the team, the toughest player he ever treated. Bryant would severely sprain his ankle, Lombardo would tell him he probably wouldn't be able to play for 10 days or longer, and Bryant would just shrug, smile, and declare that he'd be on the court in the next game.

As he sat on the floor that night while being told by the medical staff that, yes, it was his Achilles, he was already figuring out how he could take the two free throws coming to him on the foul.

"That was a no-brainer," said Bryant of his decision to get to the free-throw line.

Beyond that, he was even searching for a way to remain in the game if nothing else, as a decoy.

"[If] you tear your Achilles, you can't get up on your toes," said Bryant. "You lose that shock absorber. But, if I'm not on my toes, I don't need that absorber. So, I thought, maybe I could run on my heel, but I felt the tendon slipping farther and farther up my calf."

Shifting all his weight to his heels, he relied on adrenaline to fuel him on the short, painful journey to the line where he made both free throws.

Then reality kicked in. "[I knew] I should probably shut it down," he said. And he did, exiting to the locker room and then to the hospital for surgery the next day, his season over.

Injuries were nothing new for Bryant. He had a total of 23 over his 20-year Laker career, spending as much time with Lombardo and trainer Gary Vitti as he did with his teammates.

"I just love to play," said Bryant. "It was basic logic to me. If an injury was not going to get worse if I played, [that was what] I was going to do. If it was just painful and I could navigate through it, I was going to be fine."

But the Achilles injury marked the start of treacherous waters he ultimately couldn't navigate his way through. After years of punishment, his body finally rebelled.

Bryant joined the Lakers at age 17 and was an integral part of the team throughout his career. When Shaq was traded to the Heat after the 2003–04 season, Bryant's workload increased even more. No longer the child prodigy, he was the leader of the team.

But the work ethic remained a constant. When Caron Butler joined the Lakers along with Lamar Odom and Brian Grant in exchange for Shaq, Bryant, at the press conference welcoming the trio to L.A., asked Butler if he was ready to go to work. The newcomer quickly learned what that meant. For Bryant, a successful workout ended with a blackout.

That wasn't an exercise, but a condition.

He literally pushed himself until he passed out.

But Bryant's body could only withstand so much. The Achilles injury was his third in that game alone. Earlier, he had hyperextended a knee and hurt one of his feet.

It didn't get any easier for him. His long recovery from the Achilles injury, plus a fractured bone in his left knee, limited him to just six games in the 2013–14 season. He played only 35 games the following season because of a torn rotator cuff.

If Bryant was a used car, he would have been towed to the junkyard.

Finally acknowledging his ever-growing limitations, he announced early in the 2015–16 season that it would be his last. Although he had the usual aches and pains, he battled through as always to play in 66 games.

On April 13, Bryant stepped on an NBA court for the final time as a player to face the Utah Jazz at Staples Center. He began that night averaging only 16.9 points per game and shooting just 35.4 percent from the floor, the lowest accuracy mark of his career.

Did he have enough left in the tank for a grand farewell? That looked questionable at first as he began the game by missing his first five shots.

But there was no way Bryant was going to go quietly into retirement. A pump fake followed by his signature jumper, this one from 10 feet out, gave him his first two points with just over five minutes remaining in the first quarter. Calming his nerves and settling into a rhythm, he finished the quarter with 15 points.

By halftime, he had 22 and fans could relax. Bryant, it seemed, was at least going to go out with a 30-point performance.

He blew past that by finishing the third quarter with 37. It looked like he was going to get 40. Amazing.

No, 50!

No, 60!

Taking 50 shots from the floor, connecting on 22 of them, and adding 10 free throws, Bryant had the fifth highest scoring total of his career, was the oldest player to score 60 points in a game, and finished with the most ever by any NBA player in the last game of his career.

It wasn't as if it was an All-Star Game in which both sides wanted to enable a retiring player to exit with one last blaze of glory. "We weren't trying to let him go off on a win," Jazz small forward Joe Ingles, one of those with the unenviable task of guarding Bryant that night, told the Associated Press. "I don't think we gave him any open looks."

Bryant admitted even he was shocked at what he had accomplished.

"The thing that had me cracking up all night long," he said, "is, I go through 20 years of everybody screaming [at me] to pass the ball. And then [in the last game], they're like, '*Don't* pass it!'"

When it was over, Bryant addressed the crowd, signing off with, "Mamba out."

But it wasn't quite over. After he had showered and dressed, he returned to the floor. When the clock hit midnight, he was still there, walking around and around the court with his wife, Vanessa, and their daughters, Natalia and Gianna. Kobe didn't want to leave because he knew that he would never be back. Not in the role of a player.

He walked over to the section of hardwood where one of his jersey numbers, 24, was emblazoned and wrote *Laker for life* on it.

Finally, at 12:20, Kobe left the building.

Every athlete agonizes when it comes time to cut the cord on his career. Many find a way to stay in their game, as a coach, assistant coach, broadcaster, or somewhere in a team's front office.

Not Bryant. He had other plans, other dreams.

He formed a production company, hired a crew, and produced an animated short film, *Dear Basketball.*

Bryant once said that everyone, regardless of their chosen field, should strive to reach the top. If they play sports, their goal should be a championship. If they produce a film, they should shoot for an Oscar.

Sure enough, in 2018, *Dear Basketball* won an Oscar.

98 Revenge Is Sweet

It was the most crushing loss the Lakers ever suffered against their most hated rivals.

When they were beaten in the devastating Memorial Day Massacre by the Boston Celtics in 1985, a 34-point defeat, it was only Game 1 of the NBA Finals, a series the Lakers went on to win in six.

There were other memorable losses to the Celtics in the Finals that were at least close and competitive.

But what happened on June 17, 2008, like the Memorial Day Massacre, was neither close nor competitive, nor even salvageable. In getting shellacked by Boston 131–92 at TD Garden, the Lakers were eliminated from the Finals in six games.

What could be more painful for them than watching the Celtics dance on their beloved green parquet floor, listening to the Boston fans jeer the evil Purple and Gold, knowing that the 39-point defeat was the largest in an elimination game in the history of the Finals and realizing there was no chance to respond?

Beat L.A.? This was *Bury* L.A.

There was another humiliating loss in the series in Game 4. With a chance to tie the Finals at two games apiece, the Lakers instead blew a 24-point lead, ending in a 97–91 Celtics victory.

"Boston just was hungrier," said Kobe Bryant of the series, "and they played with much more passion. They truly deserved this championship."

Bryant made that remark through gritted teeth. He couldn't wait for a rematch.

Sure enough, the Lakers made it back to the Finals in 2009, but Boston was sitting home, having been defeated by Orlando on its way to the Finals. The Lakers knocked the Magic out in five games.

Sweet, but not sweet enough to remove the bitter taste in the Lakers' collective mouths from the season before. Only a victory over the Celtics would do that.

One year later, the Lakers got their chance to again plant their sneakers on the parquet floor in June.

It was a tough series, tough enough to stretch to seven games, the first time the Lakers and Celtics had gone that far head-to-head in more than a quarter century.

The Lakers split the first two games at home and lost two out of three in Boston, thus needing to win the last two. The Lakers took Game 6 by 22 points and appeared to have two big advantages for Game 7. It would be played on their home court and Kendrick Perkins, a key figure in the Celtics' frontcourt, would not suit up because of torn ligaments in his right knee.

Phil Jackson and his then-significant other, Jeanie Buss, had a nightly pregame ritual at Staples Center. Before they parted at the door to the locker room, they kissed.

But that night, with a huge media mob in the hallway, Jackson initially kissed off the affectionate gesture.

"You're not going to kiss me?" said Jeanie.

Jackson turned, did kiss her and then said, "You are going to stay and be here for me afterward, aren't you?"

"Absolutely," she replied. "I'll be here no matter what happens."

A lot happened in that game, not much of it good for the Lakers through two and a half quarters. They trailed by 13 with 8:25 to play in the third quarter.

Bryant was having a miserable game by his standards, uncharacteristically trying too hard. He was just 5 of 20 from the floor as the fourth quarter began.

"I just wanted it so, so bad," he said. "The more I tried to push, the more it kept getting away from me. I'm just glad that my teammates really got us back in the game."

That they did. Ron Artest, who had struggled in the regular season, scored 20 points, including a big three-pointer with 1:01 to go, and played tight defense against Boston's Paul Pierce.

"He brought life to our team," said coach Phil Jackson of Artest. "He brought life to the crowd."

And helped bring the Lakers their 16th title as they beat the Celtics 83–79.

Jackson embraced Jeanie on the sidelines, and Bryant leaped atop the scoring table to soak in the joy of the crowd.

"This one," said Bryant of his fifth title, "is, by far, the sweetest."

99 Best and Worst

Best Players

1. Magic Johnson
2. Kobe Bryant
3. Kareem Abdul-Jabbar
4. Jerry West
5. Shaquille O'Neal
6. George Mikan
7. LeBron James
8. Elgin Baylor
9. Wilt Chamberlain
10. James Worthy

Best Coaches

1. Phil Jackson
2. Pat Riley
3. Bill Sharman
4. John Kundla
5. Fred Schaus

Best Teams

1. 1971–72
2. 1984–85
3. 1999–00
4. 1986–87
5. 2019–20

Best Trades

1. Acquired Kobe Bryant from the Charlotte Hornets for Vlade Divac in 1996.
2. Acquired Kareem Abdul-Jabbar and Walt Wesley from the Milwaukee Bucks for Elmore Smith, Brian Winters, Dave Meyers, and Junior Bridgeman in 1975.
3. Acquired Pau Gasol and a future second-round draft choice from the Memphis Grizzlies for Kwame Brown, Javaris Crittenton, Aaron McKie, the draft rights to Marc Gasol, and two future first-round picks in 2008.
4. Acquired Anthony Davis from the New Orleans Pelicans for Lonzo Ball, Brandon Ingram, and Josh Hart, three first-round draft choices, plus the option of swapping picks with the Lakers in a future draft.
5. Acquired Wilt Chamberlain from the Philadelphia 76ers for Jerry Chambers, Archie Clark, and Darrall Imhoff in 1968.
6. Acquired Gail Goodrich from the Phoenix Suns for Mel Counts in 1970.

Worst Trades

1. Traded Shaquille O'Neal to the Miami Heat for Lamar Odom, Caron Butler, Brian Grant, and future first-round and second-round draft choices in 2004.
2. Traded Adrian Dantley to the Utah Jazz for Spencer Haywood in 1979.
3. Traded Caron Butler and Chucky Atkins to the Washington Wizards for Kwame Brown and Laron Profit in 2005.
4. Traded Sam Perkins to the Seattle SuperSonics for Benoit Benjamin and Doug Christie in 1993.
5. Traded Eddie Jones and Elden Campbell to the Hornets for B.J. Armstrong, J.R. Reid, and Glen Rice in 1999.

Five Biggest Head Cases

1. Spencer Haywood
2. Dennis Rodman
3. Cedric Ceballos
4. Smush Parker
5. Nick Van Exel

Ten Who Shouldn't Be Forgotten

1. Marge Hearn
2. Bill Bertka
3. Trainer Gary Vitti
4. Trainer Jack Curran
5. Former office manager Mary Lou Liebich
6. Dr. Steve Lombardo
7. Front office relief ace Linda Rambis
8. Photographer Andrew Bernstein
9. P.A. announcer Lawrence Tanter
10. Staples Center PR boss Michael Roth

100 A True Fan

You've never heard of Mark Wallach. He didn't buy a courtside seat, call talk radio, write letters to the editor or comments on websites. He didn't even attend the victory parades.

But he was there in the arena, in front of his television, or listening on his radio.

He didn't miss preseason, regular season, and certainly not postseason games.

Nothing meant more to him than his Lakers. If a game was on, he'd see it or hear it.

And even when the season was over, he couldn't turn his mind off. He'd obsess about the possibility of a trade, the signing of a free agent, or the selection of a draft choice.

Mark was the true definition of a fan, a fanatic in the best sense of the word.

It's not the corporations who buy the suites, the celebrities who fill the courtside seats, or those who follow the team only in the playoffs who are the foundation of the Lakers.

It's the Mark Wallachs, the fans who are there in good times and bad, season after season, decade after decade.

Mark died in 2011 of cancer. When he went into the hospital for the last time, he said, "I'm not going to see another Lakers season."

That was his first thought when he felt the end was near.

His loss wasn't as heralded as that of Chick Hearn. There weren't any streets, press rooms, or post offices named after Mark. There weren't any public tributes or statues.

Nor would he want any.

Mark didn't need recognition for his support. He was happy just being a true fan, one of those who have carried this franchise in their heart and soul for generations.

Every team needs a Mark Wallach.

Sources

Books

Abdul-Jabbar, Kareem, Knobler, Peter. *Giant Steps.* Bantam Books, 1983

Buss, Jeanie, Springer, Steve. *Laker Girl.* Triumph Books, 2010

Christgau, John. *Tricksters in the Madhouse.* University of Nebraska Press, 2004

Feinstein, John. *The Punch: One Night, Two Lives and the Fight That Changed Basketball Forever.* Little, Brown, 2002

Hearn, Chick, Springer, Steve. *Chick, His Unpublished Memoirs and the Memories of Those Who Knew Him.* Triumph Books, 2004

Heinsohn, Tommy. *Heinsohn, Don't You Ever Smile? The Life & Times of Tommy Heinsohn & the Boston Celtics.* Doubleday, 1976

Heisler, Mark. *Madmen's Ball.* Triumph Books, 2004

Hugunin, Marc, Thornley, Stew. *Minnesota Hoops: Basketball in the North Star State.* Minnesota Historical Society, 2006

Johnson, Earvin "Magic." *My Life.* William Novak, Random House, 1992

Kerwin, James F. *My Home Town, Carroll, Iowa.* Ferguson Publications, 1992

Ostler, Scott, Springer, Steve. *Winnin' Times.* Macmillan Publishing Company, 1986

Pearlman, Jeff. Showtime: Magic, Kareem, Riley and the Los Angeles Lakers Dynasty of the 1980s. Gotham Books, 2014.

Pluto, Terry. *Tall Tales: The Glory Years of the NBA.* Bison Books, 2000

Schumacher, Michael. *Mr. Basketball, George Mikan.* Bloomsbury, 2007

Springer, Steve. *Encyclopedia of the Lakers. Los Angeles Times*, 1998
Encyclopedia of World Biography
The Official NBA Basketball Encyclopedia, Villard Books, 1989

Newspapers and Periodicals
Associated Press
The Atlantic
Charleston Gazette-Mail
The Chicago Defender
The Sporting News, Dave Kindred
Encyclopedia Britannica
Esquire magazine
Los Angeles Times
Minneapolis Star Tribune
Orange County Register
Philadelphia Daily News
Pittsburgh Post-Gazette
San Francisco Examiner
The Sporting News Official NBA Guide
The Sporting News Official NBA Register
Sports Illustrated

Other
American National Biography Online
AOL News
Associated Press
Basketball-Reference.com
Bleacher Report
California Sports, Inc.
DePaul University website
ESPN.com
ESPN Radio
HickokSports.com

History.com
Hoopedia
Ivy League's Black History
Los Angeles Lakers media guides
Minneapolis Lakers game results by Stew Thornley
Naismith Memorial Basketball Hall of Fame
NBA.com
Net Industries—George Mikan, college ball
Reuters
This Day in History, History.com
UCLA 2005–06 Men's Basketball Media Guide

Acknowledgments

A couple of years ago, I was on a five-person panel that was formed to come up with five inductees for the first class of a Los Angeles Sports Hall of Fame. Each of us struggled to keep the number of Lakers nominees to two.

After all, L.A. is a town that can also boast of the Dodgers, Angels, Rams, Chargers, USC, UCLA, Kings, and Ducks, along with the Raiders from a previous era. Add in Oscar De La Hoya, Billie Jean King, and Rafer Johnson, to name a few, and the dilemma is obvious.

How do you limit it to a pair of Lakers when you've got Magic Johnson, Kareem Abdul-Jabbar, Jerry West, Chick Hearn, Elgin Baylor, Wilt Chamberlain, James Worthy, Gail Goodrich, Phil Jackson, Pat Riley, and Shaquille O'Neal to consider? (The candidates had to be retired, which made an extremely tough decision slightly easier, since at the time Kobe Bryant and Jerry Buss were not yet eligible.)

The difficulty of this task demonstrates just how special the Lakers have been to Los Angeles (and to Minneapolis before that).

When Tom Bast at Triumph Books approached me about writing another in their excellent series, *100 Things Fans Should Know & Do Before They Die*, I figured, considering the incredibly rich history of the Lakers, the problem would be limiting it to 100.

I was right.

I have taken the franchise from its roots in Detroit—where it was known as the Gems—to its present lofty status as, arguably, L.A.'s most celebrated team, and the second-most successful club in NBA history, with one championship fewer than the Lakers' archrivals, the Boston Celtics.

Although some descriptions of great moments on the court are necessary to tell their story, I have mainly focused on what has happened off the court, taking readers into the locker room, the front office, the practice facility, the team plane, and even players' homes. A team is judged by its wins and losses, but it is defined by its personality, the flesh and blood behind the numbers. In the case of the Lakers, there is no shortage of colorful, intriguing people, creating a rich and indelible history that will unfold in the pages that follow.

No matter how much you thought you knew about the Lakers, you are about to learn more.

Among the 100 things are the stories of the struggles of African American players like Elgin Baylor in the years before integration, the frightening night the Lakers' plane crash-landed in an Iowa cornfield, how the team got LeBron James, how the Lakers could have become the Oceaneers, how Jerry Buss amassed his fortune, how Jim Buss lost his job, how a nearly deadly bike ride drastically changed the course of team history, how Jerry West spied on Norm Nixon, how Lakers teammates once carried matchbook covers that read "Trade Kareem," how Rick Fox tried to keep Kobe and Shaq together, how Francis Dayle Hearn became "Chick," and how Jeanie Buss and Phil Jackson found true love.

There are lists in here as well, bests and worsts.

I want to thank Adam Motin and Jesse Jordan, the best basketball editors on the planet, and all the hardworking people at Triumph.

I want to thank my son, Alan Springer, the most knowledgeable Lakers fan I know, for supplying insight and good advice.

I want to thank Jeanie and Jerry Buss for generously giving their time; Chick for his memories; the inspirational Marge Hearn; Lon Rosen; all of the Lakers players, coaches, front-office personnel, and broadcasters over the last three decades who supplied material; Gary Vitti; Jack Curran; Dr. Steve Lombardo; Mary Lou

Liebich; Joyce Sharman; Bob Baker; Mark Wallach; Scott Ostler; Rich Levin; Mitch Chortkoff; Mark Heisler; Steve Bisheff; Bill Dwyre; Randy Harvey; Peter Schmuck; Jim Rhode; Barry Stavro; and the Lakers gatekeeper, John Black.